American Photographs 1900–1950

American Photographs 1900–1950

from the National Gallery of Canada

Ann Thomas

Ottawa, 2011

American Photographs 1900–1950 is the fourth in a series of publications focusing on selected masterpieces from the Photographs collection of the National Gallery of Canada. The exhibition *Made in America 1900–1950: Photographs from the National Gallery of Canada* is organized and circulated by the National Gallery of Canada.

Itinerary
National Gallery of Canada
9 December 2011 – 1 April 2012

Art Gallery of Windsor
3 June – 3 September 2012

National Gallery of Canada, Ottawa
Acting Chief, Publications: Ivan Parisien
Editors: Eugenia Bell and Lauren Walker
Picture Editor and Production: Anne Tessier

Copyright © National Gallery of Canada, Ottawa, 2011

Designed and typeset by Fugazi, Montreal
Printed and bound in Italy by Conti Tipocolor, Florence

Cover: Ralph Steiner, *Model T* (detail), 1929, printed later (cat. 59)

Library and Archives Canada Cataloguing in Publication
National Gallery of Canada
American photographs 1900–1950 from the National Gallery of Canada / Ann Thomas.
Exhibition catalogue.
Issued also in French under title: Photographies américaines 1900–1950 du Musée des beaux-arts du Canada.
"4" – Spine.

ISBN 978-0-88884-889-5

1. Photography – United States – History – 20th century – Exhibitions.
2. Photography, Artistic – History – 20th century – Exhibitions.
3. Photograph collections – Ontario – Ottawa – Exhibitions.
4. National Gallery of Canada – Exhibitions. I. Thomas, Ann II. Title.

TR23 N37 2011   770.973   C2011-986003-1

Distribution
ABC Art Books Canada
www.abcartbookscanada.com
info@abcartbookscanada.com

Contents

Foreword

American Photographs 1900–1950 is the fourth in a series of exhibitions and catalogues that presents the National Gallery's outstanding collection of international photographs. The first to be launched was *Modernist Photographs*, followed by *19th-Century French Photographs,* then *19th-Century British Photographs*. This catalogue highlights yet another important period in the history of photography.

The first half of the twentieth century marks a lively era in American art history when photography was first celebrated as an art form. The 1910 exhibition of almost six hundred Pictorialist photographs at the Albright Art Gallery (now the Albright Knox Art Gallery) was the first of its kind in an art museum. By the time the Museum of Modern Art, New York, established its department of photography in 1940, the medium was anchored firmly in American cultural life.

Canada and the United States have long been linked through ideas and artworks. In 1903 thirty works from the collection of the Photo-Secession were featured in an exhibition presented by the Toronto Camera Club. Four years later, a large international Pictorialist exhibition at the Art Association of Montreal (now the Musée des beaux-arts de Montréal) included work by American Photo-Secessionists Alfred Stieglitz, Edward Steichen, Clarence White, and Gertrude Käsebier.

American photographers and painters have also drawn inspiration from Canadian artists and landscapes. Works by Canadian-born painter Henrietta Shore motivated Edward Weston to create his stunning series of shell photographs in 1927. Many American photographers came north for inspiration in the first half of the century; Gertrude Käsebier to Newfoundland and Paul Strand to the Gaspé and Nova Scotia.

The Gallery's collection is sufficiently rich in twentieth-century American photographs that it has necessitated an exhibition and catalogue in two parts, this first presentation focuses on the period between 1900 and 1950. Our holdings of work by Photo League members Lisette Model, Walker Evans, Lewis Hine,

Aaron Siskind, Harry Callahan, Edward Weston, and Robert Frank are such that they alone can form the core for monographic exhibitions on the work of these photographers.

This comprehensive collection has been amassed in large part through the generosity of our donors. The first significant donation of gelatin silver prints came from Dorothy Meigs Eidlitz, an American who established the Sunbury Shores Arts and Crafts school in St. Andrews, New Brunswick. Our exceptional collection of two hundred and eighty-one Walker Evans prints were donated by Phyllis Lambert, a long-time supporter of the Gallery's collection of photographs; more than two hundred and sixty prints and the Lisette Model Archive came to us through the Estate of Lisette Model facilitated by the American Friends of Canada (now the Council for Canadian and American Relations), and two hundred and fifty-two works by Andreas Feininger were recently donated through the estate of his widow and facilitated by his son, Tomas Feininger, a resident of Quebec City. In addition to the extraordinary contributions of donors, annual donations by Anne Shabaga and Mark McCain and our Photography Collectors' Group have allowed us to buy great works of art to augment our holdings. This exhibition and catalogue would not be what they are without them.

Marc Mayer
Director and CEO
National Gallery of Canada

Acknowledgements

One of the benefits of producing this series of exhibitions from the National Gallery of Canada's Collection of Photographs is the opportunity that it provides to review and address the strengths and weaknesses of significant parts of the collection. Director Marc Mayer, the Board of Trustees of the National Gallery of Canada, and the Board of Trustees Advisory Committee, have played invaluable roles in this regard, offering much appreciated support and feedback. Their ongoing encouragement has led to the acquisition of several major works that are included in this exhibition and without which the exhibition would have been less richly informed. Among them are Clarence White's *Entrance to the Garden*, Edward Steichen's *Lady and the Lamp* and Alfred Stieglitz's *Miss S.R., Vienna*. In this regard Canada's Cultural Property Review Board must also be acknowledged for the critical role that it has played over the many decades that major gifts have been made to the collection. Without its presence, this collection would not have received the level of international renown that it now enjoys.

An equal debt of gratitude is owed to the extraordinary generosity of the supporters of this collection who have provided funding for purchases, given extensive donations, and offered ongoing moral support for the building of this collection: Phyllis Lambert, Anne Shabaga, Tomas Feininger, Mark McCain, and others who prefer to remain anonymous. Phyllis Lambert's great respect for the founding curator of the collection of photographs, James Borcoman, and her visionary insight led her to donate a major body of Walker Evans in 1982. Evans still inspires younger generations of photographers of all nationalities and it is because of this donation that his contribution is strongly represented. Thanks to the generous support of the National Gallery of Canada Foundation, and in particular, the Donald and Beth Sobey Chief Curator's Research Endowment, I was able to engage a curatorial assistant.

The intent of this catalogue is to highlight masterpieces from a particularly well represented period of our holdings and to contextualize them with the illustration of other images by the photographer or the photographer's peers. I thank those copyright holders who lent their support to this endeavour, which allows us a greater appreciation of the ongoing dialogue that occurs within a photographer's practice and in relation to the work of his peers. David Newman and William Ewing are owed special thanks in this regard. I regret that this does not occur in entries 8, 9, 10, 27, and 51, where copyright restrictions on works by Harry Callahan, Robert Frank and Irving Penn precluded the use of comparative figures.

Thanks also to my colleagues working internationally in museums and universities who have written so eloquently on many of the photographers represented in this exhibition and who responded to my enquiries for information and served as sounding boards with regard to potential acquisitions: Anne Wilkes Tucker, The Museum of Fine Arts, Houston; Malcolm Daniel, Curator in Charge, Department of Photographs, The Metropolitan Museum of Art, New York; Peter Bunnell, McAlpin Professor of the History of Photography and former Director of the Princeton University Art Gallery; Joel Smith, Curator of Photography, Princeton University Art Museum; Sarah Greenough, Curator of Photographs, National Gallery of Art, Washington; Peter Galassi, former Chief Curator, Photographs Collection, The Museum of Modern Art, New York; Tom Hinson, former Curator, Cleveland Museum of Art; and Keith F. Davis, Senior Curator, The Nelson-Atkins Museum of Art, Kansas City; Aaron Glass, Assistant Professor, Bard Graduate Center; Karen Duffek, Curator, UBC Museum of Anthropology; Barbara Brotherton, Curator, Seattle Art Museum; Mary Jane Lenz, Smithsonian Institution; and Peter Macnair, Curator Emeritus, Royal BC Museum.

My colleagues who have helped with this project have demonstrated extraordinary patience and collaboration, accommodating my chaotic schedule as I tried to balance both my substantive position and that of Acting Co-Chief Curator. Katherine Stauble, Sobey Curatorial Assistant, formed an invaluable member of this team, fact-checking, contacting various sources for information, and reviewing edits with unfailing perseverance and cheerfulness. Charlene Heath, Ryerson University graduate student in the Photographic Preservation and Collections Management programme,Marie Lesbats, intern from the Université de Paris XII, and Candice Hopkins, National Gallery of Canada Elizabeth Simonfay Curatorial Resident of Indigenous Art assisted in the research on individual photographs in the catalogue.

The National Gallery Library staff conducts itself with an almost invisible professionalism and dedication; without the tremendous efforts of Julie Levac, Annie Arsenault, Sarah D'Aurelio, Jo Beglo, Anna Kindl, Cyndie Campbell and their Chief Librarian, Jonathan Franklin, the catalogue would be much the poorer.

In the National Gallery's Publications department, Serge Thériault, Director of Publications, New Media and Distribution, Ivan Parisien, Acting Chief of Publications, and Lauren Walker, English editor working with external editor Eugenia Bell ushered this catalogue through its various stages with great professionalism. Anne Tessier demonstrated that she has a healthy supply of photo editor genes by remaining calm and cheerful in the face of yet another overwhelming task. François Martin of Fugazi, Montreal, produced the elegant design for the catalogue as he has done for the past three in the series.

In the Exhibitions department, Christine Sadler, Chief, Anne Troise, Project Manager and Seema Hollenberg, Senior Project Manager, ably handled the scheduling, co-ordination and touring, and are acknowledged for their efforts. I also thank Karen Colby-Stothart, Deputy Director, Exhibitions and Installations for her unwavering support.

My sincere thanks also go to the following people who worked on the exhibition: John McElhone, Chief Conservator, Shawn Boisvert, Documentations and Storage Officer, and Andrea Gumpert, Education Officer. Thanks also to designer Stefan Canuel, Mark Paradis, Chief, Multimedia Services, and the fine staff in Technical Services. Finally, I must acknowledge the enormous contribution of Kristin Rothschild, Acting Manager, Copyrights, and Emily Antler, Copyrights Officer.

Although not directly associated with the catalogue and exhibition I owe a huge debt of gratitude to members of my department Lori Pauli, Associate Curator of Photographs, and Louise Chénier, Administrative Assistant, for their exemplary professionalism as they assisted in every possible way with all the other major projects in which our department was involved.

Although he has moved on to becoming Director of the Cleveland Museum, David Franklin's initiation of this series for both the Photographs and Prints and Drawings Collections must be acknowledged.

Ann Thomas
Curator, Photographs
National Gallery of Canada

Introduction

The timeframe of this exhibition and catalogue on American photography covers five remarkably fertile decades. Each one of them is characterized by tremendous growth, change, and creative thought about the medium and its reception in the United States. This essay provides a framework of major developments in photography that will allow readers to situate the individual images in a particular context and, therefore, leaves out a great deal of the detail that defines this extraordinary period. Nonetheless, the excitement around the flowering of the medium and the pendulum swings between styles and approaches it was subject to are still conveyed, if only in snapshot form.

The century opens with Pictorialism, a style of photography that privileged the expression of mood over the transmission of visual fact. The desire to gain equal status for photography as an art form meant that for the better part of this period a debate would take place around the nature and role of photography, a discourse that reflected the lively state of American culture and would lead to a plurality of intellectual positions and photographic practices.

Photography as an art form and as a tool for social and political change came into its own in several different incarnations during these five decades. While the former addressed the poetic and transformative expression in photography, the latter supplied images of the country in its various phases of industrial development and economic growth.

On both the technical and technological levels great strides were made in America during this time. Some of these – such as Harold E. Edgerton's refinement of the strobe – were significant to the advancement of industry and science. Others proved to be pertinent on a more professional, personal, and populist level as with the introduction of 35mm cameras following the model of the German made Leica, and Ansel Adams and Fred Archer's creation of the Zone System to determine optimal film exposure and development.

This essay looks at photography as an art form, on the one hand, and as a social document on the other. That this division is porous and somewhat arbitrary is borne out by the fact that the National Gallery of Canada, like many international art museums, considers documentary and vernacular photography a vital part of its collection, and the standard practice in many cultural studies programs in academia is to include the study of art photographs.

Photography as Art
Pictorialism: A Plastic Process

The idea that photography did not have to be limited to recording visual facts but was capable of conveying complex and multiple forms of artistic and cultural expression had gained in popularity by the late nineteenth century. The aesthetic photography generated out of this way of thinking, Pictorialism, promoted a gestural and personally expressive style. Its pictorial conventions were associated with two influential movements in painting, Symbolism and Tonalism. The favoured themes were pastoral landscapes, foggy street scenes, idealized women and children, and the Hellenic past, rendered in suppressed detail, and often silhouetted or described in muted mid-tones. Dappled or softer lighting conditions such as dawn, dusk, and moonlight when shapes assume a quality of indeterminacy, prevailed. This subjection of form, place, and time to broad generalization underscored the movement's rejection of contemporary reality.

The process of making photographic prints, and particularly the attention paid to including handwork on the negative or the print, was heavily influenced by traditional printmaking techniques like lithography, etching, and engraving, as well as by the tenets of the Arts and Crafts movement. Camera clubs, international salons and photography associations dedicated to the Pictorialist aesthetic were formed among a large group of international supporters.

Fired with missionary zeal to reform what he considered to be a sluggish and random state of affairs in photography in the United States, Stieglitz, who had been publishing articles in British and German photography periodicals, remained involved on the international level after his return home, but also became active locally, joining the Society of Amateur Photographers of New York (later known as the Camera Club of New York). He served as editor of *American Amateur Photographer* from 1893–96, and then transformed the newsletter of the Camera Club of New York into the journal *Camera Notes*, which he edited from 1897 to 1902.

The spring of 1900 saw the fortuitous meeting between Edward Steichen (fig. 2) and Alfred Stieglitz, when the former stopped into the rooms of the Camera Club of New York en route to Paris to show Stieglitz his portfolio of paintings, drawings, lithographs and photographs. Impressed by what he saw, Stieglitz purchased three platinum prints[2] and included Steichen in an exhibition of American photographs he assembled for the photographic section of the Glasgow International Arts and Industrial Exposition in 1901. In the five-year period after Stieglitz and Steichen first met, the two men worked swiftly to establish a place in New York for pictorial photography.

Unhappy with the lack of standards at the Camera Club of New York, Stieglitz agreed willingly in 1902 to curate an exhibition on the premises of the National Arts Club in New York to prove that American pictorial work was as impressive as that coming out of Europe and Great Britain. He made it known to Charles de Kay,[3] founder and director of the National Arts Club, however, that he would not tolerate any vetting or interference from the Arts Club's committee.

The resulting installation of 162 works by thirty-one participants was titled *An Exhibition of American Photography Arranged by the Photo-Secession*, and marked the inauguration of the Photo-Secession. Composed of Gertrude Käsebier, John G. Bullock, William B. Dyer, Frank Eugene, Joseph T. Keiley, Edward Steichen, Eva Watson-Schütze, and Clarence H. White, with Alfred Stieglitz at the helm, the group adapted photographic processes and techniques to what they considered to be more expressive and artistic ends, proving that the medium could compete with painting and traditional printmaking. While based in New York, the Photo-Secession would become the flagship for Pictorialist photography in the United States, gaining a strong foothold for the movement at home and abroad. In 1903, Stieglitz, with the assistance of Steichen, established the high-quality quarterly *Camera Work*.

Finding this level of appreciation for photography in the United States would require the participation of determined and knowledgeable individuals, supportive institutions, and the mobilization of a considerable number of adherents. American-born Alfred Stieglitz (fig. 1), son of German Jewish immigrants, played a key role in having photography recognized as an art form in the United States. In 1890 he returned to New York from Berlin, where he had studied mechanical engineering and taken a course in photographic chemistry from Dr. Hermann Wilhelm Vogel, one of the most respected scientists in the field. Stieglitz's exposure to the European aesthetic of pictorial photography and the work of American-born, UK-based P.H. Emerson, inspired him to not only dedicate himself to photography as a form of personal expression, but also to formulate a vision of how he could establish a more vibrant and rigorous photographic culture back home, one that would resemble what he had enjoyed abroad. "In 1890 when I returned to America," he wrote, "I found that photography as I understood it hardly existed; that an instrument had been put on the market shortly before called the 'Kodak' and the slogan sent out to advertisers read, 'You press the button and we do the rest.' The idea sickened me."[1]

Fig. 1 Alvin Langdon Coburn, *Alfred Stieglitz, Esquire*, 1907, photogravure, plate VI from *Camera Work*, no. 21 (January 1908), National Gallery of Canada, Ottawa (PSC68:039:218)

Fig. 2 Edward Steichen, *Self-Portrait*, 1901, photogravure, plate III from *Camera Work*, no. 2 (April 1903), National Gallery of Canada, Ottawa, Gift of Dorothy Meigs Eidlitz, St. Andrews, New Brunswick, 1968 (34999.3)

Edward Steichen's hand could be seen in its appearance from the design of the cover to the choice of typeface and layout (fig. 3).

Camera Work was intended as much to encourage a general interest in Pictorialist photography as it was to satisfy the needs of those already invested in the aesthetic. It was also meant to provide a forum for an ongoing exchange of ideas about the medium and to develop a vocabulary that would enable this discourse to gain clarity and depth. Stieglitz made his vision for the quarterly clear in an introductory essay for the first issue, in January 1903: "Only examples of such works as gives evidence of individuality and artistic worth, regardless of school, or contains some exceptional feature of technical merit, or such as exemplifies some treatment worthy of consideration, will find recognition in these pages. Nevertheless, the Pictorial will be the dominating feature of the magazine."[4]

Two years later Stieglitz and Steichen established the Little Galleries of the Photo-Secession at 291 Fifth Avenue, which would later be known simply as "291." Steichen had initially proposed the idea of a gallery to Stieglitz by suggesting that the two rooms adjacent to his studio would serve the purpose

well, and on 24 November, Little Galleries of the Photo-Secession were inaugurated with an exhibition of one hundred photographic prints made by the members. Stieglitz's vision of both the Little Galleries and *Camera Work* incorporated a strong public education component that included the development of skills in photographic print connoisseurship.

The Photograph as an Art Object

With its emphasis on the "gestural" effect in the photographic print and its preference for painterly processes such as gum and platinum, Pictorialism emphasized the importance of an appreciation of fine printmaking. This insistence on print connoisseurship was integral to both exhibiting and publishing photographs and held particular significance for Stieglitz and Steichen, both of whom had significant experience working in the printing and engraving business.[5] Every care was taken in the production of *Camera Work* to ensure that the photographic prints were translated as truthfully and elegantly as possible from their original medium into the hand pulled photogravures on Japan tissue, that were tipped onto heavy deckle-edged paper.

Fig. 3   Cover of *Camera Work*, no. 21 (January 1908), National Gallery of Canada, Ottawa

A number of platinum and gum bichromate prints in the National Gallery's collection and featured in this exhibition (cats. 33–35) were published as photogravures in the first issue of *Camera Work*

Years later, the painter, filmmaker, and photographer Charles Sheeler, for whom Stieglitz served as a mentor of sorts, would expound on the importance of teaching people to differentiate between types and states of photographic prints:

> There should be the same sort of discrimination between fine photographic prints as between different Rembrandt etchings. Work like that of Steichen or Edward Weston should be collected in portfolios with the same zest that etchings are collected or lithographs. It's a pity this is not happening in a broad way, for much of the significant work of the camera of our time may go out, say in a hundred years, because some of the finest examples are considered only of transitory, journalistic interest and because the medium is so perishable.[6]

Bringing his experience as a painter and a printmaker to bear on photography, Steichen's images possessed an assurance and strength that resulted in their gracing the pages of the quarterly with greater frequency than those of any other photographer. In an attempt to resolve his dual commitments to painting and photography, Steichen spent two extended periods in France trying to establish himself as a painter. Nevertheless, he continued to practice photography. Up until World War I, his landscapes, like early Stieglitz images, emphasized atmospheric effects. His portraits were romantic and brooding, coming to a stunning crescendo in those that he made of Rodin in his studio (fig. 4). While based in Paris he advised Stieglitz on European artists he should consider exhibiting in the Little Galleries or publish in *Camera Work*.

Although it was Alfred Stieglitz who was pivotal to the creation of the Photo-Secession and who assumed the role of high priest of photography in New York – vetting venues that requested exhibitions of Photo-Secession work and insisting on conditions of exclusivity when it was shown with works by other Pictorialists – Steichen's role in assisting in the establishment of the gallery and *Camera Work*, as well as in setting the bar for strong Pictorialist work, cannot be underestimated.

Fig. 4 Edward Steichen, *Rodin*, photogravure, plate I from *Camera Work*, no. 2 (April 1903), National Gallery of Canada, Ottawa, Gift of Dorothy Meigs Eidlitz, St. Andrews, New Brunswick, 1968 (34999.1)

Stieglitz as Mentor

Alfred Stieglitz played an important role as a mentor to fellow and younger photographers. Käsebier's representation in the first issue of *Camera Work* testifies that he was open-minded, given the times, when it came to acknowledging quality work made by women photographers. Of all the women Pictorialists, Käsebier would push the aesthetic to its most painterly extreme (fig. 5). Other women active in the Pictorialist movement who benefitted from his support were Anne Brigman, Alice Boughton, and Eva Watson-Schütze. Just as he had validated Steichen as a young photographer, he was also highly influential in the careers of Alvin Langdon Coburn, Clarence White, Paul Strand, and Charles Sheeler, among others.

Clarence H. White (fig. 6) was also a collaborator in 1907–08 on a series of nudes, and it was he who would carry the torch for Pictorialism after Stieglitz had abandoned the cause. Following the accepted tenets of Pictorialist practice and Arthur Dow's pedagogical approach, White opened his Sequinland School of Photography on Georgetown Island, Maine, in 1910.[7] He periodically hired both Day and Käsebier to teach there. In 1914 he established The Clarence H. White School of Photography in New York, which continued up until the time of his death in 1925. Many of the most influential photographers from the first half of the twentieth century in the United States would pass through one or the other of his schools.

In 1910 Stieglitz organized a major Pictorialist show, the *International Exhibition of Pictorial Photography*. This epic display of almost six hundred Pictorialist photographs, prepared for the Albright Art Gallery in Buffalo (now the Albright Knox Art Gallery), ostensibly achieved Stieglitz's goal of placing photography on an equal footing to the other visual arts. Not only did he succeed in having photography recognized as an integral part of museum programming, but the museum purchased fifteen works and subsequently hung them in their galleries. Stieglitz's interests were, however, shifting steadily away from Pictorialism and towards avant-garde art. The *International Exhibition of Pictorial Photography* was not only Stieglitz's swansong in respect of his advocacy of Pictorialism, it also marked the end of his leadership of the Photo-Secession. His *volte face* was, to a large degree the product of growing intellectual frustration and dissatisfaction, but it also marred his relationships with leading members of the Photo-Secession. In 1912 both Gertrude Käsebier and Clarence H. White broke off their relations with Stieglitz over his autocratic and dictatorial manner. In terms of the continuation of

Pictorialism as a movement, the baton was, by default, passed on to White.

In New York, the comfortable – some might even say provincial – world of American art was about to be irreversibly changed with the opening in 1913 of an exhibition of 1,300 paintings and sculptures comprising not-so-new objects and a significant selection of radically different artworks. The *International Exhibition of Modern Art*, popularly known as the Armory Show, ran for less than a month from 17 February to 15 March 1913 at the Armory of the Sixty-Ninth Regiment in New York.[8]

With the opening of the Armory Show Stieglitz's detachment from the movement was almost complete. He praised artists who "decline to go on doing merely what the camera does better,"[9] and transformed himself from defender of Pictorialism to champion of the avant-garde, not altogether a surprising move, given his position as an early arbiter of the avant-garde through the pages of *Camera Work* and *291*. Up until its closing in 1917, his 291 gallery increasingly showed the work of European painters and sculptors. While *Camera Work* had continued to publish regularly, by 1917 it had few subscribers and folded with Strand's work appearing in the last issue.

Pictorialism: An Enduring Aesthetic

Pictorialism did not perish overnight. It was a hardy strain, going on to an ever popular reception among the general public who became adherents of Photo Clubs and subscribers to Pictorialist journals.[10] While Stieglitz remained scornful of such manifestations of photography, Clarence White set about ensuring Pictorialism its place in history. Ignoring the mannerist works and the pastiches – like the melodramatic renderings of William Mortensen – that exerted such appeal over the popular imagination, White's school taught fine photographic printmaking. Clarence White opened his New York School one year after the Armory Show. The continuation of the Pictorialist aesthetic in its more thoughtful manifestation was now largely through White. Students of the school whose work would contribute not only to late Pictorialism but also, in some instances, to Modernist practice were Dorothea Lange, Laura Gilpen, Paul Outerbridge, Ralph Steiner, and Doris Ulmann. Canadian-born photographer Margaret Watkins, a former student at the summer school, was a member of the faculty. In 1916 a new association of photographers formed, the Pictorial Photographers of America (fig. 7). Gertrude Käsebier and Clarence White were two of the former Secessionists who were at the helm of the club.

Fig. 5   Gertrude Käsebier, *Man on a Rooftop*, 1901?, gum bichromate print, National Gallery of Canada, Ottawa (31395)

Fig. 6   Alvin Langdon Coburn, *Clarence H. White (1871–1925)*, 1912, photogravure, National Gallery of Canada, Ottawa (21482)

Even with the closing of 291, the folding of *Camera Work*, and the stock market crash of 1929, Stieglitz's influence did not wane, even though he had stepped away from what had become mainstream art photography in order to reassess it relative to what was happening in avant-garde painting. Continuing to question the role of photography in art, Stieglitz started to advocate for what were now considered to be photography's intrinsic properties, writing in 1923: "My photographs look like photographs – and [in the eyes of the 'pictorial photographers'] they therefore can't be art."[11] He ruminated on the notion of "the idea photography" and its relationship to abstraction. From 1922 to 1935 he photographed clouds and structured the prints into sequences, further expanding the grammatical parsing of the medium to endow it with greater expressiveness.[12] In 1922, he solicited answers from thirty-two writers, artists, and musicians to the question "Can a photograph have the significance of art?," and published them in the short-lived journal *Manuscripts*.[13]

Included in the fresh approaches that he brought to the photographic image was his extended notion of the portrait, "To demand *the* portrait that will be a complete portrait of any person is as futile as to demand that a motion picture be condensed into a single still."[14] Both he and Strand undertook serial portrait studies of their respective partners: Stieglitz photographed Georgia O'Keeffe almost obsessively from 1917 to 1937, and Paul Strand produced a more condensed series of his first wife, Rebecca Salsbury, in the early twenties.

Despite financial pressure, Stieglitz remained undeterred, and the desire to put artwork on public view was ever present. He raised funds and became once again a gallerist, first of the Intimate Gallery (1925–29) on Park Avenue, and later of An American Place (1929–36) on Madison Avenue.

West Coast Pictorialism

Stieglitz went through various stages of being an internationalist and a nationalist and sometimes both together, but his sphere of influence was most significant in New York and on the East Coast, tending perhaps to make him more of a regionalist. Anne Brigman was one of the few Pictorialists from the West whom he brought into the Photo-Secession fold. While New York was the indisputable hub for the Pictorialist movement in America, there was an

Fig. 7   Margaret Watkins, *Pictorial Photographers of America Convention*, 1919, palladium print, National Gallery of Canada, Ottawa, Purchased 1984 with the assistance of a grant from the Government of Canada under the terms of the Cultural Property Export and Import Act (20624)

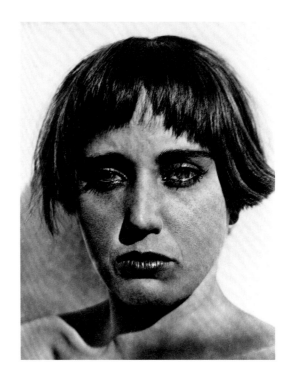

active school in California whose members took a special interest in the presence of *Camera Work.* Later, over the course of four decades, photographers from the West Coast – Johann Hagemeyer in 1916, Edward Weston in 1922, Adams in 1933, Cunningham in 1934, and Minor White in 1946 – would make the pilgrimage to Alfred Stieglitz's galleries.

In addition to Stieglitz's ongoing reconsideration of the role of photography between the time of the Armory Show and 1929, Alvin Langdon Coburn, Charles Sheeler, and Paul Strand exhibited and published work that would emphatically announce the arrival of a new aesthetic in photography. If abstraction in photography had seemed like a contradiction in terms, its exploration by Charles Sheeler in his 1917 photograph, *Side of White Barn* (cat. 52), Paul Strand's untitled abstractions in the final issue of *Camera Work* (fig. 8), and Alvin Langdon Coburn's series of Vortographs, also made in 1917 (cat. 12), proved otherwise.

Over the course of his career, Strand, who had first visited 291 as a student in 1907, moved from Pictorialism to abstraction to "straight" photographs

that were centred on man's relationship to the land and community. As his friendship with Stieglitz deteriorated in the late 1920s, Strand became increasingly politicized, a factor that would also shape the look of his work.[15] His directly composed, superbly printed images of the 1920s, like Sheelers',[16] were precise to the point of being immaculate and would leave a mark on the future of the medium as an art form.[17]

By the end of the twenties a select number of American modernists had received recognition in the international context of the landmark exhibition *Film und Foto: Internationale Ausstellung des Deutschen Werkbund*, held in Stuttgart, in 1929. American photographers included were Edward Weston and Edward Steichen, respectively West and East Coast organizers for the American section, as well as Sheeler, Berenice Abbott, Cunningham, and Outerbridge. Significantly, Sheeler's *Side of White Barn* was selected for that exhibition as was Edward Weston's portrait of Nahui Olin (fig. 9).

Fig. 8   Paul Strand, *Photograph*, photogravure, plate XI from *Camera Work*, no. 49/50 (June 1917), National Gallery of Canada, Ottawa, Gift of Dorothy Meigs Eidlitz, St. Andrews, New Brunswick, 1968 (34999.170)

Fig. 9   Edward Weston, *Nahui Olin*, 1923, printed before July 1969, gelatin silver print, National Gallery of Canada, Ottawa (33645)

The considerable developments on the East Coast influenced the formation of a group that would most effectively draw attention to art photography on the West Coast. If Pictorialism made a case for its legitimacy as an art form because of its capacity to share the textural and atmospheric effects of certain schools of painting, the Group f.64, which sprung up in the San Francisco Bay Area in the early 1930s, argued for artistic validation on quite the opposite grounds, contending that it was the inherent properties of photography's sharpness, clarity, and uniform surface that qualified it as such. This was similar to the credo that the European modernists promoted in the 1920s under the rubric of the New Vision and *Neue Sachlichkeit* (The New Objectivity), reflecting the values of sharp focus, uniform surfaces, and clearly contrasted tonalities that Strand and Sheeler promoted in their work from the late teens and twenties in New York.

Convinced that these qualities would be maximized to their best effect in an image made with a large-format view camera with its shutter closed to the smallest possible aperture and contact printed on glossy paper, the Group f.64 was with equal verve a counter movement to Pictorialism and an advocacy group for a new vision of photography. In 1933 when Ansel Adams published a description of the newly formed f.64 for *Camera Craft* magazine, he knowingly distinguished between the hothouse environment that existed in many organizations devoted to Pictorialist photography and the aspirations of openness for his group, expressing the hope that it would be free of "any of the restrictions of artistic secret societies, Salons, clubs or cliques, adding that their motive was not to impose a *school* with rigid limitations, or to present our work with belligerent scorn of other view-points, but to indicate what we consider to be reasonable statements of straight photography."[18]

Formally established in August of 1932, f.64 had seven original members: Ansel Adams, Imogen Cunningham, John Paul Edwards, Sonya Noskowiak, Henry Swift, Willard Van Dyke, and Edward Weston.[19] Although nature was a central subject for these photographers, they were not confined to it. The photographers in the group all developed distinctive styles of working but shared a crisp-edged clean-lined aesthetic. The photographs collection in the National Gallery of Canada includes images by Sonya Noskowiak (fig. 10) and Ansel Adams (fig. 11) that were represented in the group's first and only exhibition at the M.H. De Young Memorial Museum in San Francisco from 15 November to 31 December 1932.

Edward Weston, Imogen Cunningham, and Ansel Adams were key figures in the advancement of art photography on the West Coast. Cunningham is celebrated above all for her extraordinarily precise and elegantly composed botanical plant studies, but also appreciated for her portraits and nudes. Adams is heralded for his sublime landscape photographs of the Yosemite and the California coast, and Weston is perhaps equally well recognized for his nudes, still lifes, portraits, and landscapes.

Edward Weston settled in Los Angeles, and like Dorothea Lange in San Francisco, would establish his own successful portrait studio in Glendale, until such time that he decided to practice not as a commercial photographer, but as an artist. His finely crafted platinum prints, exhibited in numerous international photographic salons, were often singled out in reviews for their originality. For Weston, 1922 was a milestone year. Disenchanted with nostalgia and working in a soft-edged aesthetic, he wrote in support of British photographer Frederick H. Evans' critique of mannerist Pictorialist practices: "I groped through all the stages of 'fuzziness' and intentional over- and underexposure to get 'effects,' until I awakened to a realization of what photography really means … 'an affirmation of the majesty of the moment.'"[20] It was during this transition that he began to look more closely at modern art and read about it. He visited Stieglitz in New York and made his first industrial photographs of the Armco steel mill in Middletown, Ohio (fig. 12).

Born in Portland, Oregon, Imogen Cunningham was introduced to photography through the Pictorialist journals, *Camera Work* and *The Craftsman*, and was particularly attracted to the photographs of Gertrude Käsebier. By the time she moved to San Francisco in 1917, she had already become interested in abstraction but did not incorporate it into her work until 1921, when she started to explore her interest in patterns in nature.[21] Cunningham first met Edward Weston and Ansel Adams in 1920. Both encounters would develop into strong and mutually respectful friendships that continued throughout her life.[22]

Ansel Adams' photographs are synonymous with West Coast landscape photography. Working in the photo-finishing business and also as a warden in Yosemite National Park prepared him for the eloquent photographic capture of landscapes. When Adams made the claim that he had little concept of the expressive nature of photography until he met Paul Strand in 1930, he appeared to be separating the competency of artistic seeing from that of understanding more deeply the relationship of subject to self. That he was a highly capable maker of

Fig. 10   Sonya Noskowiak, *Sand Patterns*, 1932, gelatin silver print, National Gallery of Canada, Ottawa, Purchased from the Phyllis Lambert Fund, 1979 (32323)

Fig. 11   Ansel Adams, *Frozen Lake and Cliffs, Kaweah Gap, Sequoia National Park, California*, 1927, printed before February 1974, gelatin silver print, National Gallery of Canada, Ottawa (20525)

Fig. 12   Edward Weston, *Steel*, October 1922, gelatin silver print, National Gallery of Canada, Ottawa, Purchased from the Phyllis Lambert Fund, 1979 (no. 33716)

artfully composed landscape photographs before 1930 is evident in the work that he produced in the late 1920s, and which he published in the Parmelian portfolio. Although the kinds of processes the Photo-Secessionists were using and the aesthetic values they aimed for differed greatly from those of f.64, both groups considered technical matters and connoisseurship of great importance.

It did not take long for Adams' work to earn the respect it deserved out East. In 1936 it was exhibited by Stieglitz at An American Place, and in 1940 Adams was enlisted to help establish the Department of Photography at the Museum of Modern Art in New York, and to assist in curating its first exhibition.

Although Minor White was not a member of f.64, his association with West Coast photography is important in the 1940s. Born in the Midwest, Minor White crossed the country several times establishing himself first on the West Coast, then spending two years studying in New York. He moved to San Francisco in 1946, at the invitation of Ansel Adams, to teach in the newly established Department of Photography of the California School of Fine Arts (now the San Francisco Art Institute).[23] White and Adams were instrumental in bringing Lisette Model to teach at the school that same year. White would subsequently return to the East Coast.

It was Stieglitz's ideas regarding the metaphorical nature of the photograph and possibly Callahan's concept of sequencing (passed on to Callahan by Ansel Adams) that influenced White's complex restructuring of the syntax of the photograph and its relationship to other photographs.[24] His most significant contribution was to expand the understanding of the photograph with its particular relationship to reality as an agent of metaphorical expression, and to introduce greater complexity into the parsing of sequences.

The Institute of Design

There was yet a third force for the advancement of photography as an art form: The New Bauhaus – later known as the Chicago School of Design (today known as the Illinois Institute of Design), which based its teaching of photography on the pedagogical principles of the original Bauhaus. It advocated the merging of art and daily life through the application of clean-lined but aesthetically pleasing design principles. Unlike Pictorialism and the Group f.64, which were essentially photographer-led associations, the New Bauhaus was obviously a structured and institutionalized learning experience. The aesthetic that emerged from it was formalist and personal. Founded in 1937 by László Moholy-Nagy, the school lasted only for one year and then reopened in 1939 as The School of Design, by which it was known until 1944.

As a former teacher at the Bauhaus in Weimar and Dessau, László Moholy-Nagy brought a wealth of knowledge about the New Vision and the relationship between form and function, as well as the pertinence of art to society. He advocated fiercely for photography and film as the new literacy. His four-point approach was described as follows: "first: photography was taught as a basic understanding of light and the manipulation of light; second, it was recognized as central to modern vision, a fundamental part of what Moholy believed it meant to say that someone was literate; third, photography was integrated into a complete art and design curriculum; and fourth, it was taught experimentally, not rigidly or dogmatically or commercially."[25]

After Moholy-Nagy's death in 1946, two influential twentieth-century photographers, Harry Callahan and Aaron Siskind, would be brought to teach in the department of photography.

It was at the Detroit Photo Guild that Harry Callahan, a member since 1940,[26] first met Arthur Siegel, the man who would bring him to the Institute of Design in 1946.[27] Callahan's turning point occurred in 1941 when, as part of the Photo Guild's program, Ansel Adams came to Detroit for two weekend-long workshops.[28] Taking full advantage of the master photographer's presence, Callahan followed him around and bombarded him with technical questions, the answers to which he duly recorded in a notebook that was to become "his bible." His first viewing of Adams' *Surf Sequence* (cat. 3) occurred at this time and was a revelation for Callahan,[29] inspiring him to make sequences himself. In the same year Callahan and his wife visited Alfred Stieglitz at an American Place. While Callahan claimed not to have been impressed by the Stieglitz photographs that he saw on that occasion, he later admitted to having been strongly affected by his cloud sequences.[30] For Callahan things personal were closely linked to his photography, a quality that is apparent in his work by the formal and yet intimate syntax that he employed in the rigorous composition of his images. "I am interested," he wrote in an early statement of purpose, "in relating the problems that affect me, to some set of values that I am trying to discover and establish as being my life. I want to discover and establish them through photography."[31]

Callahan first met Aaron Siskind in New York in 1948 when he attended an exhibition at the Museum of Modern Art that included several of his works. The resulting friendship led Siskind to join Callahan at the Institute of Design.

While Callahan was interested in painting and recalled having been impressed by Stuart Davies' paintings of torn posters, Siskind was intensely inspired by painting. He formed part of a small circle of friends that included the abstract expressionist painters Adolf Gottlieb and Mark Rothko. Like Callahan, Siskind combined a highly personal style of expression with a consciously formalist approach to photography and used the flat planar surface of a sheet of film in much the same way that a painter uses a canvas to describe complex, abstract, and ambiguous formal relationships.

Documentary Photography
Capturing a Society in Flux

Outside of the intense and sheltered world of Pictorialism, the early years of the twentieth century saw world events that would sweep Western societies along inalterable courses, and social and technological changes that would transform daily life.

By 1903 the Suffragette movement was gaining momentum, the Wright Brothers had made their first flight, *Camera Work* was established, and Lewis Hine had begun to use a camera. Although Pictorialist photography garnered attention based on the merits of its own strongly developed aesthetic and through its close association with the influential Photo-Secession group and 291, it was not the only practice to leave a lasting effect on American culture in the first decades of the twentieth century.

Wisconsin-born Lewis Wickes Hine moved to New York in 1901 from Chicago, where he had been studying at the University of Chicago, and took a job as an assistant teacher at the Ethical Culture School. Under the sage and innovative leadership of social reformer Felix Adler, founder and rector of the school, Hine was encouraged to develop in his students an awareness of one of the most significant of the sweeping changes occurring in the country: the steady influx of hundreds of thousands of new immigrants that had been occurring since 1890 and would continue unabated until the outbreak of World War I. Adler wanted his students to hold these people in the same regard as they did their Americans forefathers. Hine photographed the new arrivals at Ellis Island for five years, during which time he also turned his attention to recording immigrant families after they settled. Hine also captured other events that were unfolding, such as the fallout from the 1907 market crash, known as The Panic, in his photographs of men in a bread line.

From 1906 until 1918 Hine made photographs for the National Child Labour Committee, recording children employed in cotton plantations and mills, factories, the fishing industry (cat. 32) and in the beet, berry, and tobacco fields of the South.

The demands for his photographs were such that Hine gave up teaching to devote himself full time to documenting social issues.[32] He became the principal supplier of images over the years for publications such as *The Child Labour Bulletin*, *Charities and Commons*, and *The Survey*. While he carried on Jacob Riis' tradition of photographing the underclass,[33] Hine approached his subjects with greater sensitivity to their plights.

As conscious as Hine was of the power of the camera to record social injustices, he described himself early in his career, on his photographer's stamp, as an Interpretive Photographer, and retained a respect for the camera as an instrument of artistic expression, writing in 1906: "A good photograph is not a mere reproduction of an object … it is an interpretation."[34] Although capable of making aesthetically composed works, Hine's photographs stand in stark contrast to the Photo-Secession and Pictorialist schools by appearing to be almost accidental in composition. Printed on gelatin silver paper, his images are small and unassuming. They were made without artifice and almost in a snapshot aesthetic, indicating that Hine knew that to maintain credibility with his professional audience, he could not afford to engage in artful composition or seductive printing techniques. His photographs were highly effective in mobilizing public opinion against child labour and are often cited as having been instrumental in the introduction of legislation banning the practice. It is this incidental appearance of these photographs that make the images of the immigrants and child labourers so poignant. Hine's approach would provide an important touchstone for photographers like Paul Strand and Walker Evans. His images continue to attract us with their honesty and for the fresh record that they provide of the past.

The rise of industrialization and increasing urbanization of the late nineteenth and early twentieth centuries elicited increasing interest in the documentation of the indigenous people of North America whose cultures and autonomy had been slowly eroding. While Adam Clark Vroman approached this subject in ways that, to our contemporary eye, appear less sensational and more empathetic, it was the work of Edward C. Curtis that captured the public imagination. A rather deplorable offshoot of this mood of nostalgia that surrounded the recently defeated indigenous people was Buffalo Bill's Wild West show, which also provided Gertrude Käsebier with some of her portrait subjects.

Pictorialism and the social document became subject to adaptations and new thinking as the first half of the century progressed in America. While the approach to photography as an art form became increasingly self-critical and complex, embracing sequencing and serial modes of presentation, so the documentary approach evolved into a more self-conscious form of expression, rejecting manipulation of the negative and seeking more comprehensive treatment of subjects. The notion that these two directions were irreconcilably oppositional would be mediated through the work of Walker Evans, making vernacular subject matter legitimate content for artistic exploration. This dialogue between distinct approaches yielded a fertile field of creative practices.

Photo League

American photographers' engagement with the camera as a tool for witnessing social change was probably never as acute as in the period from the mid 1930s to the late 1940s, when the country saw the socially oriented regime under President Franklin Delano Roosevelt, with its New Deal Programs, decline into a culture of mistrust with the witch hunt conducted by the House Un-American Activities Committee (HUAC) in concert with the Federal Bureau of Investigation. Two important social documentary programs were established: the Photo League, a local photographer-driven organization, and the photographic unit of the Farm Security Administration (FSA) and its parent body, the Works Progress Administration (WPA), whose reach was national and federally funded. In no other time was Lewis Hine's legacy made so apparent.

Founded in 1930, New York's Film and Photo League was a cultural wing of the Workers' International Relief and contained within it was a camera league whose members supplied photographs to publications like the *New Masses* and *Daily Worker*. In 1934 dissension developed within the film group and by 1936 the photographers had separated and established themselves as the Photo League.[35] The group would be an important force, attracting young photographers to their 21st Street space,[36] which was equipped with a darkroom, to look at the photographs they exhibited on a regular basis and to attend organized talks and workshops established to educate people about photography and its social import.

The program at the League was externally focused with group leaders taking members onto the streets of particular districts of New York to photograph life in the city. The photographs made on these outings would be critiqued back in the rooms of the Photo League. The imagery was, as to be expected, focused on the daily lives of ordinary people. Some photographers, possibly influenced by members Weegee (Arthur Fellig) or Lisette Model, revelled in social satire, as did Arthur Leipzig in his photograph of opera attendees (cat. 39). Many photographers of a younger generation who became members, or simply attended events, would later refer to the lasting influence that the organization had on their lives and their work. Arthur Leipzig, born in Brooklyn to an orthodox Jewish couple, gravitated to the League after an industrial accident, in search of a possible métier. Enrolling in a workshop at the Photo League in 1942, he claimed that Sid Grossman and Paul Strand, two of his teachers there, shaped his vision and exerted a lifelong influence over his work.

While painters might have seen everyday reality simply as good subject matter, the League photographers – perhaps because of the peculiar relationship of photography to reality – saw it as politically loaded and understood their photographs to be evidence of the need for social reform. This perhaps ingenuous view of the photograph as a purveyor of truth and catalyst for social change sometimes led to ideological strife within the organization. Aaron Siskind, a politically aware and early subscriber to the group would eventually resign from the League in opposition to the view that the attributes of a "good photograph" rested too heavily on its content and not sufficiently on its aesthetic and technical properties or print quality. Siskind's concerns were held by some members not only to be secondary, but bourgeois and irrelevant.

The House Un-American Activities Committee established in 1938 would investigate the Photo League on the grounds that it was a Communist front. Established to identify those who were affiliated with the Communist Party, HUAC took a devastating toll on human lives and taxed the ability of artists who were either blacklisted or placed on the National Security Index to make a living in their own country. The Photo League closed in 1951 after having been placed on the Attorney General's blacklist as a subversive organization.

There were photographers working in New York making documentary photographs during this period whose careers were completely independent of organizations, even when, like Berenice Abbott, they might have had a membership in the Photo League. Abbott, through her association with French turn-of-the century photographer Eugène Atget (who recorded the streets and facades of Paris), produced an important corpus of photographs that includes her renowned *Changing New York* from the

1930s as well as scientific photographs recording specimens and physical principles. Margaret Bourke-White was a driven and highly successful photojournalist. Likewise, Andreas Feininger produced a large body of work documenting New York, Chicago, industry, and natural history artefacts.

WPA and FSA: *"The Cruel Radiance of What Is"*

In the aftermath of the 1929 economic collapse and the devastation caused by a series of droughts that struck America's food bowl throughout the 1930s, the government under Franklin Delano Roosevelt established the massive assistance program known as the New Deal. Among the numerous economic relief and recovery initiatives, the Works Progress Administration (renamed Work Projects Administration in 1939), the Resettlement Administration, and the Farm Security Administration would most benefit artists and photographers.

Sharply contrasting the urban character of the work of the Photo League, the Resettlement Administration and the Farm Security Administration dispatched photographers to rural America to document life on farms and in small towns and communities.[37] While the Photo League photographers were political by nature, economist Roy Stryker hired photographers to make photographic records of rural destitution and federal government efforts to alleviate it on the basis of their skills, although they too may have felt ideological empathy with the dispossessed. Furthermore, the Photo League photographers determined the subjects they would photograph, whereas the Farm Security Administration economists such as Tugwell and Stryker set the agenda and the itineraries for those photographers. Both Tugwell and Stryker were knowledgeable about American documentary photography and if any photographer provided a model for them it was Lewis Hine. The "shooting scripts" the photographers were originally given were vague and directed largely toward production and processing of agricultural goods.[38] Rather than tell them precisely what or how to photograph, Stryker preferred to rely on the photographers' perceptiveness. "They were intelligent people reporting things that they felt and saw based upon past experience, based upon a good deal of investigation. And above all else, particularly as regards the human side of this, a sincere, passionate love of people, and respect for people."[39] Dorothea Lange and Walker Evans are the two photographers represented in this catalogue who worked for the Farm Security Administration.[40]

Both Lange and Evans were well-established photographers before joining Stryker's staff and their styles were already formed. Notorious for his independent streak, Evans resisted ideological labelling. He confessed to being politically confused, and took umbrage at the Photo League's unauthorized use of his name as a sponsor. When Roy Stryker invited him in 1935 to join his team of photographers at the FSA, Evans agreed on the condition that Stryker would not interfere in any way with his work.[41] He was apparently the only photographer allowed to dictate such terms. His friend Jay Leyda confirmed Evans' political neutrality, stating, "He had his own cause – maybe it was that of anonymous people – at heart."[42] Ultimately, it is probably fair to say that Evans was not a team player and when his employment was terminated at the FSA in 1938 it was because Stryker, forced to cut staff, had tired of what he perceived as Evans' lack of cooperation.[43]

Dorothea Lange was also an independent spirit. She had demonstrated this when she made her photograph *White Angel Breadline* (cat. 37) by responding spontaneously to the sight of homeless men lining up in a breadline. She also acted without a shooting script when she went off the beaten path to photograph pea pickers, a decision that resulted in her powerful *Migrant Mother* image (cat. 38). She too was considered uncooperative by Stryker, who fired her more than once.[44] Unlike Walker Evans, however, Lange's natural allegiances were to the left of the political spectrum. Even though she was based in California when the Photo League formed in 1936, she supported it with operating and scholarship funds, gave talks there when in New York, and remained part of its membership even when the League had been blacklisted by the Attorney General in the late 1940s.[45] Lange's brand of humanism is arguably more easily identified than Evans'. Although humanity moved him, it is not so clear that individuals – particularly those close to him – touched him in the same way. Commenting on his photograph of a Penny Picture display (fig. 13), he makes both his tenderness toward humanity and his amusement at the replicative nature of the photographic act apparent: "It's uproariously funny, and very touching and very sad and very human. Documentary, very real, very complex. All these people had posed in front of the local studio camera, and I bring my camera, and they all pose again together for me. That's a fabulous fact. I look at it and think, and think, and think about all those people."[46]

The year that he was fired from the FSA, the Museum of Modern Art in New York, soon to open a department of photographs, honoured Evans' achievements in their first one-man exhibition and published a book of his work that would prove to be seminal to the history of twentieth-century American photography: *American Photographs*.

If ever there was an antidote to Pictorialism it was in the work of Walker Evans. He is said to have hated the word nostalgic. Describing his working method, his friend Lincoln Kirstein noted how precise Evans was in his quest for clarity. "In order to force details into their firmest relief, he could only work in brilliant sunlight, and the sun had to be on the correct side of the streets. Often many trips to the same house were necessary to avoid shadows cast by trees or other houses; only the spring and fall were favorable seasons."[47] Evans scorned conventional or sanctioned subject matter. "I'm interested in what's called vernacular," Evans once said, "… educated architecture doesn't interest me, but I love to find American vernacular."[48] As far as photography as both an art and a document is concerned, Walker Evans is an essential part of the American twentieth-century photographic narrative. If there is something reminiscent of Lewis Hine in his vernacular photographs, there is a great deal of Walker Evans residual in the post-1950 generation of photographers who would be assembled under the rubric of the New Topographics.

Evans' ability to look without sentimentality or partisanship at the world around him would also leave an impression on Robert Frank, the young Swiss photographer who arrived in New York in 1947 anxious to explore the larger world, and whose poetic yet edgy 1956 publication *The Americans*, along with the work of Diane Arbus is pivotal to the evolution of American photography post-1950.

Over the five decades covered here, photography in the United States acquired a respected status in the art world, attracting the attention of critics, artists, and an art-loving public, and convincing the gatekeepers of high art. This was largely the result of a network of ideas, people, institutions and initiatives across the United States that spread from the desire to advance and explore photography in all of its manifestations: art, social document, and illustration. Each photographer who ventured into the unknown, who extended the boundaries of the medium, has left a part of a greater legacy that would nourish future generations both within and beyond the borders of the United States. Stieglitz dominated the first half of the century as a force to be both followed and rebelled against. Would Walker Evans or Paul Strand have evolved as they did without Lewis Hine? Would Diane Arbus have had the courage to journey into uncharted psychological terrain without the example of Lisette Model? Each element of these human and institutional endeavours contributed to this rich mosaic of activity and to the lively intellectual parrying that marks the period.

All of these efforts, whether organizational or discursive, political or personal, created a legacy that keeps the art form alive within the creative maelstrom of American culture today.

Fig. 13   Walker Evans, *Penny Picture Display, Savannah*, March 1936?, printed April 1969, gelatin silver print, National Gallery of Canada, Ottawa (21737)

Note to the Reader

Dimensions for prints – height × width in centi-
metres – are for the image/sheet. If the image
is smaller than the sheet, the size of each is noted
separately. Inscriptions are handwritten by the
artist; annotations are by others, or are printed
mechanically.

Abbreviations

u.l.	upper left
u.c.	upper centre
u.r.	upper right
c.l.	centre left
c.	centre
c.r.	centre right
l.l.	lower left
l.c.	lower centre
l.r.	lower right
t.	along or at the top
b.	along or at the bottom
l.	left
r.	right
[...]	an erased or illegible portion of the inscription or annotation

Catalogue

1 Berenice Abbott

Springfield, Ohio 1898–1991 Monson, Maine
What One Artist Craftsman Works With **1947**
Gelatin silver print, 23.8 × 19.3 cm
26639

Inscriptions   **verso, c., graphite,** *Berenice Abbott*

Annotations   **verso, c., magenta ink stamp,** *BERENICE ABBOTT / PHOTOGRAPH / 50 COMMERCE STREET / NEW YORK 14, N.Y.,* **l.l., graphite,** *2059.1 Box 11*

Provenance   **Purchased from Lunn Gallery, Washington, DC, 1981 (Phyllis Lambert Fund)**

The detailed and loving attention that Berenice Abbott pays to the arrangement of various saws, wrenches, clamps, drills, drill bits, pliers and mallets, among other items in the studio of Japanese-American sculptor Isamu Noguchi (1904–1988), attests to her own experience working in sculpture. In 1921, Abbott left New York for Europe, where she would spend the next two years pursuing her interests at the Académie de la Grande Chaumière, in Paris, and at the Kunstschule in Berlin.[1] Working as an assistant in Man Ray's Paris studio from 1923 to 1925, she made the acquaintance of French photographer Eugène Atget and began to pursue photography as her chosen medium. Abbott and Noguchi's paths first crossed in Paris,[2] where he worked for six months in Constantin Brancusi's studio during a two-year sojourn on a Guggenheim Fellowship between 1927 and 1929.[3] They both returned to New York in 1929.

By titling this work *What One Artist Craftsman Works With*, Abbott alludes to the community of like-minded artists she was surrounded by and whom she admired. The status of "craftsman" did not carry derogatory connotations for her. To the contrary, craftsmanship ranked high in her understanding of how a successful work of art was created. In her view, both technical skill and aesthetic intelligence were fundamental requirements in creative expression and this array of tools in Noguchi's studio – framed on the left by measuring instruments, the T-square and transparent right-angle – conveyed his astonishing ability to invent extraordinary forms in stone, wood and sheet metal, using workaday tools.

Embracing the chaotic order in Noguchi's studio – boring, cutting and shaping tools in the upper tiers, paints and solvents in the shelf underneath, and a sea of paper work in the lower third of the image – Abbott pays homage in this finely composed picture to masterpieces by Eugène Atget, as well as John Frederick Peto (1854–1907) (fig. 1.1) and Walker Evans (fig. 1.2). Continuing a tradition of American art that celebrates the things of everyday life in pictorial form, Peto and Evans were also honouring a tradition of trompe l'oeil painting that embraced the display of found objects. However, Walker Evans, who made a stunning series of photographs of tools for *Fortune* magazine, went further and saw elegance in banal objects, such as these dustpans and brooms in a hardware store window. Abbott also invites us, in her richly detailed print, to discover beauty in our experience of the everyday.

Fig. 1.1   John Frederick Peto, *Office Board*, 1885, oil on canvas.
Metropolitan Museum of Art, New York, George A. Hearn Fund.
1955 (55.176)

Fig. 1.2   Walker Evans, *Window Display, Bethlehem, Pennsylvania*,
1935, printed later, gelatin silver print. National Gallery of Canada,
Ottawa, Gift of Phyllis Lambert, Montreal, 1982 (19506)

2   Berenice Abbott
Springfield, Ohio 1898–1991 Monson, Maine
Transformation of Energy c. 1955
Gelatin silver print, 26.3 × 34.3 cm
26634

Inscriptions   secondary support, graphite, l.r. below image, *BERENICE ABBOTT*

Annotations   verso of secondary support, l.c., black ink stamp, *PHOTOGRAPH / BERENICE ABBOTT / ABBOTT, MAINE 04406*, l.l., graphite, *5153.7*

Provenance   **Purchased from Lunn Gallery, Washington, DC, 1981 (Lunn inventory # 5153.7)**

Berenice Abbott called her photographs of scientific subject matter the "gutsy stuff." This focus took hold in 1939 and she continued to experiment with it into the late 1950s. Although these works shared a similar precision and clarity with the work of some of her European counterparts, including Karl Blossfeldt and Ernst Fuhrmann, Abbott focused predominantly on the illustration of principles of physics rather than the European tendency toward botanical subjects and patterns in nature. Abbott's crisp, high contrast prints reflected an engagement with mechanical principles and an excitement about science and its relationship to photography. In her *New Guide to Better Photography*, she describes photography as the link between art and science:

> Photography is a new way of making pictures and a new way of seeing. Indeed, the vision of the twentieth century may be said to have been created by photography. Our familiar awareness of the visual world has been evolved for us not alone by the eye but by the camera, used for myriad purposes. The very character of the medium, its dualistic science-art aspects, is the index of its contemporaneity. It took the modern period, based on science to develop an art from scientific sources.[1]

By rejecting what might be called science-inspired photography as "mere by-play," and also disdaining a category of straight scientific visual documentation for being dull, she placed great value on maintaining a balance between truth to her subject matter and graphically strong composition.[2] Her first photographs of natural and mechanical objects made during the mid- to late 1940s were not made for any specific scientific purpose, but simply reflected her fascination with the forms and structures of animate and inanimate objects. An inventor, experimenter and innovator in photography's technical aspects, she devised a technique that she called "projection photography" or Supersight in the early 1940s. This involved projecting and enlarging the subject directly onto a 16 × 20-inch piece of paper or film. Her photographs of birds' wings, fish (fig. 2.1), moths and insects, enlarged to 16 by 20 inches, use this technique.[3]

Two appointments provided Abbott with the opportunity to produce a serious body of scientific photography: in 1944 she became photography editor of *Science Illustrated*, and in 1958 she was hired to work with a group of scientists and high school science teachers in a team known as the Physical Sciences Study Committee (PSSC).[4] Addressing the need to improve science education in the United States following the successful launch of the Soviet satellite Sputnik,[5] in 1957, the group selected images by Abbott similar to *Transformation of Energy* to illustrate two high school text books.[6] Several of the photographs show aspects of motion imperceptible to human vision, such as in *Cycloid* (fig. 2.2). Abbott's photographs from this period were acknowledged for their formal beauty by American historian of photography Beaumont Newhall, who noted that "all the drama, beauty, and arresting suspense of the physical laws and the natural phenomena are excitingly presented."[7]

Fig. 2.1   Berenice Abbott, *Untitled (Fish Head, Supersight)*, c. 1945, gelatin silver print. National Gallery of Canada, Ottawa, Gift of Dorothy Meigs Eidlitz, St. Andrews, New Brunswick, 1968 (20503)

Fig. 2.2   Berenice Abbott, *Cycloid: A Light Trace by Time Exposure*, 1958–60, gelatin silver print. National Gallery of Canada, Ottawa, Lisette Model Archive

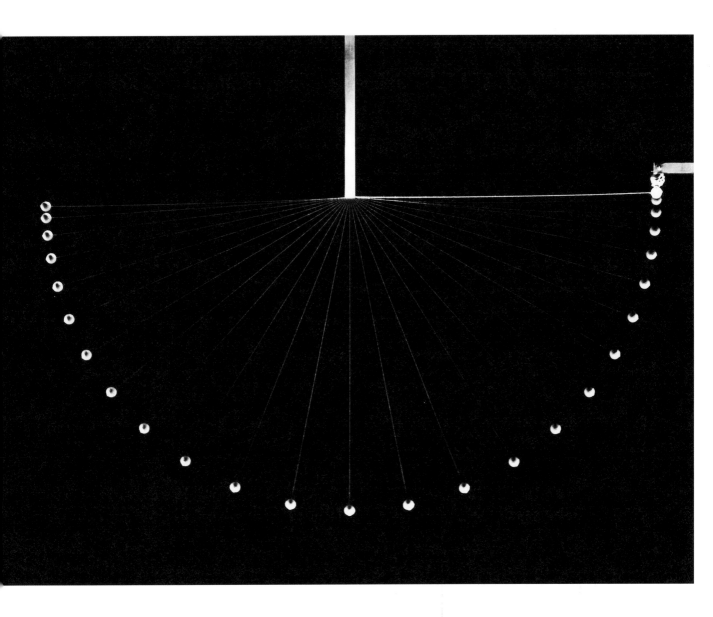

3   Ansel Adams

San Francisco 1902–1984 Monterey, California

Surf Sequence, Nos. 1–5, San Mateo County Coast, California 1940, printed 1981
27.8 × 32.6 cm, 27.9 × 32.4 cm, 27.9 × 32.6 cm, 28 × 32.5 cm, 28 × 32.3 cm
29743, 29744, 29745, 29998, 29999

(Inscriptions and annotations are identical for each image in series, with the exception of sequence and identification numbers annotated on verso.)

Inscriptions   **secondary support, l.r., graphite, *Ansel Adams***

Annotations   **secondary support, verso, c., black ink stamp with black ink additions, *Photograph by Ansel Adams / Museum Set Edition / Route 1 Box 181 Carmel, California 93923 / Surf Sequence number one / San Mateo County Coast California / Negative made c –1940 / Print made 1981 / Identification number 5301***

Provenance   **Purchased from Harry H. Lunn, Jr., New York, 1987**

By the time Ansel Adams made this sequence of photographs, his reputation as a photographer of nature was firmly established and his commitment to the preservation of wilderness affirmed through his association with the Sierra Club. He was also engaged at this time in establishing the first department of photographs at the MoMA, and had several publications to his credit. His sublime *Yosemite Half-Dome* had entered into the American imagination as the photographic equivalent of Albert Bierstadt's epic views of the landscape of the American West.

One morning, driving along California's coastal Highway One, just south of San Francisco, Adams was struck with the idea of making a sequence: "At one location I noted that below me was a nice curve of rockfall fronting the beach. The surf was streaming over the beach, barely touching the rocks and creating one beautiful pattern after another. I realized that I could perhaps make a series of images that might become a sequence …"[1]

He took nine exposures over a twenty-minute period, but in the end, only five met his aesthetic criteria. Writing about *Surf Sequence #3*, John Szarkowski notes, "This picture is one of a series of five, all made within the span of a few minutes from the same camera position. Each defines in photographic terms a momentary configuration of water and light that is unique and unrepeatable, and only half apprehensible to the most alert trained eye."[2]

Made some fifteen years after Alfred Stieglitz's pioneering *Equivalents* series (see cat. 62), *Surf Sequence* was seen by Adams as a "progressive series of images of the same general subject."[3] This meant that it differed in nature from both the series of Stieglitz and the sequences of Minor White, both of whom were less intent on exploring the progressive temporal changes than on seeking symbolic associations in their sets of photographic images. Adams cites White's comment that "a sequence of several images can be thought of as a single statement."[4] At once both cinematographic and musical in its rhythmic progression of images,[5] this sequence was perhaps more inspired by cinematography than by Stieglitz's investigations into the grouping of photographs as a way of expanding the syntax of the photograph. There is also a significant difference between the graphic, almost musical relationships between Adams' images in *Surf Sequence* and the metaphoric nature of Minor White's 1948 sequence *Song Without Words* (see cat. 77).

Adams even went so far as to ensure that, although each of the five images had different exposures due to the changing light conditions, they were tonally harmonious in the printing and were uniformly cropped. His lack of insistence on a fixed chronological order also suggests that the images were created to work graphically in any sequence.

"It is possible to determine the actual sequence of the exposures by observing the movement of the shadows on the rocks, caused by the rising sun behind me," he wrote. He also added the caveat that "the chronological sequence is not especially important, and the prints can be displayed in any order desired."[6]

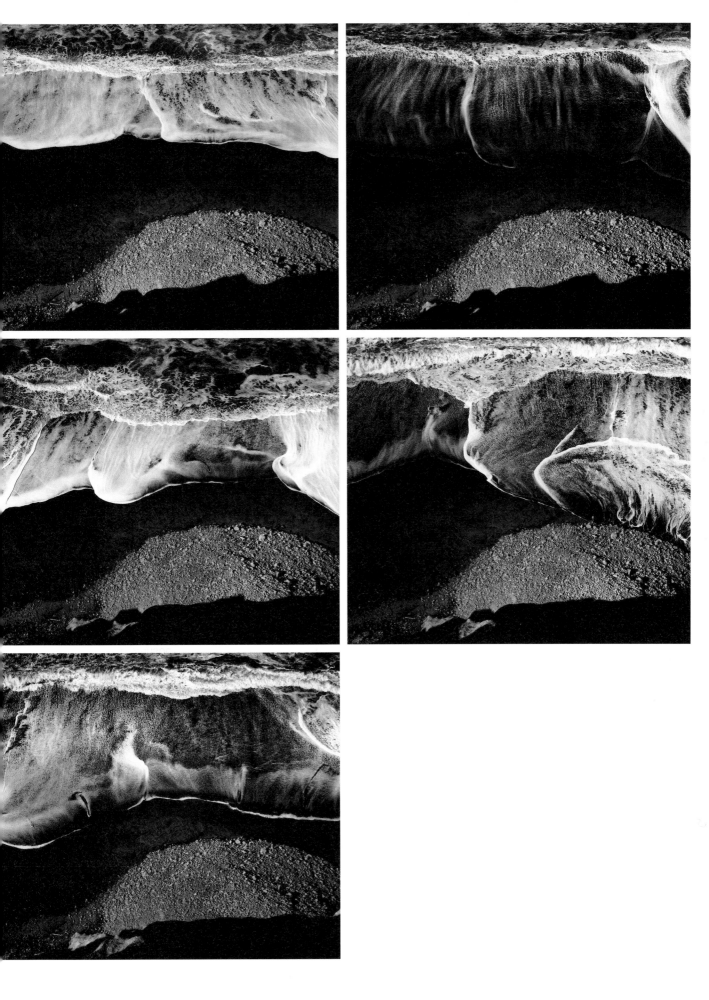

San Francisco 1902–1984 Monterey, California
Moonrise, Hernandez, New Mexico 1 November 1941, printed before February 1974
Gelatin silver print, 38.8 × 49.3 cm
20523

Inscriptions	secondary support, l.r. below image, graphite, *Ansel Adams*
Annotations	secondary support, verso, c. grey ink stamp
Provenance	purchased from the artist, Carmel, California, 1974

By far one of the most iconic images of the twentieth century, *Moonrise, Hernandez, New Mexico* attracts us not only for the brilliance of its skilful composition and its technical virtuosity but also for the haunting otherworldliness created by the combination of impending darkness and the soft illumination of a late afternoon light.

A combination of serendipity and quick-wittedness came into play one November[1] day in 1941 when Ansel Adams, en route to Sante Fe, spotted the moon making its appearance in the late afternoon sky over the Sangre de Cristo mountains. Further dramatizing the moment and transforming what might otherwise have been a commonplace scene was the darkening shadow falling over a group of houses and the adjacent cemetery.

Adams recognized how quickly he would have to assemble his large-format camera, light meter, and tripod if he were to succeed in capturing the passing gleam of sunlight on the clouds and the white crosses before the entire scene plunged into shadow. Unable to locate his light meter, he was "at a loss with the subject luminance values," as he later confessed.[2] On the verge of making several exposures at different settings and speeds, it suddenly dawned on him that he knew the luminance value of the moon (250 foot-candles) and was consequently able to make an exposure which would, at least, capture detail in the brighter parts of the scene.

Although there are reputed to be close to 1300 prints of this image made from 1941 up until the time of Adams' death in 1985,[3] Adams acknowledged how challenging it was for him to make prints from this negative that he liked and given the variables of papers and toners. "It is safe to say that no two prints are precisely the same,"[4] he wrote.

Over time his interpretation of the negative changed. The sky in later prints of *Moonrise* is darker and there is an overall increase in contrast. His assistant Mary Street Alinder recalls Adams processing the negative and making the prints from it:

> *Moonrise* was Ansel's most difficult negative of all to print. Though he kept careful records of darkroom infor-
> mation on *Moonrise*, each time he set up the negative, he would again establish the procedure for this particular
> batch of prints because papers and chemicals were always variables not constants. After determining the gen-
> eral exposure for the print, he gave local exposure to specific areas. Using simple pieces of cardboard, Ansel
> would painstakingly burn in (darken with additional light from the enlarger) the sky, which was really quite pale
> with streaks of cloud throughout. He was careful to hold back a bit on the moon. … Ansel created Moonrise
> with a night sky, a luminous moon and an extraordinary cloud bank that seems to reflect the moon's brilliance.
> Moonrise is sleight of hand. Moonrise is magic.[5]

It was around the time Adams made *Moonrise* that he began to concentrate on a series of landscapes taken in US national parks, in part sponsored by the Department of the Interior. Working on this project over several decades, he spent much of his time in the Southwest making photographs of its sublime and more intimate features (fig. 4.1). In so doing, he recapitulates the drama that his American painter predecessors experienced before their easels some eighty years earlier (fig. 4.2).[6]

Fig. 4.1   Ansel Adams, *Pinnacles, Alabama Hills, Owen Valley, California*, 1945, printed c. 1970–73, gelatin silver print. National Gallery of Canada, Ottawa (20522)

Fig. 4.2   Frederick Edwin Church, *Twilight in the Wilderness*, 1860, oil on canvas. The Cleveland Museum of Art, Mr. and Mrs. William H. Marlatt Fund (1965.233)

5 Margaret Bourke-White

New York 1904–1971 Stamford, Connecticut
Woman Who Has Just Obtained Meat after Waiting in Line, U.S.S.R. 1931
Gelatin silver print, 33.6 × 23.4 cm
20977

Annotations   secondary support, verso, u.c., typewritten label, *U.S.S.R. / - woman who has / just obtained meat after /
waiting in line*, u.c., black ink stamp, *A / MARGARET BOURKE-WHITE / PHOTOGRAPH*

Provenance   purchased from Elizabeth Stern, Ottawa, 1981 (Phyllis Lambert Fund)

The daughter of Joseph White, an engineer and designer employed in the printing industry, and Minnie Bourke, who taught blind children to read,[1] Margaret Bourke-White studied at the Clarence White School of Photography at Columbia University,[2] and in 1927 graduated with a degree in biology from Cornell.[3] During her student years Bourke-White took pictures for the school papers and photographed people's homes on commission.[4] Later, at the age of twenty-six, she opened her own studio in the newly erected Chrysler Building and hired a number of studio technicians.

Bourke-White embraced a wide range of subject matter, from industry, New York architecture of the 1930s, scenes of human deprivation during the Depression, the Second World War, the independence of India, and apartheid in 1950s South Africa. Some of her most enduring images, however, describe pre-World War II Europe. In 1930, she undertook her first of many visits to the Soviet Union. She also travelled to Germany and to the areas around Poland, Hungary and Czechoslovakia that became political pawns in the heightening power struggle between Germany, the USSR and the neighbouring countries.

Published in the first of six articles on the Soviet Union, written and illustrated by Bourke-White for the *New York Times Magazine*, this image was made during her second trip, in 1931. For the magazine, it was curiously titled *Daughters of the Soil – Women of the Changing Soviet Order*, which would seem to illustrate the elevation of peasant life in the service of ideology, rather than evoking ideals of the "new women."[5] Artists such as Lyubov Popova and Varvara Stepanova come to mind when one thinks of the liberated Russian women of the period. Bourke-White's article was primarily devoted to the role of women's fashion and its place – or lack thereof – under the Five Year Plan,[6] and thus neglects to mention that the women in *Woman Who Has Just Obtained Meat after Waiting in Line, U.S.S.R.* were photographed in the steel manufacturing centre, Magnitogorsk, which Bourke-White visited in 1931. Like many idealistic, socially minded young intellectuals from Europe and the United States, Bourke-White was interested in the social revolution occurring under Communism.

During her first (self-financed) five-week trip in the summer of 1930, Bourke-White so impressed Soviet officials with her photographs of industry that they invited her back in 1931 under the auspices of the Soviet government. A cropped version of a variant showing a larger group (fig. 5.1), this image and *State Farm No. 2, Verblud, U.S.S.R.* (fig. 5.2)[7] illustrate how effortlessly Bourke-White could accommodate the new realist style favoured in the Soviet Union at the time, a significant factor in her acquisition of a travel visa to that country.[8]

Unbeknownst to Bourke-White, as her enthusiasm for the social experiment taking place in the Soviet Union grew, so did American mistrust and fear of the USSR. Her trips there would, within a decade, be viewed with suspicion and, under the powers invested in the House Un-American Committee (HUAC), these forays and the photographs that she brought back with her would eventually be used to brand her as a Communist sympathizer.[9]

Fig. 5.1   Margaret Bourke-White, *Russian woman grimly holding a slab of meat as other peasant women staunchly stand by*, 1931, gelatin silver print. Time & Life Pictures/Getty Images (50621810)

Fig. 5.2   Margaret Bourke-White, *State Farm No. 2, Verblud, U.S.S.R.*, 1930, gelatin silver print. National Gallery of Canada, Ottawa (20975)

6 Margaret Bourke-White
New York 1904–1971 Stamford, Connecticut
George Washington Bridge 1933
Gelatin silver print, 34.6 × 22.6 cm
41282

Inscriptions   secondary support, l.r., graphite, *Bourke / White*

Annotations   secondary support, verso, u.c., black ink stamp, *A / MARGARET BOURKE-WHITE PHOTOGRAPH*, l.c., graphite, *#26 Geo. Washington Bridge / PF43624H*

Provenance   St. Louis, Missouri, thrift shop, bought by Linda Hartman, c. 1997; e-Bay auction, bought by Lee Gallery, Winchester, Massachusetts, c. 1999; bought by Howard Greenberg Gallery, New York, 2001; purchased from Howard Greenberg Gallery, 2003

In January 1933 Ralph McAllister Ingersoll, associate editor of *Fortune* magazine, asked Margaret Bourke-White to consider making a series of photographs of some of the structures under the jurisdiction of the Port of New York Authority, to appear in the September 1933 issue of the magazine.[1] This extraordinary image of the George Washington Bridge, taken just two years after its opening, was a result of that assignment. At the time of its completion in 1931, the George Washington Bridge, was one of the longest single span suspension bridges in the world. Designed by Swiss-American engineer Othmar H. Amman, it connected Fort Lee, New Jersey and Upper Manhattan across the Hudson River, and the Port of New York Authority was justifiably proud of it.

The choice of Bourke-White as the photographer best suited to capture the "engineering miracle" of the Port Authority's sites, was based on her earlier work in industrial settings. In fact, it might be said that she had become pigeonholed as an industrial or corporate photographer and not typically called upon to capture the "human content" of a story.[2] In correspondence that followed their discussion of the terms of the assignment, Ingersoll informs Bourke-White, "We shall also use photographs of individuals, but as I explained to you, we will get these elsewhere."[3]

In 1928, when she was just twenty-four and starting her career as a professional photographer, Bourke-White received a commission to document the Otis Steel Mills in Cleveland. This assignment established her reputation as an able and adventurous photographer of industrial subject matter. It was followed by commissions to photograph for Detroit automobile companies around 1929 and by self-initiated trips to Russia undertaken in 1931 and 1932.

Subjects of industry and massive engineering feats were popular amongst poets, writers and visual artists in North America during the 1920s. Bridges held a particular fascination for American artists of this period, as evidenced by Joseph Stella's paintings of the Brooklyn Bridge, made from the teens through to the 1940s, and Hart Crane's epic poem *The Bridge*, published by Black Sun Press in 1930. Stella's highly abstracted view of the Brooklyn Bridge painted in 1936 (fig. 6.1) complements the clean-lined severity of the Bourke-White image. Like the Brooklyn Bridge, the George Washington Bridge offered artists the opportunity to explore extreme perspectives and complex geometry. Renowned French architect Le Corbusier (Charles-Édouard Jeanneret) was rhapsodic in his description of it, declaring it, "the most beautiful bridge in the world… the only seat of grace in the disordered city."[4] Andreas Feininger (see cats. 23–25) a photographer whose oeuvre celebrated equally the microcosm of nature and the macrocosm of the built environment, was equally captivated by the bridge's dynamic perspective and vibrant linear forms (fig. 6.2).

40 Catalogue

Fig. 6.1   Joseph Stella, *Bridge*, 1936, oil on canvas. San Francisco Museum of Modern Art, The United States General Services Administration, formerly Federal Works Agency, Works Projects Administration, allocated to the San Francisco Museum of Modern Art (3760.43)

Fig. 6.2   Andreas Feininger, *George Washington Bridge*, January 1948, gelatin silver print. National Gallery of Canada, Ottawa (42732)

7 Margaret Bourke-White
New York 1904–1971 Stamford, Connecticut
Boys Studying Talmud, Orthodox Jewish School, Uzhorod 1938
Gelatin silver print, 25.8 × 33.8 cm
41745

Inscriptions   secondary support, l.r., graphite, *Bourke / White*, verso, c., graphite, *Carpatho-Ruthenia / Orthodox Jewish school / at Uzhorod. / Boys studying Talmud*

Annotations   secondary support, verso, u.c., red ink stamp, *A / MARGARET BOURKE-WHITE / PHOTOGRAPH*

Provenance   Swann Galleries, New York, 2003; purchased from Jane Corkin Shopland, Toronto, 2006

Margaret Bourke-White, one of the most versatile photographers of the twentieth century, was capable of switching from a dynamic modernist style in her photographs of industrial machinery and state-of-the art bridges to a less artful and more contextual approach when documenting workers and events in the Soviet Union during the three trips she made there in the 1930s.

This image dates to Bourke-White's documentary phase, when she privileged the illustration of content over purely formalist exploration, an approach that differed from the Pictorialist or modernist styles of photography, both of which were popular at the time. Made in 1938 when Bourke-White was once again travelling in western and central Europe, this photograph refers back to an image that she made in 1932 (fig. 7.1) of school children seated in a classroom in Kolomna in the western Soviet Union. While the children in the 1932 photograph, with their solemn ghost-like faces, stare fixedly at the photographer, *Boys Studying Talmud* captures not only the look of absorption in the children's faces but also their relationship to one another as they read under the watchful guidance of their teacher. *Boys Studying Talmud* transcends straightforward reportage and becomes an expressive group portrait.

In its indiscriminate capture of visual data, the camera often records "sub-plots" that the photographer is unaware of until the negative is scrutinized later. A careful inspection of this image rewards us with just such a moment. In the far right of the picture along the bank of windows, we can see half the face of a young boy pressed against the window pane (fig. 7.2). He stares with intent curiosity into the classroom.

Munkacs (also known as Mukachevo), where this photograph was taken, lay within the administrative district of Uzhorod at the time. Located in Carpatho-Ruthenia (between Hungary and Poland), it was home to a thriving community of Galician and Hungarian Chasidic Jews, who made up almost half of the population up until 1944, when the city was pronounced *Judenrein* (cleansed of Jews). As much as we may enjoy the image for the moment it captures, in light of what we know about the history of the Jews of Carpatho-Ruthenia, it becomes a poignant, even painful, record.

Fig. 7.1   Margaret Bourke-White, *Village School, Kolomna, Volga Region,* 1932, gelatin silver print. National Gallery of Canada, Ottawa (20968)

Fig. 7.2   Margaret Bourke-White, *Boys Studying Talmud, Orthodox Jewish School, Uzhorod* (detail) 1938, gelatin silver print. National Gallery of Canada, Ottawa (41745)

8 Harry Callahan
Detroit 1912–1999 Atlanta, Georgia
Eleanor, Chicago **1949, printed before 1979**
Gelatin silver print, 18.2 × 16.8 cm, sheet 25.2 × 20.3 cm
23922

Inscriptions   l.r, graphite, *Harry Callahan*; verso, u.c., graphite, *Harry Callahan EM2*

Provenance   gift of Benjamin Greenberg, Ottawa, 1980

Born and raised in Detroit, Harry Callahan graduated from high school during the Depression. Finding himself without employment prospects, he enrolled at Michigan State College for engineering. Quickly deciding against a career in engineering, Callahan did not complete the program, taking instead a menial position at Chrysler Motor Parts Corporation. It was while he was employed there in 1938 that he was introduced to photography. This led to his joining the Detroit Camera Guild and a fortuitous encounter with photographer Todd Webb, who like Arthur Siegel, another Guild member, would remain a close friend. The appearance of Ansel Adams at the Guild for a workshop would focus Callahan's thinking about photography in a remarkable way. Callahan clearly hung on to the master photographer's every word: "I took a notebook and asked him every technical question I could think of – [the] kind of papers he used, the developers and film. Everything."[1] Adams convinced Callahan of the merits of working with a large-format camera, inspiring him to trade in his enlarger for an 8 × 10 camera. There is no evidence, however, that Callahan attempted to adopt Adams' heroic style of picture-making.

A naturally reserved individual, Callahan found in photography another avenue of expression. It offered him a way to give substance to his place in the world, both in his familiar relationship to his family and in a larger, more anonymous social milieu.

By the late 1940s Callahan, who had been very impressed by the sequential nature of Ansel Adams' *Surf Sequence* (see cat. 3), was deeply engaged in producing a series of photographs of his wife, Eleanor. As Paul Sherman has noted, "Any presentation of Callahan's work must begin with studies of his wife Eleanor, the primary inspiration of his art."[2] This practice of posing Eleanor – and later, Eleanor with their daughter Barbara – in a variety of settings that ranged from the intimacy of the bedroom to the open spaces of the Chicago lakefront, street corners and parks, would continue into the 1950s.

Eleanor, Chicago is an iconic image from this series, evoking the idea of the woman as a primordial force as her form emerges from the surface of the water. It is not only the simplicity of the composition that is so striking, but also the photographer's ability to find within the experience of the everyday a moment of eternal import. Callahan was a most astute observer of what might be called "ordinary" life. He was at the farthest remove from the preordained subject matter of the Pictorialists, or the event driven culture of photojournalism, savoring every instant for its particularity and for the visual interest it could yield.

9 Harry Callahan

Detroit 1912–1999 Atlanta, Georgia
Chicago 1949
Gelatin silver print, 19.3 × 24.4 cm
26756

Inscriptions secondary support, l.r., graphite, 7662; verso, c., blue pencil, *Harry Callahan / Chicago 1949*

Annotations secondary support, verso, l.r., all on label, in letterpress, *VAN RIPER & THOMPSON, INC. / EL MOCHUELO GALLERY / 703 ANACAPA STREET / SANTA BARBARA, CALIFORNIA / 93101,* typewritten, *HARRY CALLAHAN / "Chicago 1949" / no.37*

Provenance purchased from the Yarlow/Salzman Gallery, Toronto, 1981

By the time Callahan made this striking image of the facade of a Chicago building in 1949, he was three years into what would become a fifteen-year teaching career at the Institute of Design in Chicago. As a result of the strong friendship that he had developed with fellow Detroit Camera Guild member, Arthur Siegel, Callahan was invited to join the faculty of the photography department in 1946. The school, originally established by László Moholy-Nagy in Chicago in 1937, was based on the model of the avant-garde German art school, the Bauhaus.[1]

Although Callahan's path would cross only briefly with that of Moholy-Nagy (the Hungarian-born artist died in 1946 just six months after Callahan had joined the staff) it is evident that these two individuals, albeit from disparate backgrounds, shared a common commitment to the concept of the new vision. Colleagues, students, friends and family remember Callahan as an almost compulsive photographer. He believed passionately in the kind of learning experience that close examination of the world around us offers, thus subscribing to at least two of Moholy's principles for the New Camera Vision – abstract seeing and exact seeing – as outlined in "The Eight Varieties of Photographic Vision," published in *Telehor* in 1936.[2]

Chicago was a city rich in architecture and street life, and it rewarded its observers handsomely. *Chicago,* a study of the rhythmic design of rounded window openings and their lively interplay with the linear geometry of fire escapes, is a photograph that reminds us of Callahan's love of music and its influence on his work.[3] While he specifically stated music as an influence in his photographs of pedestrians of the early 1940s, it is clear that he has transferred some of his appreciation of syncopation into the tonal and linear relationships found in this facade. Minor White noted that Callahan's building facades had an anthropomorphic quality to them, an observation that is borne out by a comparison between this image and the flattened-out, highly linear portrait of Eleanor made around 1947.

Although *Chicago* is an expression of the Institute's formalist approach to image-making, it retains qualities that are characteristic of Callahan's vision: direct composition, slightly eccentric focus on detailing, and his superb printmaking skills.

10 Harry Callahan
Detroit 1912–1999 Atlanta, Georgia
Chicago 1952, printed c. 1978–80
Dye transfer print, 22.3 × 34.2 cm, sheet 28 × 35.4
19666

Inscriptions   l.r. below image, graphite, *Harry Callahan*
Annotations   verso, u.l., graphite, *D6 / L3*, u.l., red pencil, diagonally, *15*
Provenance   gift of Donald Fraser, Ottawa, 1981

One of the first sustained photography projects that Callahan made was of pedestrians on Detroit sidewalks in the early 1940s. Callahan maintained that he had difficulty conversing with people and he found strangers even more of a challenge. Photographing pedestrians was not only one of his first conscious efforts at working in a series but also his exploration of a subject that held personal significance for him. In part wanting to overcome his reserved nature, Callahan set about photographing pedestrians against the blurred and anonymous facades of downtown buildings.

The photographing of strangers on the street was not an innovation on Callahan's part but a practice that has its roots in the nineteenth century and was directed toward commercial ends from early in the twentieth century up until the 1950s. Recognizing the aesthetic value of vernacular and snapshot photography, photographers, such as Paul Strand in the second decade of the twentieth century, and Ben Shahn and Walker Evans in the 1920s and 1930s, began to photograph strangers in urban settings. Evans made photographs in the 1940s of people hurrying along the sidewalks of Detroit, Chicago and elsewhere.

As Callahan was embarking on his photographs of pedestrians, he was also exploring colour photography. "Around this time I began shooting in color. When I photographed people walking down the street I did that as a freeing process. And I wanted to carry that further, so I started moving the camera on streetlights at night. Then I realized it would be nice on color slides. They were never really printed, they were just Kodachrome slides."[1]

What makes this photograph so memorable is the way in which Callahan has turned an image of a passing stranger into a portrait that isolates the woman from what was in all likelihood a stream of passing human traffic. Unguarded, yet engaged in private thought, the anonymous woman has stepped out in her colour-coordinated finery. By virtue of the photographer's sensitivity toward colour and composition, and his awareness of human gesture, he has turned a snapshot into a masterpiece. A black-and-white street portrait by Callahan made just two years earlier, is much more a study of emotions, emphasizing his subject's introspective mood and illustrating Callahan's initial attraction to this subject, which he summed up succinctly: "I liked the way they were lost in thought."[2]

11 Alvin Langdon Coburn
Boston 1882–1966 Colwyn Bay, Wales
Mission, San Fernando Valley 1911
Platinum print, 40.7 × 30.5 cm
21500

Inscriptions   previous mat, verso, graphite, u.c., *"Palm Trees" / (California Mission) 1911*
Annotations   previous mat, verso, all in graphite in different hands, c.r., *P74.169*, l.l., *Acc. 67:157:50 (Copy B)*, l.r., *C658*
Provenance   purchased from George Eastman House, Rochester, New York, 1974

Whether photographing people or places, Coburn's gift for identifying the most evocative features of his subject is always in evidence. The precocious son of a successful Boston shirtmaker, Coburn started taking photographs at the age of eight with a 4 × 5-inch Kodak camera[1]. Recognition of his talents came early. In 1900 his work was included in the landmark New School of American Pictorial Photography exhibition (London, Royal Photographic Society), organized by his cousin and fellow photographer, Frederick Holland Day.[2] In short succession, he was elected a member of the Photo-Secession (1902); joined the Brotherhood of the Linked Ring (1903);[3] contributed to a 1904 exhibition in the Department of Fine Arts of the Carnegie Institute, Pittsburgh;[4] and had an exhibition of his work mounted at the Royal Photographic Society, London, in 1906.

Coburn made this striking image of two soaring silhouetted palm trees on the grounds of a mission station in the Californian desert during a trip to Yosemite National Park, taken between 23 June and 13 July 1911. A consummate romantic, Coburn captured the scene at dusk, when the setting sun mellows the starkness and hard edges of the topography and a gentle monochromatic haze settles over the land. His virtuoso introduction of dark verticals into an otherwise tonally flat and featureless landscape recalls another extraordinary night scene that Coburn made two years earlier of a fog enshrouded Broadway, lined with lampposts and illuminated by electric signs (fig. 11.1). Coburn's ability to embrace equally the challenge of wide-open horizontal spaces, such as in *Long Beach, California* (fig. 11.2), taken during the same trip as *Mission*, demonstrates his admirable versatility as an artist.

Coburn, like Gertrude Käsebier, studied art with Arthur Wesley Dow.[5] He was also a great admirer of the simplicity of Japanese art and understood the crucial relationship between the syntax of image making and the choice of process that would give life to the picture. His use of gum bichromate Coburn to further soften the edges of his forms, to emphasize the indistinct atmospheric effects and to retain strength in the mid-tones of his composition.

Fig. 11.1 Alvin Langdon Coburn, *Street Lights*, c. 1910, photogravure. National Gallery of Canada, Ottawa (21471)

Fig. 11.2 Alvin Langdon Coburn, *Long Beach, California*, 1911, platinum print. National Gallery of Canada, Ottawa (21494)

12 Coburn, Alvin Langdon
Boston 1882–1966 Colwyn Bay, Wales
Vortograph 1917
Gelatin silver print, 27.6 × 20.3 cm
41656

Inscriptions   secondary support, l.r., graphite, *Alvin Langdon Coburn*

Provenance   gift of the artist to Leonard Arundale, London; his grandson, Leon Arundale, London; Christies, London, bought by Edwynn Houk Gallery, New York, May 2003; purchased from Edwynn Houk Gallery, 2005

Difficult as it may be to think of a photographer whose aesthetic was nurtured during the high point of the Pictorialist era as a "radical," the ability to question and challenge the accepted conventions of photography was one of Coburn's great contributions. "[W]hy," he asked, "should not the camera also throw off the shackles of conventional representation and attempt something fresh and untried? Why should not its subtle rapidity be utilized to study movement? Why not repeated successive exposures of an object in motion on the same plate? … Think of the joy of doing something which it would be impossible to classify, or to tell which was the top and which the bottom!"[1]

Although Coburn issued this challenge in 1916, a year before he produced his Vortographs, there is evidence of his interest in Cubist composition in earlier works such as *Bridge with Three Men* (fig. 12.1), *The Rudder*, (fig. 12.2) and the 1912 photographs *New York from Its Pinnacles* and *The Thousand Windows, New York*.[2] Made between October 1916 and January 1917, the Vortographs are the result of a collaboration with his friend, the poet Ezra Pound. They became key examples of photography's transition from Pictorialism to modernism. Constructing a device dubbed a "Vortoscope"[3] – which consisted of three mirrors (reputed to be the remnants of Pound's broken shaving mirror)[4] joined together in a triangle around a camera lens[5] – Coburn photographed objects, transforming them into dynamic and complex facets of light and shade. The general outrage that the eighteen Vortographs elicited, when exhibited along with thirteen of Coburn's paintings at the London Camera Club in February 1917, was an indication of the conservative attitudes that prevailed toward the role of photography in the visual culture of the time. One reviewer suggested that Coburn's creations were the result of "poseuritis."[6] Even Coburn's friend and fellow photographer Frederick Evans joined the crowd of detractors, calling for the return of "sane art" and implying that these unprecedented images were probably merely evidence of a misguided youth.[7]

Pound, who had been invited by Coburn to write the introduction to the show's catalogue, characterized the Vortograph as "an excellent arrangement of shapes, and more interesting than most of the works of Picabia or of the bad imitators of Lewis."[8]

Coburn's experiments with Vortographs did not last long. Within a few months he abandoned them and returned to making more conventional images, while becoming increasingly interested in mysticism and comparative religion.

Fig. 12.1 Alvin Langdon Coburn, *Bridge with Three Men*, c. 1910, photogravure. National Gallery of Canada, Ottawa (21473)

Fig. 12.2 Alvin Langdon Coburn, *The Rudder*, c. 1905, printed January 1908, half-tone. National Gallery of Canada, Ottawa (PSC 68:039:222)

13 Imogen Cunningham
Portland, Oregon 1883–1976 San Francisco
Frida Kahlo 1931, printed later
Gelatin silver print, 29.2 × 23.7 cm
43259

Inscriptions secondary support, l.r. below image, graphite, *Imogen Cunningham 1937*

Accompanied by a letter from the artist to the original purchaser

Provenance gift of the artist to a San Francisco public radio station, after 1970; unknown purchaser; consigned to Butterfield Auction House, San Francisco, mid-1980s; purchased by Arthur Ollman, San Diego, California; purchased from Arthur Ollman 2011.

An iconic figure in the feminist history of twentieth-century photography, and in the history of photography, Imogen Cunningham (named after the Shakesperean heroine in *Cymbeline*)[1] studied chemistry at the University of Washington. Introduced to photography during her student years, through the Pictorialist journals *Camera Work* and *The Craftsman*, she was particularly attracted to the photographs of Gertrude Käsebier. From 1907 to 1909 Cunningham was employed as a technician in the Seattle studio of Edward Curtis, who earned his reputation as a photographer of the aboriginal peoples of America's West Coast. After printing for Curtis, she accepted a one-year scholarship to study platinum printing, art history and life drawing at Dresden's Technische Hochschule, which had a long and esteemed history in the study of photographic processes. Cunningham returned in 1910 to Seattle, where she operated a portrait studio. In 1917 she moved with her husband, the etcher Roi Partridge, to San Francisco, where she formed a working relationship with modernist photographer Francis Bruguière.[2]

Cunningham rapidly evolved into a photographer of exceptional talent. She belonged to a generation of photographers whose artistic inclinations were nurtured during the Pictorialist and modernist eras, and her oeuvre reflects both stylistic expressions at different times in her career. This portrait of the legendary Mexican painter Frida Kahlo is a superb example of her transition from a softer-edged, more romantic aesthetic to a more direct style.[3]

Made in the studio of San Francisco photographer Roger Sturtevant, in the same year that Diego Rivera was completing his murals for the San Francisco Stock Exchange, this image has been widely reproduced, but it is rarely seen in such a fine print form.

Cunningham left little doubt about her admiration for Kahlo when she noted in a letter that accompanies this portrait: "this photograph represents a woman whose work I greatly admire, more than I admire her husband!" (fig. 13.1). There is, however, no evidence at all of sentimentality in this direct, frontal view in which Cunningham endows her subject with both dignity and elegance. Posed in the ambience of a soft modulating light and wearing a traditional shawl around her shoulders, Kahlo rests her left arm lightly on the back of a wicker chair. She looks frankly at the photographer with much the same expression of strength and stoicism that we see in her self-portraits (fig. 13.2), but without the sense of internal anguish.

Although Cunningham would become well-known for her outstanding botanical studies, as well as for abstractions and landscapes, the 1930s was a decade during which she reconnected with portraiture as an artistic, rather than commercial, subject, focusing increasingly on the integration of subject and setting.[4]

Fig. 13.1 Imogen Cunningham, letter to original purchaser on verso of *Frida Kahlo*, after 1970. National Gallery of Canada, Ottawa

Fig. 13.2 Frida Kahlo, *Self-portrait with Thorn Necklace and Hummingbird*, 1940, oil on canvas. Harry Ransom Center, University of Texas at Austin

Imogen Cunningham PHOTOGRAPHER
1331 GREEN STREET,
SAN FRANCISCO, CA. 94109
(415) 776-4014

This photograph of Frieda Kahlo Rivera was made in the studio of
Roger Sturtevant on Montgomery St in 1937, which was the year in which
Diego Rivera , her husband did the murals in the Stock Exchange.
Since that time a local cinematographer has made a film on her- unfortuneat
after her death. Never the less it is remarkable and may have been shown
by KQED, and if not, should be. His name is Cromie of 936 Wisconsin St. S

And now I, Imogen Cunningham am digging into my past, trying to make
myself worthy of the Guggenheim award, to print some things unprinted.
I could send you # something more recent, but this photograph represents
a woman whose work I greatly admire, more than I admire her husbands;
Few people in this country know it.

Price $50.—

14 Edward S. Curtis

near Whitewater, Wisconsin 1868–1952 Los Angeles
The Catcher (The Snake Priest) 1906
Gelatin silver print, 15.5 × 20.7 cm, sheet 16.5 × 21.5 cm
21419

Inscriptions   u.l., vertical, reversed, in negative, *B174*
Annotations   verso, graphite, t.l., *(see 2109)*, u.l., grey ink, *The "Catcher" (195)* / violet ink, *(X-1999 – '06)* / graphite,
The Snake Priest / grey ink, *(small)*
Provenance   purchased from Andrew Smith, Santa Fe, New Mexico, 1978

The Snake Dance in one of the most revered rituals of the Hopi, a Pueblo tribe from the Southwestern United States. Sixteen days of preparation precede the snake dance, a ceremony in which snakes (predominantly rattlesnakes) are captured from locations that represent the four cardinal points on the compass. The snakes are washed, de-fanged and quieted before being housed in a specially constructed shelter from which they are removed on the sixteenth day for a ceremony that is performed in gratitude for the fruits of the earth, and in the hope of bringing future prosperity to all people. Revered because of their reputation as having brought life to all living creatures, the snakes are held between the teeth of dancers as they perform. The moment that Curtis has captured here shows the ritualistic washing of the snakes.

Initially seen as a private and highly solemn occasion, the Snake Dance attracted such intense interest from non-aboriginal people that the size of its audiences increased to uncontrollable numbers, causing its performers to prohibit public access. Curtis is reputed to have been made an honorary member of the Snake Dance.[1]

The snapshot-like quality of *The Catcher (The Snake Priest)* contrasts starkly with Curtis' larger and more epic compositions that were printed in photogravure or orotone and clearly intended to be published and exhibited. In *The Catcher* as well as in *Coastal Salish – Cowichan Masked Dancer* (1912) and *Ulala Dancer – Kaskimuli* (c. 1910–14), also in the Gallery's collection, the blurred backgrounds, lack of formal composition, and indifferent print finish – although enhancing the authenticity and intimacy of the photograph – suggest an informality and perhaps even a certain furtiveness on the part of the photographer. Curtis, known for his theatrical style, was perhaps permitted to photograph the private Snake Dance only in certain ways. This would certainly have been true of his recording of the Cowichan people's Sxwayxwey ceremony, a ritual of such sacred import that today their elders rarely grant permission for the exhibition or reproduction of any part of this ceremony.[2] It is also important to note that at the time Curtis was photographing these ceremonies, they were prohibited by federal legislation in both the United States and Canada.

15 Harold E. Edgerton

Fremont, Nebraska 1903–1990 Cambridge, Massachusetts
Baton Multiflash 1953, printed later
Gelatin silver print, 44.2 × 36.9 cm, sheet 50.5 × 40.8 cm
38485

Inscriptions   verso, l.r., graphite, *HAROLD EDGERTON*
Annotations   verso, b.l., graphite, *5301.2017*, l.r., graphite, *17/50*
Provenance   donated by the Harold and Esther Edgerton Family Foundation, Santa Fe, New Mexico, 1997

There are limits to what the human eye can see, the detailed trajectory of rapidly moving objects being beyond our visual capability. Fortunately, human curiosity and inventiveness are not in short supply and existed in abundance in the person of the young Harold "Doc" Edgerton – also affectionately known to his peers and students as "Papa Flash." Edgerton came to the problem of how to record imperceptible movement with a passion for, and an advanced education in electrical engineering. An early interest in photography, nurtured by an uncle who taught him the basics, and a fascination for electric power, gained from summers spent working for the Nebraska Power and Light Company, served him well in pursuing his goal of traversing the threshold between invisibility and visibility in the recording of motion.[1]

Drawing on the existing knowledge about strobe lighting – explored for the first time in 1832[2] – Edgerton devised a synchronized camera and flash system that subjected moving objects to a series of short, rapidly emitted bursts of high-intensity light. This was done at controlled intervals appropriate to the speed at which the subject was moving and recorded on a single sheet of film.

Harold Edgerton's advancement of our understanding of the phases of acceleration and change that happen in time in space would have important consequences for science and its disciplines of medicine, zoology and kinesiology, among others. The technology he invented was immediately appreciated for its industrial and military applications.[3] Edgerton's photograph of Harvard coach Wesley E. Fesler's boot kicking a football (fig. 15.1) was the impetus for investigating a wider range of athletic activity. Not only could actions such as a tennis serve (fig. 15.2), football kick-off or golf drive be scrutinized and improved as a result of the strobe imagery he introduced, but so could the durability and effectiveness of athletic equipment.

His contribution to sports was widely recognized almost immediately. Beginning in 1940, newspapers regularly illustrated their sports sections with stop action photographs.

In this image of drum majorette Muriel Sutherland throwing her baton into the air, her figure is represented by a blur of white, while the baton's trajectory appears as a filigree of intersecting and arcing lines. The image itself is reminiscent of the intricate linear structures that sculptor Naum Gabo based on parabolic curves and other abstract geometric configurations. Edgerton was, however, adamant that his photographs were not made with artistic intention, countering any suggestion to the opposite with the assertion, "I am an engineer. I am after the facts. Only the facts."[4]

As insistent as Edgerton may have been on the scientific nature of his work, contemporary reception of it went beyond the acknowledgment of its scientific contribution. Reviewing his 1939 publication, *Flash, Seeing the Unseen by Ultra High Speed Photography* in the *New York Times*, E. F. Hall exclaimed that the book not only covered "the fields of nature, sport and industry," but was also "a compilation of magic and of things undreamed, calculated to excite the most sluggish mind."[5]

Fig. 15.1 Harold Edgerton, *Wes Fesler Kicking a Football*, 1934, printed later, gelatin silver print. National Gallery of Canada, Ottawa (38446)

Fig. 15.2 Harold Edgerton, *Gussie Moran, 1949 (Tennis Serve)*, 1949, printed 1977, gelatin silver print. National Gallery of Canada, Ottawa (23894.4)

16   Rudolf Eickemeyer, Jr.

Yonkers, New York 1862–1932 Yonkers, New York
Spider c. 1890–1929
Bromoil print, 21.9 × 17.9 cm, sheet 23.2 × 18.7 cm
19201

Inscriptions   l.r., graphite, *Spider*

Annotations   verso, u.l., graphite, in two different hands, inverted, *700* [?] / *7775*

Provenance   purchased from Daniel Wolf Gallery, New York, 1982

This bromoil print by Rudolph Eickemeyer is a fine example of the Pictorialist tendency to relegate subject matter to secondary importance in picture-making. In this instance the photographer has seen the spider as an opportunity to explore the well-camouflaged relationship between it and the gauzy intricacies of its web and general habitat. In addition, and above all, he has concentrated on how far he can push the scene's legibility by using the surfaces and textures of the various printing techniques recently made available to photographers. The result is a subtle and seductive print that renders a vast range of silvery greys and a delicate tracery of lines out of which the observant viewer will slowly perceive – and finally be rewarded with – a picture of the spider and its web. The idea of living things being integrated into their environment was popular among the Pictorialists, and was a tendency also illustrated in the works of pioneering Secessionist photographers Anne W. Brigman and Alice Boughton, who showed the female body as an integral part of the landscape (figs. 16.1 and 16.2).

Eickemeyer's experience as a draughtsman in his father's machine production company and then at two New York advertising firms, served his career as a Pictorialist photographer well. It gave him an unusual proficiency in technical matters and mastery over graphic composition. It has been suggested that "Eickemeyer used every printing process available over the course of his career."[1]

Picking up photography first as a means of recording his father's inventions, Eickemeyer became a passionate advocate for its expressive capabilities: "… when I tried photography as a means of pictorial expression, its possibilities so engrossed me that my camera was my constant companion and then a part of me."[2]

Although he was one of the early practitioners of Pictorialist photography and enjoyed more than a passing association with Alfred Stieglitz, he gradually distanced himself from Stieglitz and the group of photographers around him. He did not ally himself with the Photo-Secession but preferred to join the ranks of its detractors. With the introduction of a broad range of modernist styles into the United States at the time of the Armory Show in 1913, many photographers began to question their reliance on a visual vocabulary adapted from painting and traditional printmaking. Instead of engaging with Stieglitz's vision of a photographic aesthetic independent of painting and traditional graphic art and true to its own properties, Eickemeyer remained steadfastly committed to the original tenets of the Pictorialist school. He continued to make his portraits and gentle landscapes and to exhibit widely in International Salons up until 1926, garnering an impressive number of awards and medals in the process.[3]

Fig. 16.1 Alice M. Boughton, *Sunshine*, c. 1902–11, platinum print. National Gallery of Canada, Ottawa (20937)

Fig. 16.2 Anne W. Brigman, *The Dying Cedar*, before 1907, printed January 1909, photogravure. National Gallery of Canada, Ottawa (PSC68:039:255)

17 Frank Eugene

New York 1865–1936 Munich
Portrait of a Man c. 1890–1900
Toned platinum print, 20.9 × 16.3 cm, sheet 24.4 × 17.5 cm
21680

Annotations   secondary support, verso, graphite, *FRANK EUGENE*
Provenance   purchased from Hastings Gallery, New York, 1979

Frank Eugene Smith was born in New York to a German immigrant family and worked as a carpet designer[1] before leaving for Munich, where he studied painting at the Royal Bavarian Academy of Pictorial Art (Bayerische Akademie der Bildenden Künste). It was then that he recognized his commitment to being an artist and established a new identity for himself, dropping his more run-of-the-mill surname in favour of the more exotic "Frank Eugene." On his return to New York in 1894,[2] Eugene turned his attention to photography, a medium with which he had been familiar since the 1880s and had more than likely used as an aide-memoire for his painted portraits.

By the late 1890s Eugene was fully engaged in the international Pictorialist movement, becoming a member of the Camera Club in 1899 and a year later joining the influential Pictorialist Photography circle of the Linked Ring, making the acquaintance of Pictorialism's most prominent practitioners – Frederick Holland Day,[3] Edward Steichen, Gertrude Käsebier, Clarence H. White, and Alfred Stieglitz.[4] A founding member of the Photo-Secession, he was soon exhibiting with fellow Secessionists, publishing in *Camera Work*, and showing his work in international exhibitions. Despite his integration into the New York Secessionist group (fig. 17.1), the formative experience of his Munich years continued to be vital to Eugene's evolution as an artist; in 1906 he returned to Germany, where he remained for the rest of his life. There he resumed painting, making portraits in both media, and working from 1907 to 1913 as a teacher at the Institute of Photography in Munich-Schwabing. From there he moved to Leipzig where he taught at the Royal Academy of Graphic Arts and Book Design.

Established in Europe, Eugene set about establishing contacts with prominent photographers working in the same soft-focus style, meeting up in 1907 with the great Austrian Pictorialist Heinrich Kühn in Innsbruck and maintaining a correspondence with him.[5]

Like the French photographer Robert Demachy, Frank Eugene indulged heavily in the manipulation of his negatives, using dry-point to feather out the edges of forms in the negative, thus making his prints appear more like drawings, etchings, or paintings. Even Demachy, on viewing Eugene's prints in the Photo-Secession exhibition at the Photo-Club of Paris in 1903, noted his treatment of the negative and was inspired to describe him as a creator of "mellifluous and delicate effects."[6] This radical reworking of the negative is nowhere more strongly illustrated than in his *Adam and Eve* (fig. 17.2). To some critics and colleagues this license constituted something close to a violation of photography, causing one of them, Dallett Fuguet, to write in a review of an exhibition of Eugene photographs: "Mr. Eugene does not work on the prints in any way, but his negatives must be in a state which the ordinary photographer would consider shocking."[7]

Although we do not know the identity of the subject of this melancholy portrait,[8] Eugene made numerous photographic portraits of artists, and it is possible that this is one of them.

Fig. 17.1 Frank Eugene, *Stieglitz, Steichen, Smith and Kuehn Admiring the Work of Frank Eugene*, 1907, platinum print. Metropolitan Museum of Art, New York, Rogers Fund (1972.633.132)

Fig. 17.2 Frank Eugene, *Adam and Eve*, 1898, printed April 1910, photogravure. National Gallery of Canada, Ottawa (PSC68:039:300)

18 Walker Evans

Saint Louis, Missouri 1903–1975 New Haven, Connecticut
Moving Truck and Bureau Mirror 1929
Gelatin silver print, 11.4 × 16.4 cm
19316

Annotations verso, l.l., graphite, #850, l.c., black ink stamp, with graphite additions, *Walker Evans / II 32*
Provenance gift of Phyllis Lambert, Montreal, 1982

Raised in Kenilworth, a suburb just outside of Chicago, Walker Evans moved with his mother to New York in 1919, after the divorce of his parents.[1] There is little in Evans' youth to indicate that he would eventually dedicate his life to photography. In fact, his early inclinations showed him to be more literary than visual. Going to Paris in 1926 with the intention of becoming a writer, he attended classes at the Sorbonne[2] and used his camera to record friends and sights in a casual and diaristic manner. It was during this period of travel in Europe that his interest in photography was piqued. The medium offered him expressive opportunities that were not fulfilled in his writing. Upon his return to New York in 1927,[3] Evans began to explore the nature of the medium and to test its capacity to render the world in ways that matched his perception of it.[4] Three years later he decided to become a professional photographer, equipping himself with both large format and hand-held cameras, and soon enjoyed early recognition. His work was shown in the landmark international exhibition *Film und Foto*, and in 1930 his photographs illustrated Hart Crane's *The Bridge*.[5]

Evans' wide-ranging experimentation in the first five years of his career is remarkable: he explored sharply angled viewpoints, as seen in classic modernist views by Rodchenko and Moholy-Nagy, and tried his hand at architectural photography, producing a series of uninflected views of Victorian houses, Greek revival buildings and southern plantation mansions.

Moving Truck and Bureau Mirror is among his most inspired and original avenues of exploration, one that would influence generations of American photographers. Made in 1929, it is not only a radical representation of how he is seeing the world, it also exemplifies his redefinition of the potential of the medium. It shows how the camera could capture the complexity of spatial arrangement, and our perception of it, in a way that anticipates the confounding and engrossing later images of Lee Friedlander.

In May of 1932, Julien Levy, one of the most forward-looking of gallerists to have set up shop in New York at this time, mounted the exhibition *New York by New Yorkers* and included *Moving Truck and Bureau Mirror* in it.[6] The *New York Times* critic singled it out as an "incredible study of chaos."[7]

Evans's fascination with vernacular America manifested itself even earlier in the summer or fall of 1929, when he made *Roadside Gas Sign* (fig. 18.1), an image that celebrates the enigmatic nature of road signs.[8] Around the same time, his insatiably curious mind and eye were caught by the complex forms of debris on building sites, resulting in photographs of crushed metal trim and ornamentation (fig. 18.2).[9]

Fig. 18.1 Walker Evans, *Roadside Gas Sign*, 1929, gelatin silver print. National Gallery of Canada, Ottawa, Gift of Phyllis Lambert, Montreal, 1982 (19259)

Fig. 18.2 Walker Evans, *Stamped Tin Relic*, 1929, printed later, gelatin silver print. National Gallery of Canada, Ottawa, Gift of Phyllis Lambert, Montreal, 1982 (19502)

19 Walker Evans
St Louis, Missouri 1903–1975 New Haven, Connecticut
Citizen in Downtown Havana **1933**
Gelatin silver print, 25.1 × 20.1 cm
19328

Inscriptions   verso, c.r., graphite, *Havana / 1932*,

Annotations   verso, c., graphite, *I-20 / II-20* [crossed out], l.l., graphite, *#1303*, l.c., black ink stamp, with graphite additions, *Walker Evans / I 48*

Provenance   gift of Phyllis Lambert, Montreal, 1982

When Walker Evans left for Havana in May 1933 he was still trying to establish himself as a professional photographer. Balancing his artistic inclinations and his need to earn a living was proving a challenge when Evans accepted the commission to provide photographic illustrations for Carleton Beals' *The Crime of Cuba*. Reflecting on this period, in 1971, he observed, "It was a job. It was commissioned. You must remember that this was a time when anyone would do anything for work."[1] The commission called for Evans to stay in Cuba for only two weeks, but thanks to a loan from Ernest Hemingway, whom he is reputed to have met in a Havana bar, he was able to extend his stay.

Although Evans had already started working with an 8 × 10 view camera by 1933, he chose to use, for reasons of portability, a hand-held camera as well as a view camera. This image and the series from which it comes were made with a 2 ½ × 4 ¼ roll-film camera,[2] while his close-up portraits of dockworkers (fig. 19.1) were made with a 6 ½ × 8 ½-inch view camera.[3]

This tightly cropped portrait of a well-dressed Havana citizen could be mistaken for a New York street photograph, except, perhaps, for the Spanish magazines on the racks of the news kiosk. Even the print from the National Gallery's collection showing the subject full-length (fig. 19.2) speaks more to life on the streets of a busy metropolis than it does to the experience of a young American confronting a foreign culture. With its larger context, it was this latter image that was selected to illustrate the article "Cuba Libre" in the final issue of Lincoln Kirstein's respected literary quarterly *Hound and Horn*, in 1934.[4]

It is the man's slightly guarded expression, the tentativeness of his hand gesture, and the overall complexity of the composition that make this portrait arresting and that give the subject elegance and presence. We cannot know the degree to which the subject was aware of being photographed for the simple reason that Evans, like Paul Strand, was known to use a false lens placed on the camera at a right angle to the normal lens, as he did in his subway portraits. Could this be an early example of Evans exploring this technique?

Evans insisted that he never wanted his photographs to illustrate Beals' book in a literal sense and this is borne out by its organization. Twenty-eight of Evans' images – mainly of workers, street life and building facades – and three photographs documenting political violence, which were selected by Evans from contemporary newspapers, appear as photogravures in a separate section at the end of the book. Despite Evans' later insistence that he was politically neutral,[5] the fact that he omitted *Citizen in Downtown Havana* from the book is possibly an indication of his thinking at the time. He wanted his choice of images to reflect the political reality of Cuba and to give some visual evidence of the need for social revolution without making an overtly political statement.

Fig. 19.1 Walker Evans, *Dock Worker, Havana*, 1933, printed later, gelatin silver print. National Gallery of Canada, Ottawa, Gift of Phyllis Lambert, Montreal, 1982 (19331)

Fig. 19.2 Walker Evans, *Citizen in Downtown Havana*, 1933, printed later, gelatin silver print. National Gallery of Canada, Ottawa, Gift of Benjamin Greenberg, Ottawa, 1981 (20380)

20 Walker Evans

St Louis, Missouri 1903–1975 New Haven, Connecticut
Church of the Nazarene, Tennessee 1936, printed later
Gelatin silver print, 19.1 × 24.2 cm, sheet 20.2 × 25.2 cm
19290

Inscription   verso, l.r., in graphite, *Walker Evans*

Annotations   verso, all in graphite, u.c., *Church of the Nazarene, Tennessee, 1936.*, l.l., *V* [erased] + *A 63* [circled],
l.r., *Walker Evans*, l.l., *I-142*

Provenance   gift of Phyllis Lambert, Montreal, 1982

Architecture was an important part of Walker Evans' repertoire of image-making from the beginning of his career. As early as the spring of 1931, Evans traveled with Lincoln Kirstein, first to photograph Lyman Paine's ultra-modern house at Naushon,[1] and then to Boston to photograph Victorian houses for John Brooks Wheelright's project on Victorian Architecture.[2] In late 1934, Gifford Cochran hired Evans to photograph his Greek Revival home in Croton Falls, New York.[3] This led to a larger Cochran-financed project to have Evans photograph extant Greek Revival architecture in the South.[4] This in turn was followed by a trip to New Orleans, where he photographed the city's distinctive French and Spanish colonial-style architecture and Louisiana plantation architecture.[5]

Evans' interest in the vernacular would also inspire him to photograph domestic interiors. In the fall of 1931, while visiting Ben Shahn and his family in Cape Cod, he photographed the rooms of a house owned by a family of Portuguese fishermen, the De Luzes.[6] It could be argued that it was as much the corners crammed with random objects that drew his attention as it was the house's architectural elements.

What really fascinated Evans about the built environment, however, was not high art architectural style, with its conventions of proportion and ornamentation, as derived from handbooks and treatises. Rather, it was structures built by ordinary people, constructed with whatever tools were available.

Church of the Nazarene was probably taken when Evans was photographing for the Resettlement Administration (later the Farm Security Administration), in the South, in the winter of 1936.[7] It is an image that he regarded highly enough to include in his 1962 article, "Primitive Churches," published in *Architectural Forum*.[8] *Church of the Nazarene* is very much a visual narrative about the spiritual life of a community at a particular time in history. Similarly, *Country Store and Gas Station, Selma, Alabama* (fig. 20.1), with its facade adorned with torn posters and advertisements, is an index of the culture shaping it.

Never one to shy away from recording things as they were, Evans made perhaps his greatest contribution in his photographic homage to the vernacular, expressed through his careful attention to the humble buildings that he encountered while travelling in the deep south from 1935 to 1937.

Evans' claim that he was not interested in conventional architecture, but rather in the kind of unstudied structures that we call "vernacular," is borne out by the number of photographs he took in the same year, and possibly on the same trip, that touched on this subject matter. *Corrugated Tin Facade* (fig. 20.2) is typical of the kind of archetypal form that he sought out, reminiscent of the schematic simplicity of drawings that children make of buildings. Shortly before his death, Evans confirmed this tendency toward the ordinary and everyday, saying, "I lean toward the enchantment, the visual power, of the esthetically rejected subject…. I got a lot of my early momentum from disdain of accepted ideas of beauty …."[9]

Fig. 20.1 Walker Evans, *Country Store and Gas Station, Selma, Alabama*, January 1936, printed later, gelatin silver print. National Gallery of Canada, Ottawa (19416)

Fig. 20.2 Walker Evans, *Corrugated Tin Facade, Moundville, Alabama*, c. July–August 1936, printed later, gelatin silver print. National Gallery of Canada, Ottawa (19421)

21 Walker Evans
St Louis, Missouri 1903–1975 New Haven, Connecticut
Floyd Burroughs and his Family, Hale County, Alabama c. July–August 1936, printed later
Gelatin silver print, 19.2 × 24.1 cm, sheet 20.2 × 25.2 cm
19365

Annotations **verso, c., vertical, in grease pencil, *215*, l.l., in graphite, *#1494*, l.r., black ink stamp with graphite addition, *Walker Evans / II 88***

Provenance **gift of Phyllis Lambert, Montreal, 1982**

There is perhaps no single sentence written on Evans' photographs that sums up this photographer's vision as cogently as Colin Westerbeck's remark, "It exacts beauty from the ungainliness of life."[1] Faced with the vast and complex reality of human existence and the world of material things that has been created around it, Evans chose to narrow his field of visual enquiry to strangers in New York subways and on the streets of Chicago, and to three farming families in the Deep South. He accomplished this with a mixture of dispassionate interest and tenderness. He avoided filtering his experience through any of the current photographic conventions and chose instead to engage with, and record, the vernacular in all of its grittiness, transparency and vulgarity.

Evans made this photograph of Floyd Burroughs and his family in the summer of 1936 while working on assignment for *Fortune* magazine with American writer James Agee. A year earlier, on 15 July 1935, Evans had met in Washington DC with Roy Stryker, the head of the Division of Information for the Resettlement Administration, a New Deal agency that was formed both for job creation and for documenting the plight of the country's rural poor.[2] Stryker had hired Evans as a Senior Information Specialist.[3] Although Evans was able to obtain a leave of absence from the Resettlement Administration to work on the *Fortune* commission, all work he made on the assignment would remain the property of Stryker's department.

This portrait of the Burroughs' family has all the attributes of an ordinary snapshot. Each member of the family has been posed against an outside wall of their home. Floyd stands in the back row, one arm around his wife, Allie Mae, and the other draped over the shoulder of his sister-in-law, Emma; the four Burroughs children are in front. Captured in strong sunlight, the curving shadows cast at their feet and sides, the neatly ordered family is thrown into relief, enhancing their individual presences and making the viewer aware of how carefully they have groomed themselves for the occasion. Evans was working with two cameras on this trip, a 35mm Leica and an 8 × 10, and it comes as a bit of a surprise to learn that it was the latter, more formal apparatus, that he elected to use for this portrait.

He also took photographs of objects around their home, such as the simple still life of a washbasin, a bucket, and a towel (fig. 21.1), and individual portraits (fig. 21.2).

Agee's text and Evans's photographs would eventually be united in the highly influential and now controversial publication, *Let Us Now Praise Famous Men* (1941).[4]

Fig. 21.1 Walker Evans, *Washroom in the Dog Run of Floyd Burrough's Home, Hale County, Alabama*, c. July–August 1936, printed later, gelatin silver print. National Gallery of Canada, Ottawa, Gift of Phyllis Lambert, Montreal, 1982 (19366)

Fig. 21.2 Walker Evans, *Lucille Burroughs, Hale County, Alabama*, c. July–August 1936, printed April 1969, gelatin silver print. National Gallery of Canada, Ottawa (21742)

Saint Louis, Missouri 1903–1975 New Haven, Connecticut
New York Subway Portrait c. 1938–1941
Gelatin silver print, 13.6 × 19.7 cm, sheet 20.2 × 25.2 cm
20387

Inscriptions   l.r. below image, graphite, *2*

Annotations   verso, l.l., graphite, *#1587*, l.r., graphite, *10*, l.r., black ink stamp with graphite additions, *Walker Evans / VI 68*

Provenance   gift of Benjamin Greenberg, Ottawa, 1981

For a photographer described by some of his closest friends as "not too interested in people,"[1] Walker Evans showed an intense curiosity about strangers, at least for the truths their faces revealed in unguarded moments. Pedestrians (fig. 22.1), subway passengers and sharecroppers would, in the first decade of his career, all fall subject to his frank scrutiny.

Evans considered his subway series an important undertaking. He started it in the winter of 1938, and was obliged to leave it aside, returning to it in the winter of 1940.[2]

Evans loved travel for its suspension and displacement of one's normal sense of being in the world. Even journeys between US cities set his imagination free. While the subway series was his first extended body of work on people in transit, he would go on to produce a number of portfolios on travel for *Fortune*, the business magazine that he worked for between 1934 and 1965.[3] Evans even commissioned Robert Frank in 1955 to make the photographs for one *Fortune* article for which he wrote the text.

In September 1950 he published seven photographs and a short essay on his experience of the landscape as seen through train windows, part of which read: "In Roomette 6, Car 287, the light has not yet been switched on. For an hour the train has swayed and rattled across the land. ... Now if ever, in this place and in this mood, the traveler can abandon himself to the rich pastime of window-gazing."[4] An extended caption he wrote a few years later for a portfolio on rail travel reveals more precisely the liberation he experienced when journeying by train: "He who travels by rail over the lesser lines of the U.S.A. clangs and shunts straight into his own childhood."[5]

It seems logical, then, to wonder whether he was looking for some shared expression of the momentary freeing of the imagination when he photographed the faces of subway riders. These excursions into what Evans called the "swaying sweatbox"[6] carried all the trappings of a stealth mission. Indeed, he called himself "a penitent spy and an apologetic voyeur."[7] Evans surreptitiously snapped the travellers' pictures with a 35mm Contax – the chrome painted black and loaded with high speed film – concealed under his overcoat, the lens peeking out "between two buttons...,"[8] the cable release running down his right sleeve.[9] The two female subway riders captured in this image appear oblivious to his presence, their attention caught by other goings-on.

Mia Fineman, writing on this body of Evans' work, observed that this great compendium of portraits of ordinary Americans went further than an expression of personal curiosity to show Evans' interest in exploring and challenging in every respect the accepted conventions governing photographic portraiture.[10] The work Evans viewed as seminal in the creation of this series was in all likelihood that of a woman on 42nd Street, made in 1929 (fig. 22.2).[11]

Although a selection of these photographs was published in *Harper's Bazaar* in March 1962, the first full record of the series occurred in the 1966 book *Many Are Called,* with an introduction by William Agee.[12]

Fig. 22.1 Walker Evans, *Corner of State and Randolph Streets, Chicago*, August 1946, printed later, gelatin silver print. National Gallery of Canada, Ottawa, Gift of Phyllis Lambert, Montreal, 1982 (19459)

Fig. 22.2 Walker Evans, *42nd Street, New York*, 1929, gelatin silver print. National Gallery of Canada, Ottawa, Gift of Phyllis Lambert, Montreal, 1982 (19235)

23 Andreas Feininger
Paris 1906–1999 New York
Rockefeller Center, The RCA Building Reflected in Shop Window c.1940–42
Gelatin silver print, 24.6 × 20 cm, sheet 25.3 × 20.4 cm
42819

Inscriptions   verso, l.c., black ink, *RCA Building, reflection / in shop window*, l.l., graphite, *A. Feininger / 1940*, l.r., black
ink, *©1940 by Andreas Feininger*
Annotations   verso, c., black ink stamp, repeated, *PHOTOGRAPH BY / ANDREAS FEININGER*, l.l., green ink, *37* [circled],
l.c., graphite, *1309*, l.r., red ink, *6* [circled] *-2*
Provenance   gift of the Estate of Gertrud E. Feininger, New York, 2009

Perhaps the most well known of Feininger's photographs are his dynamic studies of New York and Chicago.
Spanning a period from the 1940s through to the 1980s, the images show Feininger's modernist roots and
illustrate his excitement at the visual complexity of city life, a subject that never ceased to inspire him.

The first of three sons born to Lyonel Feininger and Julia Lilienfeldt,[1] Andreas studied at the Bauhaus in
Weimar (1922–25) where his father was a teacher of painting. Inspired by his proximity to Walter Gropius,
the founding director of the Bauhaus, Weimar, from 1919 to 1928,[2] Andreas continued his studies in architecture at the Bauschule in Zerbst in 1927, graduating in 1929. Following a series of odd jobs, he moved
to Paris in 1932 where he worked as an assistant in the office of the legendary architect Le Corbusier.
One year later he had settled with his Swedish-born wife in Stockholm, where he earned a living as an
architectural photographer. The pre-war tensions and subsequent occupation of Sweden forbade foreigners
from practicing as photographers, resulting in the family's emigration to the United States in 1939.

Once in the United States, Feininger was attracted to the skyscrapers and infrastructure of New York and
Chicago, capturing the mood of these cities, as well as the geometry of their fire escapes, alleys, and
towering office blocks. The play of light on the building facades, whether silhouetted at dusk or brightly
reflected in the midday sunlight, was of endless fascination to him. Perfectly framing the reflection of the
celebrated Art Deco RCA building (1933), Feininger plays with the illusionary nature of the medium itself in
Rockefeller Center, The RCA Building Reflected in Shop Window. At first glance the photograph appears
to be a direct, but dramatically angled, rendering of two symmetrical towers created by the reflected fire
escape, under which the photographer has positioned himself. The studied arrangement of strong diagonals that thrust the composition into deep perspective is sufficiently captivating to deflect the viewer's
attention from any thought that this might be a flattened-out reflection of reality onto a glass window surface.
Feininger did not confine himself to working in daylight, also making night views with syncopated rhythms
of lit windows such as *Night View of New York* (1946).

Feininger consistently selected views with exceptional picture-making potential that would rivet the viewer's
attention, a talent that endeared him to the photo editors of magazines such as *Life*, *Harper's Bazaar*, and
Vanity Fair. His aerial view of New York's financial district (fig. 23.1) and *Elevated Trestle on Division Street,
Lower Manhattan* (fig. 23.2) are just two such examples.

Prior to moving to New York, Feininger had already published a number of technical books on photography.
He went on to publish several books on New York architecture, including *New York* (1945), *The Face of
New York* (1954), and *New York* (1964). He continued to publish his photographs and by the end of his
life had an impressive fifty-plus publications to his name.

Fig. 23.1 Andreas Feininger, *Financial District*, 1940, gelatin silver
print. National Gallery of Canada, Ottawa (42820). Gift of the Estate
of Gertrude E . Feininger, New York, 2009

Fig. 23.2 Andreas Feininger, *Elevated Trestle on Division Street,
Lower Manhattan*, 1940, gelatin silver print. National Gallery of
Canada, Ottawa (42818). Gift of the Estate of Gertrude E . Feininger,
New York, 2009

24 Andreas Feininger
Paris 1906–1999 New York
Self Portrait 1946
Gelatin silver print, 24.1 × 19.3 cm, sheet 25.4 × 20.6 cm
42616

Inscriptions   verso, l.c., black ink, *Andreas Feininger / Self-portrait / c. 1948*
Annotations   verso, c., black ink stamp, *PHOTOGRAPH BY / ANDREAS FEININGER*, l.c., graphite, *0129*, l.r., graphite, *63*
[circled and crossed out]
Provenance   gift of the Estate of Gertrud E. Feininger, New York, 2009

The tradition of self-portraiture showing artists engaged in their practice goes back many centuries, at least to the Renaissance. Early in the history of photography we find examples not only of consciously posed self-portraits but also of photographers representing themselves in a variety of unorthodox ways, such as capturing their presence in a landscape with their shadows cast onto the ground. In other settings we see them reflected in store windows or in mirrors, obscured by either the requisite black cloth when working with a large format camera or (during a later period) their hand-held cameras obscuring parts of their faces.

Faces intrigued Andreas Feininger, especially when their eyes were covered by goggles, visors, and masks in the course of undertaking work requiring acute observation, as in *Diamond Cutter* (fig. 24.1). He also photographed artists at work, such as Alexander Calder – in a rare colour print – and photographer Carl Mydans – shown with his camera. Starting as early as 1927, Feininger made a number of self-portraits, including one that shows him listening to a homemade radio[1] (fig. 24.2).

This self-portrait, made almost twenty years later, explores the visual trope of the photographer with his eyes partly obscured by transparent objects: a strip of film and a magnifying glass. Feininger was also an amateur scientist. He had an abiding and detailed curiosity about the world around him, and this is reflected here in the emphasis that he placed upon the power of observation, through the presence of the magnifying glass. An essential accompaniment for the photographer intent on obtaining legible and tonally balanced images, the loupe plays a dual role in this print. Although Feininger initially trained the magnifying glass upon himself in a mirror as if engaged in the careful inspection of his negatives, it becomes, in its print form, the instrument through which the viewer is examined and through which we, in turn, scrutinize the photographer. In this image we are also led to understand that the magnification Feininger applied to specimens of nature was used equally to his own countenance and his own behavior. Ultimately, it can be read as an allusion to the constructed and illusionary nature of the image and of the image-making process, in a similar way that Escher depicted himself as an artist (fig. 24.3).

Fig. 24.1 Andreas Feininger, *Diamond Cutter*, January 1955, gelatin silver print. National Gallery of Canada, Ottawa (42684). Gift of the Estate of Gertrude E . Feininger, New York, 2009

Fig. 24.2 Andreas Feininger, *Self-portrait, Dessau*, 1927, printed later, gelatin silver print. National Gallery of Canada, Ottawa (42614). Gift of the Estate of Gertrude E . Feininger, New York, 2009

Fig. 24.3 M.C. Escher, *Hand with Reflecting Sphere*, January 1935, lithograph on silver-coated wove paper. National Gallery of Canada, Ottawa (30519)

25   Andreas Feininger
Paris 1906–1999 New York
Chambered Nautilus Shell 1948
Gelatin silver print, 24.7 × 19.1 cm, sheet 25.8 × 20.2 cm
42749

Inscriptions   verso, c.l., vertical, graphite, *77-5/2 #6*, l.r., black ink, *AF 2* [circled]
Annotations   verso, all stamped diagonally in black ink, u.l., *STUDYPRINT*, c., *PHOTOGRAPH BY / ANDREAS FEININGER*
Provenance   gift of the Estate of Gertrud E. Feininger, New York, 2009

Andreas Feininger's photographs of natural objects, such as this chambered nautilus shell (*Nautilus pompilius*), are critical to understanding the underlying principle of structural interconnectedness that is common to all of his work. This was a subject that engaged his interest in a highly personal way, exceeding the more pedestrian demands of magazine commissions. Feininger explored with intensity the microcosmic and macrocosmic patterns, rhythms and material values of shells, crystals, bones, leaves (fig. 25.1) feathers and other objects from nature, because he saw in them aspects of the natural world that had inspired the creation of man-made objects. This sensibility was most certainly shaped between 1908 and 1931, when Feininger lived in Germany, listening to discussions about ideas and art in the circle of artist friends and colleagues of his father, Lyonel Feininger, a painter of international repute, as well as within his own circle of younger students at the Bauhaus. The two most influential art movements in Germany at that time, the Neue Sachlichkeit (New Objectivity) and the New Vision, had been founded on the precept of precise representation of the external world. László Moholy-Nagy, who shared a house with the Feininger family in Dessau,[1] published the highly influential book, *Painting, Film and Photography* (1925), in which he encouraged artists to expand their subject matter by exploring scientific objects, techniques and processes. In photography, this aesthetic manifested itself in the works of a number of photographers, but perhaps nowhere was it as convincingly or comprehensively expressed as in Albert Renger Patzsch's *Die Welt ist Schön*, a 1928 publication that appeared in the same year that Feininger started to take photography seriously.

> Contemplating the structural design of these different types of shells, and exploring their finer points with eye and camera, provides me with a never-ending source of enjoyment," wrote Feininger. "I'm fascinated by the fact that, for example, the shell of the nautilus … is constructed in the form of a logarithmic spiral embodying the principles of both the Fibonacci Series and the Golden Section, that classic canon of beauty.[2]

Feininger never tired of examining shells, wondering at their endless variety and the complexity of their forms and patterns. There is sometimes a Surrealist element in his interpretation of natural artifacts. Feininger occasionally captured his shells or small animal skeletons against ambiguously scaled backdrops that enhanced their anthropomorphic qualities or suggested a relationship to surrealist painting, as in *Skeletons of Two Small Birds* (fig. 25.2), which brings to mind work by French painter Yves Tanguy. Similarly, in his photographs of divers, photographers and watchmakers, he transforms their faces into something alien by showing their masks, goggles, shields, cameras and lenses (see cat. 24).

Fig. 25.1 Andreas Feininger, *Leaf*, 1936, gelatin silver print. National Gallery of Canada, Ottawa (42639)

Fig. 25.2 Andreas Feininger, *Skeletons of Two Small Birds*, c. 1960, gelatin silver print. National Gallery of Canada, Ottawa (42637)

Zurich, Switzerland 1924–
Paris 1952, printed 1969
Gelatin silver print, 22.8 × 34.9 cm, sheet 29.8 × 39.7 cm
21885

Inscriptions   **all below image, black ink, l.l., *PARIS 1949*, l.r., *Robert Frank 69***
Provenance   **purchased from Galerie Yajima, Montreal, 1978**

"Something must be left over for the onlooker. He must have something to see."[1] *Paris,* photographed by Robert Frank in 1952, shows a woman and man radiant with excitement as they careen around a bumper car track. Against the inky blackness of night, the artificial light that bounces off the smooth, metallic surface of the cars and guardrail poles illuminates their faces. By composing the image with blunt emphasis on the pleasure-seeking couple and reducing the background to a blur of dark tones interspersed with highlights, Frank allows the viewer to share the experience that initially moved him to trigger his camera shutter.[2]

Intense, engaging and unforgettable, *Paris* can be understood as symbolizing the exhilaration of postwar Paris, or as reflecting the personal happiness of the young photographer himself, who lived there at the time with his new wife, Mary and their infant son, Pablo.

These are both possible but unlikely narratives, however, because Frank is a photographer whose images challenge single readings. *Paris* takes on another possible layer of meaning when we learn that it was one of twelve images that made up the "Black" part of his 1952 handmade book, *Black, White and Things.*[3] By interposing this image of unrestrained joy in a sequence of emotionally dark images, was Frank reminding us that the experience of unfettered pleasure, like all other intense feelings, is dependent upon our knowing its opposite?

Eager from an early age to escape Switzerland because of its sense of predictability – or, as he put it, "You're inside. You know the future."[4] – Frank first moved to the United States in 1947 and found that his new home freed him to engage with his photography in a more deeply personal way. Pictures like this anticipate the strong, moody tenor of his later landmark photographs published in *The Americans*.

Frank undoubtedly was familiar with Evans' *Parked Car Small Town, Main Street* (fig. 26.1), as it was published in Evans' 1938 book, *American Photographs,*[5] and his own image appears to have been mindfully produced to counterpoint Evans'. Obvious compositional similarities and common subject matter notwithstanding, everything else in Frank's *Paris* is in the opposite tonal and emotional register. Whereas Evans' image exudes clarity, distance and a curiosity bordering on mistrust on the part of his subjects, Frank's communicates mystery, intimacy and an air of such abandoned thrall in the demeanour of his couple that they appear oblivious to him. The legacy of Frank and Evans has been of paramount importance in influencing the next generation of American photographers.

Fig. 26.1 Walker Evans, *Parked Car, Small Town, Main Street*, 1932, printed later, gelatin silver print. National Gallery of Canada, Ottawa (19238)

27 Robert Frank
Zurich, Switzerland 1924–
London **1952**
Gelatin silver print, 22.4 × 34.1 cm, sheet 27.9 × 35.3 cm
21881
Provenance **purchased from the artist, New York, 1969**

This picture, like many others made by Robert Frank in London,[1] captures life on the fog-enshrouded streets in the winter of 1951–52. Deep perspectives capture either working class neighbourhoods, where rows of council houses line the sidewalks, or the city's financial centre, with its imposing commercial facades. Whether his eye has been attracted to bankers strolling past brightly lit storefronts or to the daily routines of Welsh coal miners, Frank invites the viewers of these photographs to be participants as much as onlookers in the daily dramas, games and routines that are played out before his camera's lens.

Having left Switzerland in 1947 to settle in the United States, Frank became restless, travelling abroad in South America and Europe intermittently during the period between mid-1948 and 1953. From late 1951 to the end of March 1953, he lived in London, Paris and Valencia.[2]

London is one in a sequence of images that Frank took showing a parked funerary vehicle with its rear doors wide open. A young girl runs up the sidewalk, while a street cleaner with the tools of his trade walks toward the hearse on the opposite side of the street. Frank selected to print this image, in which the child is at the greatest distance from the hearse and her small figure, dwarfed by her surroundings, gives the impression of being in flight from the vehicle and what it symbolizes. By capturing the figure of the street cleaner just as he has moved into the frame of the car's back window, Frank has made a complex mosaic of meta-narratives on the subject of human mortality amidst the unfolding of daily life.

Philip Brookman, writing on Frank's photographs taken in London and Wales, describes this photograph as "an image of stillness, conjunction, and fate."[3] Frank is a master of black-and-white photography who uses all aspects of the medium to its most gritty and poignant effects. His ability to address the passage of time in immediate and spontaneous ways, as well as in its more eternal manifestation, is complex and exceptional.

It is not surprising to learn that Frank worked with filmmakers when he still lived in Switzerland. Hired in 1941 as a still photographer on location for Leopold Lindtberg's *Landammann Stauffacher*, he clearly absorbed the ways in which moving images capture time.[4] Six years after making this photograph he started to make films, an area in which he would be as highly regarded as he is in photography.[5]

28 Laura Gilpin

Colorado Springs, Colorado 1891–1979 Santa Fe, New Mexico
Ranchos de Taos Church 1930
Platinum print, 19.1 × 24 cm, sheet 19.9 × 24.9 cm
22079

Inscriptions   tertiary support, l.r., below image, graphite, *Laura Gilpin / 1930*
Provenance   purchased Witkin Gallery, New York, 1974

Despite the subtle ways in which Clarence White's (see cats. 74–76) teachings guided and helped to develop Laura Gilpin's vision, the evolution of her career owes much to her strong individual artistic direction. Gilpin adopted the architecture, the native peoples and the expansive landscape of the southwestern United States, and New Mexico in particular, as the subject of her generous and timeless visual narrative. In these photographs she emphasizes the harmonious formal relationships and spiritual affinities between the man-made structures and the natural environment of the region. Above all, it is her ability to translate the pure light that falls on the buildings and landforms that makes her images so unforgettable. While Gilpin's career came to maturity in the 1940s during a period in which the dominant schools of photographic practice, Pictorialism and the Group f.64, had given way to a plurality of photographic practices, the compositional elegance and careful printing so evident in her work reflect these earlier aesthetic movements.

In this work from an earlier period in her career, Gilpin responds to the architectural simplicity and integrity of her subject as much as she does to its spiritual significance.

Spanish missionaries constructed San Francisco de Assisi, popularly known as Ranchos de Taos Church, in the late eighteenth century, using the adobe building technique and style of the local aboriginal people. Located in a small village north of Taos, in the south central part of New Mexico, the church, with the sculptural forms of its rear facade and its generous buttressing, attracted not only Gilpin but also her contemporaries Ansel Adams and Paul Strand, as well as the painter Georgia O'Keeffe. Gilpin's love of indigenous architecture was intimately connected to her interest in and respect for the aboriginal people of the Southwest, whom she associated with the properties of the landscape and the native architecture (fig. 28.1). The desire to capture this architecture in pictures never really left her.

Gilpin's introduction to taking photographs was in 1903 when she was given a Brownie box camera by her parents for her twelfth birthday. Of equal significance was meeting Gertrude Käsebier in 1905, when as a teenager she sat, with her sisters, for a group portrait by her.[1] This would result in a lifelong friendship and mentorship.[2] Later in her career Gilpin would fall under the influence of a more modernist aesthetic, finding inspiration in pattern and dynamic composition, and creating images that were graphically powerful but emphasized surface over three-dimensionality, such as *American Church at Picuris* (fig. 28.2), made in 1963.

Fig. 28.1 Laura Gilpin, *Figure Study at Mesa Verde National Park*, 1925, platinum print. National Gallery of Canada, Ottawa (22080)

Fig. 28.2 Laura Gilpin, *American Church at Picuris*, 1963/pre-1978, gelatin silver print. Joslyn Art Museum, Omaha, Nebraska, Museum Purchase, 1997 (JAM 1997.22)

29 Sid Grossman
New York 1913–1955 New York
Black Christ Festival 1945
Gelatin silver print, 31.1 × 39.2 cm
28649

Annotations   auxiliary support, verso, all in graphite, t.l., *B-2*, u.l., *Black Christ / major neg. 21.2 / 0.*
Provenance   purchased from Miriam Grossman Cohen, New York, 1984

Deeply engaged in the establishment and running of the Photo League, Sid Grossman like many of his fellow Leaguers, found most of his inspiration in New York City, particularly on the Lower East Side. A New York–based organization devoted to using photography as a tool to record and critique social conditions, the Photo League was founded in 1936 by Grossman and Sol Libsohn as a breakaway group of the earlier Film and Photo League. Its members held and participated in exhibitions and workshops. A particularly interesting initiative of Grossman's was the Feature Group, which involved the systematic documentation by members of the street life and architecture of Manhattan's working-class neighbourhoods such as Hell's Kitchen, Harlem and the Lower East Side.

As a key figure in this organization, Grossman designed and directed the league's school, teaching there from 1938 to 1949.[1] Eventually, while under surveillance by the FBI for his alleged Communist allegiances, he taught photography classes at his home, first in Chelsea and then in Provincetown, Massachussetts. He participated in the Chelsea Feature Group in 1938 and 1939, and undertook an extensive documentary project in Harlem in 1939 under the auspices of the WPA's Federal Art Project.

Stationed in Panama from 1945 to 1946 on a tour of duty with the United States Army Air Corps,[2] and removed from the context of his Manhattan surroundings, Grossman produced some of his most compelling images in a series that he took of the Black Christ Festival. He encountered the Festival in October of 1945 when visiting Portobelo, a town located along the Caribbean Sea. The town's predominantly Catholic population eagerly anticipated the festival, which was heavily attended by celebrants who carried candles while following the cross-bearers (fig. 29.1). Grossman responded to the intense drama of the pageant, which took place in darkness in the hours before midnight; the climax was marked by the entrance of men carrying a life-size wooden effigy of the "Black Christ." A consistent feature of many of the photographs in the series is Grossman's framing of the faces of the participants in the procession. In this photograph he creates a dynamic arrangement of diagonals and verticals from the hand-held candlesticks and the bars of a wooden cross, and draws attention to the solemn expression of the woman in the centre of the composition, whose features are rendered legible only by the lighted candles.

Among other memorable photographs that Grossman took in Panama is his iconic image of a young girl at play, caught in mid-motion (fig. 29.2).

Fig. 29.1 Sid Grossman, *Black Christ Festival (women with candles)*, 1945, gelatin silver print. National Gallery of Canada, Ottawa (28648)

Fig. 29.2 Sid Grossman, *Jumping Girl, Aguadulce, Panama*, [1946], gelatin silver print. National Gallery of Canada, Ottawa, Gift of Miriam Grossman Cohen, New York, through the American Federation of Arts, 1986 (29481)

30 Lewis W. Hine
Oshkosh, Wisconsin 1874–1940 Hastings-on-Hudson, New York
Italian Family Hunting Lost Baggage, Baggage Room, Ellis Island 1905 printed after 1919
Gelatin silver print, 16.9 × 11.9 cm
22901

Inscriptions   verso, on dry-mount adhesive, t.c., in graphite, *Italian Family / Hunting Lost baggage / Baggage room Ellis Island / 1905*

Annotations   verso, on dry-mount adhesive, u.c., black ink stamp, *LEWIS W. HINE / INTERPRETIVE PHOTOGRAPHY / HASTINGS-ON-HUDSON, NEW YORK*; all in graphite, l.l., # / 3982, l.r., 132

Provenance   purchased from George Eastman House, Rochester, New York, 1973

A few years after starting to work as a teacher at New York's Ethical Culture School in 1901, Lewis Hine picked up a camera for the first time and began to document some of the most significant social issues confronting American society at the turn of the century. The principal of the school, Felix Adler, is reputed to have thrust a camera in Hine's hands in 1903 and asked him to make a photographic record of the new immigrants pouring into the United States through Ellis Island. His reasoning was that Hine would thus teach his students to be aware of and to respect the newcomers.

At the time that Hine was making his photographs of new immigrants, around 5,000 people a day were arriving at Ellis Island.[1] After a trans-Atlantic crossing fraught with difficulties, immigrants were confronted with bureaucratic measures that severed families. Men with an approved amount of money were free to leave, while their families had to remain behind until they could be processed by the authorities. This is seen in another Hine image, in which a young mother and her child are separated from their fellow travelers, who peer at the photographer from behind a chain-link fence (fig. 30.1).

This photograph shows a newly arrived Italian family in the baggage room on Ellis Island, in front of a wall of trunks and suitcases. The family stands frozen in the intense light of Hine's magnesium flash, ticketed and tagged for easy identification and possibly some onward destination. In his accompanying caption, he notes that the family was "Hunting Lost Baggage." Indeed, the family of four seems to have only a bundle and bag with them. Bundles borne over the shoulders, as in Hine's photograph of a young Slovak immigrant (fig. 30.2), were a familiar sight at Ellis Island and often contained all of the person's worldly goods.

Writing in 1940 about a selection of Hine's immigration prints, art critic Elizabeth McCausland eloquently sums up the plight of many of Hine's subjects and suggests that by his efforts, they escaped being a mere table of statistics:

> Here is a great drama of American history, the mingling of many peoples to bring forth on this continent a new nation. … Luckily for history Lewis Hine was present at this great drama – wangling his way in despite refusals, burning off his eyebrows with over-enthusiastic doses of flashlight powder, photographing, setting down the visual record of the greatest migration in history. The photographs of Hine give a face to those cipher millions, make them come alive for us today, so that we perceive them not as the "wretched refuse" of some teeming foreign shore, but as human beings with hopes and aspirations, with dreams to be free and happy, seeking a new life in the promised land of freedom and opportunity, courageously braving the new world. This could be a story read with the mind, not speaking to the heart. But the Hine photographs add vital experience; they make history human and real.[2]

Fig. 30.1 Lewis W. Hine, *Ellis Island When 10,000 to 12,000 Passed Through Each Day*, 1903, printed after 1919, gelatin silver print, National Gallery of Canada, Ottawa (22884)

Fig. 30.2 Lewis W. Hine, *Slovak Woman, Carrying All her Possessions on her Back, Ellis Island*, 1905, printed 1975, gelatin silver print, National Gallery of Canada, Ottawa (22902.1)

31 Lewis W. Hine

Oshkosh, Wisconsin 1874–1940 Hastings-on-Hudson, New York
Marie Kriss, Seven Years Old, Shucks Oysters ... Biloxi, Mississippi February 1911
Gelatin silver print, 10.7 × 15.5 cm
19548

Inscriptions   verso, all in graphite u.l., *2025*, u.c., *Biloxi, Miss.*, u.r., *Feb. 1911.*

Annotations   verso, u.r., graphite, *#66*; c., typewritten in black ink on label, *Marie Kriss, seven years old, shucks / oysters and picks shrimp at Biloxi / Canning Co., when not* [word crossed out with 7 Xs] *tending / the baby. Makes 25 cents some* [word crossed out with 5 Xs] *days.*

Provenance   gift of Max Serlin, Winnipeg, 1981

Two years after he had started to photograph immigrants arriving at Ellis Island, Lewis Hine embarked on a project that would see him travelling across the United States to document young children being exploited as cheap labour in cotton fields, mills and canning factories, or picking tobacco, shucking oysters, and selling newspapers.

An international tradition of social documentary photography had already been established by John Thomson (1837–1921), a British documentarian of London's street life in the late 1870s,[1] and Jacob Riis (1849–1914), an American photographer who published his influential *How the Other Half Lives: Studies Among the Tenements of New York* in 1890. Hine followed this tradition by advocating for social change through his photographs and writings.

Hine's photographs illustrated publications such as *The Child Labour Bulletin*, *Charities and Commons*, and *The Survey*, as well as posters mounted by the National Child Labour Committee (fig. 31.1). In the view of Owen Lovejoy, the executive secretary of this agency, Hine's photographs were "more responsible than any or all other efforts to bring the facts and condition of child employment to public attention."[2]

Hine varied his approach to recording child labour. Sometimes he captured the children at work, standing shoulder to shoulder with adults, or emphasizing their vulnerability by showing their diminutive size relative to that of the machinery. He also made full or three-quarter length portraits of them, ostensibly as a way of drawing our attention to them as individuals, as illustrated by *Marie Kriss, Seven Years Old*. All aspects of childhood other than her size seem to have disappeared from the girl's demeanour. She looks quizzically at the photographer, her hands perhaps holding an oyster or just the empty shell. Behind her right shoulder, a cat's head peers out from what is probably a fish shed and in the far left we see the cropped figure of a woman. In contrast to the gravity of his mission and the official nature of his assignment, it is startling to see the snapshot style of Hine's photographs (fig. 31.2). Using a short focal length lens, he often allowed the middle and far grounds of his images to fade into blurred impressions of children, foremen and buildings. This has the effect of riveting our attention on the young subject of the picture. His pictures, in their informality, often appear to have been taken with a Brownie box camera, although he was probably using a glass plate camera.[3] Hine's visual narrative is simple. In *Marie Kriss* he has captured the wary and worn out presence of a seven-year-old victim of economic greed and the appalling conditions in which her childhood was being spent. Perceptive enough to know that a photograph alone could not serve as evidence, he wrote in 1906, "A good photograph is not a mere reproduction of an object ... it is an interpretation of nature."[4] Elizabeth McCausland noted also that " ... pictures alone will not tell all of history; and Hine has wisely supplemented [his images] with documents of other sorts, photostats of newspaper clippings, labels with typed data relevant to the photograph's subject, identifying information, as place, date, etc."[5]

Fig. 31.1   Lewis W. Hine, *The National Child Labour Committee (Exhibit Panel)*, c. 1915–17, gelatin silver print. National Gallery of Canada, Ottawa, Gift of Max Serlin, Winnipeg, 1981 (19567)

Fig. 31.2   Lewis W. Hine, *The Girl and Boys are Spinners, Sweepers etc., in Valley Queen Mill, River Point, Rhode Island. Very Little English Spoken*, April 1909, gelatin silver print. National Gallery of Canada, Ottawa, Gift of Max Serlin, Winnipeg, 1981 (19539)

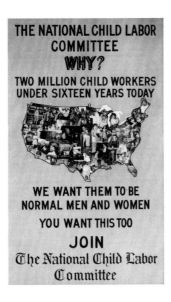

32   Lewis W. Hine
Oshkosh, Wisconsin 1874–1940 Hastings-on-Hudson, New York
Composite photograph of child labourers made from cotton mill children 1913
Gelatin silver print, 12 × 9.5 cm; sheet 12.2 × 9.5 cm
22903

Inscriptions   removed, c.r., in graphite, *3257*; verso, all in graphite, u.c., *3257*, c.r., vertical, *3257*, graphite, *1913*

Annotation   verso, removed label, c., typewritten, *Composite photograph of child / laborers made from cotton mill children.*, l.r., *18*

Provenance   purchased from Visual Studies Workshop, Rochester, New York, 1978

The great industrial expansion that the United States underwent in the late nineteenth and early twentieth centuries created a need for cheap labour. In response to this imperative, state and federal governments, in addition to adopting an open door immigration policy, turned a blind eye to the employment of young children. A large enough groundswell against this practice would occur only under the pressure exerted by humanist leaders such as Florence Kelley, Edgar Gardner Murphy, and Felix Adler – the founder of the Ethical Culture School, in New York, where Hine taught – and by the National Child Labour Committee, established in 1904.[1] This resulted in a 1924 Constitutional amendment that banned child labour and in the more effective Fair Labor Standards Act of 1938.[2] Hine's photographs for the legislative report are widely accepted as being highly instrumental in effecting these changes.

The idea that photography could be used as a tool both to understand and to manipulate social behaviour was not new. In 1877 Francis Galton, a Victorian polymath and cousin of Charles Darwin, began to combine photographic negatives of individuals in an attempt to develop a pantheon of societal types (ranging from criminals to families and, finally, mentally and physically compromised individuals) that could be used to transform future societies. While Galton rephotographed members of a family on a single plate to obtain his results, Hine sandwiched negatives together – in this instance at least two – in the hope of arriving at a portrait of a generic female child labourer. One of the negatives used in this composite was the well-known photograph of a young spinner in a cotton mill (fig. 32.1). While we know that Hine was drawing upon late nineteenth- and early-twentieth century photographic experiments that were intended to improve efficiency in the labour force or to provide proof of feeble or aberrant "types," it is unclear how he planned to use these composite images. Only a small number of his composites appear to be extant; two are in the collection of the National Gallery (fig. 32.2).

Fig. 32.1 Lewis W. Hine, *Young Spinner in Carolina Mill: Child Labour*, 1908, gelatin silver print. National Gallery of Canada, Ottawa (22899)

Fig. 32.2 Lewis W. Hine, *Composite Photograph of child labourers lade from cotton mill children*, 1913, gelatin silver print. National Gallery of Canada, Ottawa (22908)

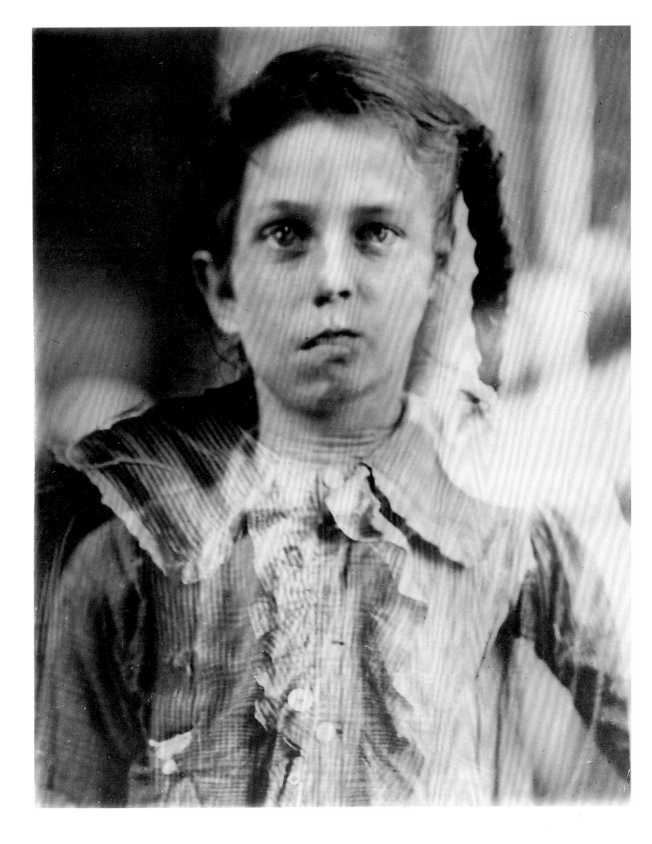

33 Gertrude Käsebier
Fort Des Moines (now Des Moines), Iowa 1852–1934 New York
The Red Man c. 1900
Platinum print, 34.4 × 25.6 cm, sheet 35.9 × 25.7 cm
31394

Inscriptions **verso, u.l., graphite, *35. / renp.* [?] *25***
Provenance **purchased from Mina Turner, New York, 1973**

Born in Iowa and raised in Colorado, Gertrude Käsebier[1] had an early association with Plains aboriginal people, the memory of which was rekindled in 1898 when she witnessed, from the Fifth Avenue window of her studio,[2] the passing parade of Buffalo Bill's Wild West Show. Issuing a formal invitation to the participants to join her for tea, she took the opportunity to make studio portraits of a good number of the performers who took up her offer. The connection that she forged with many of her Sioux sitters would continue over the succeeding years by way of both correspondence and occasional visits.[3]

The subject of *The Red Man* was apparently the last of around one hundred visitors to come to her studio over these occasions. In spite of the many portraits Käsebier had taken up to this time, some of which involved stripping sitters of traditional regalia in order to reveal what she called the "real raw Indian," she felt that she had failed to capture the essential ethnic character of the Sioux. Until, that is, she was faced with the unidentified young man in this picture. "I never could get what I wanted," she claimed. "Finally, one of them, petulant, raised his blanket about his shoulders and stood before the camera. I snapped and had it."[4]

There was complexity and certainly contradictory behaviour in Käsebier's documentation of members of the cast of the Wild West Show. She was, on one hand, appalled at the way in which these people were being used for entertainment purposes and wanted to show the humanity of her sitters. Yet, she was unable to free herself of the notion that there was merit in picturing a representative type.

We learn through published contemporary accounts that these visitors to Käsebier's studio went by the names of Red Bird, Iron Tail, Philip Standing Soldier, Lone Bear and so on, and her portraits of them were usually titled as such. In her desire to find the ideal type, she abandoned, in this instance, her mission to individualize her subjects through her portraits, instead choosing to give this work a title that is generic and has the effect of emphasizing the subject's otherness over his distinctiveness. Thus, she becomes complicit in the perpetuation of the mythical "Indian." The generic title of this work notwithstanding, there is a frank contact between the sitter and photographer in *The Red Man* and in *Joe Black Fox* (fig. 33.1), a quality that is not apparent in *Whirling Horse* (fig. 33.2), which is a more ethnographic portrait.

Käsebier took every effort, nonetheless, to express through her work the respect she held for her sitter and to acknowledge the importance of this encounter to her. We see this in the resulting print, which is warm-toned and generous in its format. The negative was apparently not easy to print from,[5] making this platinum print relatively rare.

Fig. 33.1 Gertrude Käsebier, *Joe Black Fox*, 1898–1901, platinum print, Gertrude Käsebier Collection, Photographic History Collection, Division of Information Technology and Communications, National Museum of American History, Smithsonian Institution

Fig. 33.2 Gertrude Käsebier, *Whirling Horse*, 1898–1901, platinum print, Gertrude Käsebier Collection, Photographic History Collection, Division of Information Technology and Communications, National Museum of American History, Smithsonian Institution

34 Gertrude Käsebier

Fort Des Moines (now Des Moines), Iowa 1852–1934 New York
Serbonne 1901 printed later
Gum bichromate print, 24.2 × 18.3 cm
31390

Annotations   **verso, u.r., black wax pencil, 9**

Provenance   **purchased from Mina Turner, New York, 1973**

Serbonne, with its syncopated blocks of monochromatic tone, its strategically placed verticals, and its broad, painterly gestures, recalls Gertrude Käsebier's early training as a painter at Brooklyn's Pratt Institute between 1889 and 1893. It not only illustrates her ability to incorporate these principles into her photography, but also demonstrates her facility for using the gum bichromate process to its maximum effect by reducing detail in favour of broad textured areas. Made one year before she became a founding member of the Photo-Secessionists, *Serbonne* is one of the most masterful and daring of Käsebier's compositions. It has the same bold and reduced composition as another work from the same period, *Man on a Rooftop* (fig. 5, p. 17).

In the summer of 1901, seven years after apprenticing with a chemist in Germany, in order to learn photographic chemistry, Käsebier was once again in Europe. By the time of this later visit she had become integrated into the Pictorialist photography community and visited F. Holland Day, Frederick Evans, and Steichen at his home in Voulangis, France. This scene depicts a moment during a picnic in the French countryside not far from Steichen's home.[1] Steichen stands on the left side of the composition assuming a casual pose with his hands in his pockets. He wears a beret and what appears to be painter's smock. The three seated figures are Käsebier's daughter Hermine, the artist-illustrator Frances Delehanty – who sometimes modelled for Käsebier – and Charlotte Smith,[2] Steichen's future sister-in-law. One of them has a palette on her lap.

Although the scene exudes an air of casual social interaction, it is clearly a staged group portrait. It is significant that there are numerous references to the art of painting, including the smock and palette. The photographer seems to have set out to upset the convention of the photograph as a carrier of information by relegating the photographic element to the appearance of a mere under-painting for the image. As a picture-taking opportunity, the outing was clearly a success, providing Käsebier with a number of variant views (figs. 34.1 and 34.2). The first American woman to become a member of the Linked Ring, in 1900, Käsebier was able, with *Serbonne*, to show not just her allegiance to the pictorialist school of photography, but also the degree of proficiency she had developed in making photographic prints that were broad and gestural.

Fig. 34.1 Gertrude Käsebier, *Art Students, Paris (daughter, Hermine, Frances Delehauty, Charlotte Smith, Eduard Steichen)*, 1899, platinum print. Private Collection, New York

Fig. 34.2 Gertrude Käsebier, *"Serbonne" variant*, 1901, platinum print. Private Collection, New York

Fort Des Moines (now Des Moines), Iowa 1852–1934 New York
Portrait – Miss N. (Evelyn Nesbit) c. 1901–02
Platinum print 20.5 × 15.6 cm
31391

Provenance **purchased from Mina Turner, New York, 1973**

Without the benefit of knowing what the future held for her sixteen- or seventeen-year-old sitter, Gertrude Käsebier seems to have foreseen the havoc that Nesbit's presence would wreak on the New York social scene five years after this photograph was taken. By placing Evelyn Nesbit (1884–1967) in this three-quarter-length pose with a small pitcher in her right hand leaning seductively towards the photographer, Käsebier alludes to a centuries-old allegory of Pandora and the box. In High Renaissance paintings of this subject, urns or pitchers often substitute for the latter object (fig. 35.1).

Seated on a sofa, Nesbit leans forward into the space between herself and the photographer, the small narrow-mouthed jug – a symbol of womanhood – brought into the foreground of the picture as if it were being offered. The bodice of her dress is lowered suggestively to reveal her shoulders. Nesbit's expression is simultaneously bold and dreamy. The creamy colours and smooth surface of the platinum print add sensuality to the image.

Nesbit was highly sought after by New York painters and photographers as a model. Other renditions of her, such as those by Rudolf Eickemeyer (fig. 35.2 and 35.3), also cast her in languorous poses. At the time that *Portrait – Miss N* was published as a photogravure in the premier issue of *Camera Work* (January 1903), Käsebier was forging a reputation for herself as an important Pictorialist photographer, while Nesbit, an acclaimed beauty, was gaining fame not only as a model, but also as a chorus girl and the lover of Stanford White, a renowned New York architect, friend of Käsebier's, and thirty years Nesbit's senior. By the spring of 1905, her short-lived affair with White was in the past, as was her romance with the more age-appropriate actor John Barrymore, and Nesbit married the troubled millionaire Harry Kendall Thaw. Barely a year later, an insanely jealous Thaw leveled three shots at White, killing him instantly. The murder and the subsequent trials not only caused a sensation at the time, but spawned newspaper accounts, books and films for a good part of the twentieth century.

Among the artists for whom "Florodora Girl"[1] Nesbit modelled in New York were the painters Frederick S. Church, Herbert Morgan, and Carle Blenner.

Fig. 35.1 Nicolas Régnier, *Allegory of Vanity – Pandora*, c. 1626, oil on canvas. Staatsgalerie, Stuttgart (154)

Fig. 35.2 Rudolf Eickemeyer, Jr., *Evelyn Nesbit*, 1902, platinum print. Photographic History Collection, Division of Information Technology and Communications, National Museum of American History, Smithsonian Institution (4135.B5.30)

Fig. 35.3 Rudolf Eickemeyer, *Evelyn Nesbit*, 1901, platinum print. Photographic History Collection, Division of Information Technology and Communications, National Museum of American History, Smithsonian Institution (4135.B5.24)

36 Gertrude Käsebier
Fort Des Moines (now Des Moines), Iowa 1852–1934 New York
Quidi Vidi, Newfoundland 1912
platinum print, 19 × 23.6 cm
40979

Provenance   purchased from Keith De Lellis Gallery, New York, 2002

Gertrude Käsebier is one of a small group of American artists and photographers who came to Canada during the first half of the twentieth century to paint and photograph. Among those who made the journey were Paul Strand, Margaret Bourke-White, Milton Avery, and Georgia O'Keeffe. Käsebier's visit to Newfoundland in 1912 apparently came about through her friendship with Newfoundlander John Murray Anderson, who ran an antique shop near Käsebier's New York studio, located on the corner of Fifth Avenue and 32nd Street.[1]

Although precise dates of Käsebier's trip to Newfoundland are not known, she was still there at the end of August, when she wrote an account of her experience for the periodical, *Bulletin of Photography.* In this almost ethnographic report on the habits of Newfoundland natives, Käsebier described Newfoundland as a "paradise for the sportsman or painter, and, as far as material goes, for the photographer." The light, however, struck her as "weird, like looking through smoked glass. In consequence," she wrote, "the coloring is unlike anything I ever saw in nature. I am haunted by the idea that it is all a stage setting."[2] While she was there, Käsebier photographed the harbour of St. John's, this view of Quidi Vidi, a village just north of St. John's, Petty Harbour, coves (fig. 36.1), fishing banks, boathouses and children (fig. 36.2), among other subjects. A reviewer for the *New York Times* noted: "Her fine little harbor scenes, with their distant horizons and their subtly graduated planes are landscapes of a quality that might be envied by many a modern painter attempting to lure from nature the secret of her charm."[3]

The dream-like quality of light that Käsebier noted in her writings is expressed superbly in this platinum print of *Quidi Vidi*, as are the forbidding silhouettes of the outcroppings of land. In no other photographic process could Käsebier have achieved the same degree of subtlety of distinction in the mid-tones.

Fig. 36.1 Gertrude Käsebier, *Newfoundland*, 1912, platinum print. George Eastman House, Rochester, New York (19536)

Fig. 36.2 Gertrude Käsebier, *Petty Harbour Water Rats*, 1912, platinum print. George Eastman House/Getty Images (83929177)

Hoboken, New Jersey, 1895–1965 Marin County, California
White Angel Breadline winter 1932–33, printed c. 1945
Gelatin silver print, 34 × 26.5 cm, sheet 35.3 × 27.9 cm
41560

Annotations   verso, c., black ink stamp, *PHOTOGRAPHY BY / DOROTHEA LANGE / 1163 EUCLID AVENUE / BERKELEY / CALIFORNIA*

Provenance   given to Arvid Anderson by a friend of the artist; purchased from Edwynn Houk Gallery, New York 2005

Photographed outside her San Francisco studio during the winter of 1932–33,[1] *White Angel Breadline* illustrates Dorothea Lange's ability to engage in the social issues of the day and to create an aesthetically powerful composition.

Born Dorothea Nutzhorn in Hoboken, New Jersey, she assumed her mother's surname in 1918 in protest against her lawyer father's abandonment of the family during the "1907 Bankers' Panic." After graduating from high school in 1912, Lange became interested in pursuing a career in photography, although she had never used a camera.[2] Discouraged from following this path, she instead enrolled at, and soon dropped out of, the New York Training School for Teachers. Intent on learning photography, she went to train with the portrait photographer Arnold Genthe in his New York studio. While her duties consisted of general administration, she also learned "to change the glass plates quickly, to make proofs, to spot photographs, … to retouch the plates with an etching knife and to mount pictures."[3]

Determined to learn more, Lange enrolled at the Clarence White School, which in 1917 was linked to Columbia University Teachers College. In 1918 she settled in San Francisco where she worked in the photographic supply section of Marsh's department store. She joined the San Francisco Camera Club, became friends with photographers Imogen Cunningham and Edward Weston and established her own studio, which brought her a good clientele and a respectable reputation.[4]

By 1932 Lange's income, gained from photographing wealthy San Franciscans and their families, had dropped to almost one-third of her earnings in 1930.[5] Yet this decrease bore no resemblance to the devastation around her. The effects of the crash of 1929, occurring across the country, were soon visible to Lange on the streets of San Francisco. Seeing a line of destitute men in front of a soup kitchen near her studio,[6] she felt compelled, for the first time, to take her camera into the street.[7] Many years after making the image, Lange reflected on her response to the scene: "I can only say that I knew that I was looking at something. You know there are moments such as these when time stands still and all you do is hold your breath and hope it will wait for you."[8]

In 1934 she photographed the strikes and protests on the streets of San Francisco, an indication of her steady transformation from studio photographer to that of a chronicler of her times.

Lange was not alone in making social destitution in America a subject for her art. In 1907, Lewis Wickes Hine captured the effects of the same crisis that had caused Lange's father to flee the family home. In contrast to *White Angel Breadline*, where the individual identity of the men is subsumed by the compositional dynamic, Hine's haunting group portrait, *Bowery Mission Bread Line, 2 A.M.* (fig. 37.1), reveals the faces of the hapless subjects. Another American artist, Reginald Marsh, focused on the plight of the common man. In his ironically titled print, *Bread Line – No One Has Starved* (fig. 37.2), Marsh, like Lange, captures a collective portrait of men lining up for food.

Fig. 37.1 Lewis W. Hine, *Bowery Mission Bread Line, 2 A.M.*, 1907, printed posthumously 1946, gelatin silver print. National Gallery of Canada, Ottawa (22871.2)

Fig. 37.2 Reginald Marsh, *Bread Line – No One Has Starved*, 1932, etching on paper. Whitney Museum of American Art, New York, Katherine Schmidt Shubert Bequest (82.43.1)

38 Dorothea Lange
Hoboken, New Jersey, 1895–1965 Marin County, California
Migrant Mother 1936
Gelatin silver print, 33.1 × 26 cm
37848

Inscriptions l.c., black ink, *For Charlie Rotkin / from Dorothea Lange*

Provenance acquired from the artist by Charles E. Rotkin, 1963; Neikrug Gallery, New York; purchased by Howard Greenberg, New York, c. 1989; purchased from Howard Greenberg Gallery, 1995

After making *White Angel Breadline* (cat. 37) in 1932–33, Lange began to use her formal training and experience in a new way. Intrinsic to her composition was her desire to communicate something other than conventional beauty, social standing or sentimentality. She wanted to craft a contemporary narrative about the plight of her fellow human beings.

In mid-1934, Lange's work came to the attention of Paul Schuster Taylor, Professor of Economics at the University of California at Berkeley, who had seen an exhibition of her images at Willard Van Dyke's Oakland gallery. After Taylor used one of Lange's photographs to illustrate an article he had co-authored, the two formed a partnership in work. In late 1935, Lange divorced her husband, Maynard Dixon, and married Taylor.[1]

Together Lange and Taylor made an illustrated report on the creation of a worker's cooperative, marking a shift in her focus to the matter of documenting the migration of hundreds of thousands of unemployed people from Northern California and the Midwest. In September 1935, she joined Roy Stryker's photographic unit in the Resettlement Administration (later the Farm Security Administration),[2] a position she would hold on and off until 1939.[3] Lange was returning home from an assignment when she passed a hand-lettered marker indicating the presence of a migrant pea-pickers' camp:

> I was on my way and barely saw a crude sign with pointing arrow which flashed by at the side of the road, saying Pea-Pickers Camp. But out of the corner of my eye I *did* see it. I didn't want to stop ... I was following instinct not reason; I drove into that wet and soggy camp and parked my car like a homing pigeon.[4]

When she closed her shutter on the scene of Florence Thompson – whom she described as having been attracted to "by a magnet"[5] – and four of her seven children sheltered in a lean-to, Lange blended a centuries-old pictorial tradition of representing motherhood as symbolic of compassion and sacrifice with a younger photographic tradition of portraying the mother as a Madonna (figs. 38.1 and 38.2).

Migrant Mother was one in a short series of negatives that Lange created as she searched for a definitive statement of her experience of these destitute families. It progresses from the capture of more distant elements to a highly self-conscious explication of form, seizing essential gesture and endowing the image of the mother with a depth of meaning.

The publication of two of these images mobilized not only public opinion but also political action: federal funds were immediately diverted for the construction of two emergency migrant camps and food was rushed to the starving pea-pickers.[6]

Stryker acknowledged the propaganda value of Lange's photographs in his comment: "To me, it was *the* picture of Farm Security."[7]

For Charlio / Rotte.

from Dorothea Lange

Fig. 38.1 Jacques Callot, *Mother and her Three Children*, c. 1622, etching on laid paper. National Gallery of Canada, Ottawa (15106)

Fig. 38.2 Lewis Hine, *A Madonna of the Tenements*, 1905, printed later, albumen silver print. National Gallery of Canada, Ottawa (22895)

Brooklyn, New York 1918–
Opening Night at the Opera, New York 1945
Gelatin silver print, 27 × 34.1 cm
31469

Inscriptions   secondary support, verso, u.c., blue ink, *Opening Night / at the Opera*, u.c., graphite, *1945*, c.r., graphite, *Arthur Leipzig*, l.r., graphite, *AL2*

Annotations   secondary support, verso, c., all stamped in blue ink, *An ARTHUR LEIPZIG PHOTO / 378 Glen Avenue / Sea Cliff, N.Y. 11579 / 516-676-6016*, l.c., *PHOTOGRAPH NOT TO BE / REPRODUCED WITHOUT / EXPRESS PERMISSION OF / THE PHOTOGRAPHER.*

Provenance   purchased from the Visual Studies Workshop, Rochester, New York, 1979

In many respects Arthur Leipzig's background was similar to that of a number of the young New York photographers who roamed the streets and hallowed institutions of the city looking not just for a good picture, but also for a way to confirm their social identity.

Born in Brooklyn to an Orthodox Jewish couple, it was only after an industrial accident[1] that Leipzig, in search of a possible métier, enrolled in a workshop at the Photo League in 1942. Two of his teachers there, Sid Grossman and Paul Strand (see cats. 29 and 64–67) would shape his vision and exert a lifelong influence over his work.[2] W. Eugene Smith, who came to talk and show his work at the Photo League, was another important figure in Leipzig's development, validating his interest in the human condition as a worthy subject for his photography. "Photography," Leipzig wrote, "has been a kind of path for me toward understanding the inner self and the outer world. It has been my way of making order out of chaos, finding meaning in life's seemingly random contours."[3]

"Making order out of chaos" contrasted with Alfred Stieglitz's view of his own photographs as serving to create "a picture of the chaos in the world."[4] Whereas the older photographer saw the medium functioning as a mirror of nature, Leipzig perceived it as a tool with which to comment upon and, ideally, to change society.

In *Opening Night at the Opera* a woman reaches her hand behind the nape of her neck to contain an unruly lock of hair, or perhaps aware of the photographer's lens, to unconsciously draw attention to her elegant profile. Her companion, cigarette holder dangling from his mouth, holds his jacket with one hand as he gropes in his pocket with the other, perhaps for his cigarette lighter. He returns the photographer's gaze unflinchingly.

Arthur Leipzig is a photographer attuned to familiar body language and it is his masterful portrayal of gesture in *Opening Night at the Opera* that creates a narrative about the manners of social class. Unlike many of the Photo League photographers who focused on working class neighbourhoods, Leipzig takes a satirical look at New York's affluent set, demonstrating at once an affinity with the work of both Lisette Model and Weegee (see cats. 43–47 and 69), but also giving the work a stamp of his own.

In spite of the undertone of criticism, Leipzig's images of the well-to-do were tempered with humour (fig. 39.1). Where both Model and Weegee's images were unforgiving in their ridicule, Leipzig's are gently mocking. He was also capable of making pictures of the utmost tenderness, such as that of the curled up form of a sleeping child, captured from above (fig. 39.2).

Fig. 39.1 Arthur Leipzig, *Tammany Hall*, 1947, gelatin silver print.
Howard Greenberg Gallery

Fig. 39.2 Arthur Leipzig, *Sleeping Child, Levittown, New York*,
1950, gelatin silver print. Howard Greenberg Gallery

40 Rebecca Lepkoff
New York 1916–
Clothesline out Jerry G's Window, 20 Prince Street, New York 1946
Gelatin silver print, 28 × 26.8 cm
31449

Inscriptions   secondary support, all in graphite, l.l., *Clothesline out Jerry G. Window 1946*, l.r., *Rebecca Lepkoff*, verso, l.r., graphite, *Rebecca Lepkoff – Vintage Photo. / 20 Prince St. N.Y.C. – 1946 / "out the back window from / Jerry G. apt. / Clothesline pics reprod. In Camera Magaz. 1950 / R.L.*

Annotations   l.r., graphite, *RL12*

Provenance   purchased from the Visual Studies Workshop, Rochester, New York, 1979

New York in the 1940s was a vibrant and culturally mixed city that provided photographers with a rich reservoir of iconography. Fully alive to the graphic opportunities that it offered, Rebecca Lepkoff captured skyscrapers, store windows, billboards, elevated railways, the passing feet of hurrying pedestrians, children playing on the street, and laundry lines. Lepkoff did not have to travel very far for her inspiration, frequently finding it by simply peering out of her apartment window, where a view of her husband's shirt hanging on the line, or the pattern of windows and fire escapes animating the facades of the buildings opposite inspired her to reach for her camera.

Looking out from a friend's apartment window into a courtyard in Soho, Lepkoff spotted a lively ready-made composition. The intersecting laundry lines, converging from adjacent and opposite porches, walls, fire escapes and window frames, were hung with clothing and linen of varied sizes and transparencies, creating an animated composition of lines, rectangles and squares. When modern art opened the door to the exploration of the subjects of everyday life, few would have imagined that a subject as mundane as drying laundry would appeal so strongly to the artist's imagination. Particularly instrumental in making banal subjects such as this acceptable material for artists in the United States was the Ash Can School, a loosely associated group of painters who came together in the first decade of the twentieth century and committed themselves to chronicling the less sanitized aspects of urban life such as alleyways, tenement houses, bars, as well as the local prostitutes and drunks.

While both Lepkoff and Walker Evans (fig. 40.1) were fascinated by arrangements of items hanging on laundry lines, Evans chose to photograph billowing shirts, shorts and other pieces of clothing being transformed by a vigorous wind into barely recognizable shapes. Berenice Abbott's multiplicity of clotheslines (fig. 40.2), on the other hand, radiate, like branches of a tree, from many levels off of a central pole. Rather than a picture of washing day, it looks as if the neighbourhood has been festooned in honour of some holiday, or like a totemic array of prayer flags.

Affiliated with the Photo League and raised on the Lower East Side by her immigrant family, Lepkoff knew the neighbourhood well. The act of photographing the terrain and its people was to a large extent autobiographical.

Clothesline out Jerry G. Window   1946

Fig. 40.1   Walker Evans, *Wash Day, New York City*, before October
1930, gelatin silver print. National Gallery of Canada, Ottawa (21771)

Fig. 40.2   Berenice Abbott, *Court of the First Model Tenement,
New York City*, 16 March 1936, printed later, gelatin silver print.
National Gallery of Canada, Ottawa, Gift of Rosemary Speirs,
Ottawa, in memory of Alan John Walker, Toronto, 1996 (38423.3)

41 Helen Levitt

Brooklyn, New York 1913–2009 New York
New York City **c. 1940**
Gelatin silver print, 18.5 × 24.1 cm
41072

Inscriptions   secondary support, u.r., graphite, *N H 41*, verso, c., graphite, *N.Y.C. 1940 Helen Levitt / 101 / 9*
Annotations   secondary support, verso, all in graphite, u.r., *guide* [check mark], c., *Book 37a* [crossed out] / *use this*
Provenance   purchased from Laurence Miller Gallery, New York, 2002.

Born and raised in Brooklyn, Helen Levitt showed no evidence of an early passion for image making. She was introduced to the medium in 1931[1] when she began working as an assistant to portrait photographer, J. Florian Mitchell.[2] Levitt learned the technical aspects of the medium and received an introduction to Pictorialist photography, an aesthetic that held little appeal for her. After seeing an exhibition of the work of Henri Cartier-Bresson at the Julian Levy Gallery in 1935,[3] then meeting Walker Evans three years later,[4] Levitt understood the direction she wanted to follow in photography. Evans began to mentor her – as did the writer James Agee[5] – and soon invited her to accompany him on his subway photography excursions in 1938–39 (see cat. 22).[6]

The influence of these two major figures in photography notwithstanding, Levitt established her own style and a distinctive approach to her subject matter. *New York City* was created during one of the most prolific periods in Levitt's career when she began photographing the rich street life of Yorkville, Harlem, Spanish Harlem, and sometimes the Lower East Side, Brooklyn and the Bronx.[7]

In contrast to the exchange between Jerome Liebling and his subject in his photograph, *Butterfly Boy, Knickerbocker Village* (see cat. 42), the young boy in Levitt's *New York City* appears oblivious to the photographer's presence. Engrossed in his private experience – possibly of pain – external reality has momentarily disappeared for him. Levitt, on the other hand, is transfixed by the child's behaviour and anchored in the exterior world. She records this odd moment in daily life with the same sharp and uncompromising clarity of all of her other street pictures.[8] Like the title of her image, Levitt's picture does not yield information that leads the viewer to a greater understanding of the circumstances that caused the boy to contort his body to a point where it is transformed into something more feral than human in appearance, but that was not her intention.

Neither a photojournalist nor a documentary photographer, Levitt leaves viewers in a state of suspended speculation. From the simple backdrop of a slightly ominous empty vehicle, an angled, planar sidewalk littered with a piece of cardboard, and the figure of the boy, she assembles, with an exceptional economy of form, an image charged with beauty and mystery. With an astute aesthetic sense that included radical framing, and razor-sharp insight into what is both ordinary and moving about human behaviour, she, as Max Kozloff has noted, was able to make the momentary look momentous.[9]

Children, who live in the moment and who play with unparalleled vigor and brilliance, offered Levitt the most rewarding opportunities to see the world afresh (figs. 41.1 and 41.2)[10]. They were the stars in the theatre of street life to which she so intensely responded, yet she professed no special affection for them. "People," she once said, "think I love children, but I don't. It was just that children were out in the streets."[11]

Fig. 41.1 Helen Levitt, *New York*, 1980, c-print, Laurence Miller Gallery, New York

Fig. 41.2 Helen Levitt, *New York*, c. 1940, gelatin silver print. Laurence Miller Gallery, New York

42   Jerome Liebling
New York 1924–
Butterfly Boy, Knickerbocker Village, New York City 1949
Gelatin silver print, 24.4 × 24.3 cm, sheet 25.5 × 25.2
30354

Inscriptions   secondary support, verso, u.l., graphite, *Jerome Liebling – / Butterfly Boy NYC 1949 / Paul Strand Photo League Project*

Provenance   purchased from the artist, Amherst, Massachusetts, 1989

Butterfly Boy records a chance encounter between Jerome Liebling and a young boy on a New York City sidewalk one day in 1949. At the time Liebling was attending a workshop led by Paul Strand at the Photo League. One assignment was to document Knickerbocker Village, a two-block area between the Brooklyn and Manhattan bridges, developed in 1933[1] as low-income housing by a private entrepreneur with federal funding (Reconstruction Finance Corporation). By 1949 it was known as part of "The New Ghetto" and showing signs, as Liebling expressed it, of "new decay."[2]

Captured at the moment when he has spread open his jacket as if empowered to take off in flight, the boy is riveted by the photographer's attention. Reality interrupts his reverie and, as curiosity makes claims on his awareness, the boy gazes upward for a second into the camera's lens. Unlike his subject, the photographer's focus is outward, his imagination propelled by what the external world offers him. The picture freezes for all time this momentary contact of two private consciousnesses: the boy distracted from doing what children do to shape their independent realities, and Liebling searching to inscribe his experience of the world and his relationship to this boy. *Butterfly Boy* tellingly illustrates John Szarkowski's observation that "the camera shows us a particular cone of space during a specific parcel of time."[3]

Trained in art and design at Brooklyn College when the design department was under the direction of Serge Chermayeff, an advocate of Bauhaus constructivist principles, Liebling composed *Butterfly Boy* as an arrangement of triangulated shapes. The "wings" of the coat carve up the plane of the sidewalk into similar shapes. The fender and the wheel of the car in the background serve as a kind of semi-halo, focussing attention on the boy's face and his expression of earnest inquisitiveness. This composition evidently appealed to Liebling, as he employed a similar composition when photographing another young boy for the same project (fig. 42.1).

Estelle Jussim, perceptively, sees a recurrent tension in Liebling's desire to "accommodate the seemingly academic aspects of design – line, tone, composition – within the documentary photograph."[4] This would apply to *Butterfly Boy*.[4]

Like so many members of the Photo League, Jerome Liebling was born in New York City to immigrant parents. His study of art and design at Brooklyn College began in 1942 but was interrupted by military service in Europe and North Africa; he returned in 1945 to complete his studies under Ad Reinhardt, Milton Brown, Burgoyne Diller, and Walter Rosenblum for photography.[5] Rosenblum avowed that Liebling "was immediately able to take pictures."[6] In 1947 Rosenblum persuaded him to join the League, he would be active in it for two years.[7]

Fig. 42.1 Jerome Liebling, *Boy and Car, New York City*, 1949, gelatin silver print. Howard Greenberg Gallery, New York (pf 85080)

43 Lisette Model
Vienna 1901–1983 New York
Promenade des Anglais 1934, printed c. 1940–49
Gelatin silver print, 34.2 × 27.8 cm
29041

Inscriptions   secondary support, verso, t., green ink, *Lisette Model*, t., blue ink, *Promenade des Anglais Nice*

Annotations   secondary support, verso, b., graphite, *CLM 1083.60 / 500.*

Provenance   Lisette Model estate; purchased from Sander Gallery, New York, 1985

A great deal changed in Lisette Model's life in the ten years between her leaving Vienna after her father's death to live in France in 1924 and the making of this photograph, not the least of which was her decision to become a photographer rather than a musician or singer. It was on one of the many occasions that Model was visiting her mother, who had settled in Nice, that she made this iconic image of a man lounging on a chair on the Promenade des Anglais, a boardwalk that skirts along the edge of the Mediterranean's Baie des Anges. Part of a series, it was made during a politically turbulent period in the early 1930s when hotel workers were agitating for higher wages in the resort towns of the Côte d'Azur. A popular hangout for the idle rich from all over Europe who came there to "people watch" and enjoy the sunshine, the Promenade des Anglais was like a gigantic plein-air studio with an endless supply of sitters lulled into inactivity by the soporific climate. Model was attracted to the sheer variety of those who planted themselves for hours on end in the chairs, among them this gentleman with the tanned skin and an inscrutable expression. Although it is easy to see why a viewer might sense an air of confrontation in this image, the man is more watchful than affronted by the photographer.

As we can see from a full-frame contact print of one of the 120-format negatives Model made with a hand-held Rolleiflex (fig. 43.1), the impression that she was invading his personal space is illusory. Model composed her pictures very tightly in the darkroom, eliminating surrounding space and often foreshortening their perspective by tilting her negative, thereby investing her images with a greater sense of drama. In this instance the entire backdrop of umbrellas, hotel facades, and rooftops has been removed to focus more fully on the face, the figure, and the body language of the sitter.

A selection of photographs from Model's *Promenade des Anglais* series accompanied a vitriolic article by Lise Curel in the 28 February 1935 issue of the Communist illustrated periodical *Regards* (fig. 43.2), a biographical detail that Model avoided mentioning when she moved to the United States in 1938.

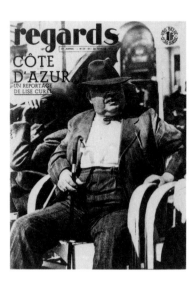

Fig. 43.1 Lisette Model, *Promenade des Anglais, Nice*, 7 August 1934, full-frame enlargement by Justin Wonnacott from original negative, 1989. Lisette Model Fonds, National Gallery of Canada, Ottawa

Fig. 43.2 Back cover of *Regards*, vol. 4, no. 59 (28 February 1935). Photograph by Lisette Model, Bibliothèque nationale, Paris

44   Lisette Model
Vienna 1901–1983 New York
Coney Island Bather c. 1939–July 1941
Gelatin silver print, 34.5 × 27.2 cm
29055

Annotations   secondary support, verso, c., black ink stamp with graphite addition, © *ESTATE OF LISETTE MODEL / 1983*
ARCHIVE NUMBER – D1/1 NY-CI-1

Provenance   Lisette Model estate; purchased from Sander Gallery, New York, 1985

When Lisette Model arrived in New York in September 1938 with her husband, the Russian painter Evsa Model, she encountered not only an unfamiliar political climate but also a different culture, one less inclined at that time to an appreciation of social satire and often with a more solemn moral reading of the photographic image. Perhaps because of the freshness of her photographs, fellow photographers and influential photo editors for magazines nonetheless greeted her appearance on the photography scene in New York with great interest. *PM's Weekly* art editor, the photographer Ralph Steiner, recognizing the exceptional qualities of Model's vision, published contrasting images of street vendors and Promenade des Anglais frequenters under the somewhat disingenuous rubric "Why France Fell," in January 1941.[1] While this provoked an angry rebuttal from an officer of the French consulate, this flurry of excitement did not deter Alexey Brodovitch, the legendary art director for *Harper's Bazaar*, from asking her to make a series of photographs for the magazine that would have the same audacity as the *Promenade* series, this time using Coney Island as her "plein-air" studio.[2]

Attracted by generous and extreme forms in humans and animals, Model presents an encounter with this Coney Island bather that was rich with the kind of lively incident she relished. In response to the snickers and giggles from a gathering crowd around the photographer and her voluptuous subject, the bather, full of verve and challenge, asked the onlookers whether they had "never seen a fat woman before!"[3]

Years later an emerging young photographer and student of Model's, who would become one of the most celebrated artists of the late twentieth century, Diane Arbus, would be spellbound by the other version of Model's bather (fig. 44.1) taken on the same summer's day. After scrutinizing the print, exhibited at the Museum of Modern Art in November 1960 in the exhibition "A Bid for Space – Part 2," Arbus sent Model a postcard with the message "What a beautiful photograph that is."[4] In their celebration of the tangible commonplace of the flesh as well as in their capture of the extroverted spirit of the subject, both photographs are vivid, life-embracing and unapologetic reflections of reality.

Fig. 44.1 Lisette Model, *Coney Island Bather, New York*, 1939–July 1941, printed later, gelatin silver print. National Gallery of Canada, Ottawa, Gift of the Estate of Lisette Model, 1990, by direction of Joseph G. Blum, New York, through the American Friends of Canada (35196)

45 Lisette Model
Vienna 1901–1983 New York
Running Legs c. 1940–41
Gelatin silver print, 34.6 × 27.1 cm
29036

Inscriptions   verso, u.l., blue ink, *Lisette Model*
Annotations   verso, l.r., graphite, *32 / R1184.705*, l.c., graphite, *RMG #880-126*
Provenance   **Lisette Model estate; purchased from Sander Gallery, New York, 1985**

Unlike Rudolf Eickemeyer (see cat. 16) or Frank Eugene (see cat. 17) of the Pictorialist school, who saw composition as an element applied from an external set of conventions, Model believed that the subject predetermined it. "Whenever we pick up the camera and look," she would say, "we force composition."[1] In others words, the camera reduced the world to a rectangle or square, depending on what type of equipment one worked with. Model found both the 2 ¼-inch and 35 mm formats frustrating and admitted to fighting against their restraints in whatever way she could. This involved cropping her images, exaggerating angles and generally using her negatives as rough sketches from which to arrive at a desired pictorial statement. Consequently, it is not unrealistic to look at her as functioning more as an artist than a candid photographer when at work in her darkroom.

In her *Running Legs* series Model found a subject that provided her with a lively syncopated composition and allowed her to express the vitality of her newly adopted home of New York, a city which had enthralled her at first glance. The angles from which she captured the truncated legs and feet of passing pedestrians varied from downward views taken from the higher perspective of upper storey windows to subterranean vantage points, where she might position herself on the stairs leading down to a basement entrance. The latter location allowed her to view the rapidly moving feet of passers-by at eye level in much the same way that a seated beggar on a Manhattan sidewalk would be viewing the world of rushing pedestrian traffic. The camera allowed Model to describe the fragmentary nature of being part of the life of New York City: "When I came to New York, I tried to photograph the skyscrapers, and with my Rolleiflex, all the lines fell down, fell down and fell down [sic], and I got terribly bored. Suddenly I pointed my camera down and I said something must happen right down there, and then for several weeks and since, I photographed the running legs."[2] New York inspired Model in many ways. Although she first gravitated towards Delancey Street and the Lower East Side, where many newly arrived European immigrants lived, it was the experience of the city's tall buildings, crowded streets and its varied types of people that entranced her and forced her to look differently – not only at what she photographed but how she did it. Through her *Running Legs* and her *Reflections* series (fig. 45.1), Model creates a narrative about the pace and life of the city, but also about altered visual experience. This was true also for her artist husband, Evsa Model, who insisted on isolating figures in the urban landscape and showed single walking figures dwarfed by towering skyscrapers (fig. 45.2).

Fellow New Yorkers and photographers were enthusiastic in their reception of this work and the Photo League, of which she was a member, exhibited a selection from both the *Running Legs* and her *Reflections* series.[3]

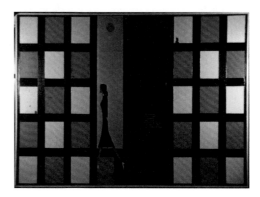

Fig. 45.1 Lisette Model, *Reflections, New York*, c. 1940–45, gelatin silver print. National Gallery of Canada, Ottawa (29039)

Fig. 45.2 Evsa Model, *Oceanside II*, 1943, oil on canvas. National Gallery of Canada, Ottawa, Gift of the Estate of Lisette Model, 1990, by direction of Joseph G. Blum, New York, through the American Friends of Canada

46 Lisette Model
Vienna 1901–1983 New York
Sammy's, New York c. 1940–44
Gelatin silver print, 34.9 × 26.9 cm
29034

Inscriptions   **verso, c., black ink, *Lisette Model***
Annotations   **verso, l.l., graphite, *5137.0***
Provenance   **Lisette Model estate; purchased from Sander Gallery, New York, 1985**

From her earliest European images it is apparent that Lisette Model was drawn to capturing people representative of opposite ends of the social spectrum. Coming from a wealthy Viennese family who, like many bourgeoisie, suffered an irreversible loss of their fortunes at the end of World War I, Model felt that she understood the plight of the less fortunate. The prohibitions and isolation of a privileged and sheltered upbringing meant that photography became a tool for her to explore all aspects of society. While her images of the rich are lacerating, she often infuses those of ordinary or dispossessed people with unusual tenderness. This photograph shows a moment of intimacy and affection shared between a sailor and a young woman dressed for a night out on the town. Amidst the hustle and bustle that typified the ambience at the immensely popular nightclub, Sammy's Bowery Follies, these two patrons appear oblivious to the photographer and indeed to anything other than their moment of shared warmth.

Introduced to Sammy's in the early 1940s by George Davis, the fiction editor for *Harper's Bazaar*, Lisette Model talked about feeling completely at home there. Like Model and Weegee (see cat. 69), Sammy Fuchs, the owner of Sammy's, was an Austrian immigrant. He started Sammy's as a simple deli in 1934 and turned it, reputedly on the advice of a visiting British Lord, into a cabaret. Described as a poor man's Stork Club, it was renowned for its wide appeal to all social levels. At Sammy's, well-heeled uptown denizens mingled with the socially marginalized from the Bowery.

Model not only photographed its patrons and the performers extensively (fig. 46.1), but took her students there as well, probably as a way of breaking down their inhibitions about photographing strangers. Model was not alone in being attracted to the cast of characters that frequented or entertained at Sammy's. Weegee's *Naked City* has a chapter devoted almost entirely to the nightclub, (fig. 46.2), and Alfred Eisenstadt published his photo essay, "Sammy's Bowery Follies," in *Life*[1] in the same year that Model published her "Sammy's on the Bowery" spread in *Harper's Bazaar*.

Fig. 46.1 Lisette Model, *Sammy's, New York*, c. 1940–44, gelatin silver print. National Gallery of Canada, Ottawa, Gift of the Estate of Lisette Model, 1990, by direction of Joseph G. Blum, New York, through the American Friends of Canada (35201)

Fig. 46.2 Weegee, *Norma Devine is Sammy's Mae West*, 4 December 1944. International Center for Photography, New York

47 Lisette Model
Vienna 1901–1983 New York
Woman with Veil, San Francisco 1949
Gelatin silver print, 49.2 × 40.1 cm
20488

Annotations   secondary support, verso, typewritten on label, *LISETTE MODEL, American – Woman, San Francisco*, graphite, *Eidlitz Coll.*

Provenance   gift of Dorothy Meigs Eidlitz, St. Andrews, New Brunswick, 1968

New Yorkers first encountered Lisette Model's *Woman with Veil, San Francisco* crisply lit against a white wall at the opening exhibition of Helen Gee's Limelight Gallery in 1954. This is the same print donated to the National Gallery of Canada by Dorothy Eidlitz, the American founder of the legendary arts and crafts school, Sunbury Shores Arts and Nature Centre, in St. Andrews, New Brunswick, and one of the lone patrons of Gee's Gallery and coffeehouse who actually bought the photographs on the walls.

Fascinated by the concept of glamour, of which identity and the masking of identity are intrinsic elements, Model sought out strangers whose appearances aspired to, or countered, mainstream ideals of glamour (fig. 47.1). She was especially pleased if the grooming that was done in service of this ideal was exaggerated to a point that exceeded accepted conventions, as in this portrait. In an interview in which Model said that she would have liked to make this photograph in colour, she recounted that the woman wore a pale blue suit and a white lacy blouse, while her lips and cheeks were painted red. The rest of her face was powdered white. A study of the negatives from this series shows that there was an equally elaborately attired young woman sitting alongside the veiled lady (fig. 47.2). The older woman, whose picture Model appeared to favour, seems to have hit a chord, revealing as she does the tragic-comic aspects of fighting off the ravages of age.

Model's interest in revealing, and simultaneously stripping away, the trappings of outward appearance and affectations was shared with the most celebrated of her students, Diane Arbus. Arbus' observation "Everybody has that thing where they need to look one way but they come out looking another way,"[1] describes the fierce and almost defiant pride in appearance manifested by Model's subject in this photograph.

This was the first Lisette Model photograph to enter the holdings of the National Gallery of Canada and takes pride of place in the generous collection of works by this influential twentieth-century photographer.

Fig. 47.1 Lisette Model, *They Honor their Sons, New York*, c. 1939–14 June 1942, printed c. 1942–49, gelatin silver print. National Gallery of Canada, Ottawa (29032)

Fig. 47.2 Lisette Model, *San Francisco*, 1949, gelatin silver print. National Gallery of Canada, Ottawa, Gift of the Estate of Lisette Model, 1990, by direction of Joseph G. Blum, New York, through the American Friends of Canada (35293)

48 Barbara Morgan
Buffalo, Kansas 1900–1992 North Tarrytown, New York
Martha Graham, Letter to the World (Kick) 1940
Gelatin silver print, 38.5 × 48.2 cm
42338

Inscriptions   secondary support, l.r., graphite, *Barbara Morgan*

Provenance   purchased by Bruce Silverstein Gallery, New York, through Sotheby's, New York, 17 October 2006 (lot 67); Wach Gallery, Avon Lake, Ohio; purchased from Wach Gallery, 2011

Morgan's photographs of the celebrated modernist dancer and choreographer Martha Graham have survived the test of time, eclipsing images made of her by photographers Imogen Cunningham and Philippe Halsman. Her anointment as the chronicler of Graham's repertoire of the 1930s and 1940s was warranted not only by the thoughtful consideration that the photographer gave to her role as an interpreter of movement, but also by the sheer graphic power of her images.

Letter to the World, (Kick) is a classic Morgan image. Indeed it is so iconic that it takes an unusual print such as this to renew one's appreciation of the mastery of all aspects of the picture, from its composition to its execution as a print. By taking the transitory experience of a Graham performance and fixing a single movement from it in space and time – capturing the gesture, the volumes of her body and the lines of the drapery folds – Morgan succeeds in creating a permanent and timeless image from an essentially ephemeral experience.

Based on an Emily Dickinson poem, *This is My Letter to the World*, Graham's choreography expresses the interiority of the poet's world. It is tempting to interpret her dance in such a way that she is a messenger to the outside world bringing "The simple news that Nature told, With tender majesty." The isolation by Morgan of this one movement exemplifies majesty, grace and a degree of despair. In capturing the dancer extending out into space and yet retaining the mood of inwardness by showing her head in a downward somewhat melancholic pose, Morgan has distilled the essence of the dance and its tribute to the poet.

The photographer and dancer worked in close collaboration. The photographs were not made during scheduled performances, but were staged either in the theatre after hours or in Morgan's studio. Morgan's unusual ability to immerse herself completely in the performance, and yet be sufficiently detached as to recognize precisely the right moment to release the shutter, won Martha Graham's praise: "It is rare," the dancer wrote, "that even an inspired photographer possesses the demonic eye, which can capture the instant of a dance and transform it into a timeless gesture.… Barbara Morgan through her art reveals the inner landscape that is a dancer's world."[1]

49 Barbara Morgan

Buffalo, Kansas 1900–1992 North Tarrytown, New York
Martha Graham, War Theme 1941, printed c. 1945
Gelatin silver print, 45.5 x 64.6 cm
42337

Inscriptions   secondary support, b.l., graphite, *Martha Graham – War Theme*, l.r. below image, graphite, *Barbara Morgan 1941*; verso, t.r., graphite, *329*, u.c., black ink, *Martha Graham – War Theme – 1941 – © – 1972 / Barbara Morgan –*

Provenance   given by the artist to Craig Krull, San Francisco; purchased by Bruce Silverstein Gallery, New York, c. 2002; purchased by Eric Ludtke, Houston; purchased by Bruce Silverstein, 2003; purchased 2008

Like *Letter to the World* (see cat. 48), *Martha Graham, War Theme* is a powerful image of the legendary modernist American dancer, captured mid-movement. Reaching out expressionistically into space with the thrust of her body, Graham suggests the shape of a machine gun. Morgan has captured Martha Graham as the "taut and apparently willful revolutionary; a language and a stage presence that repelled as often as it attracted."[1]

War Theme, like *Letter to the World*, is based on a poem – a poem in progress, to be exact. The verso inscription of an 8 × 10 print in the New York Public Library reveals the inspiration behind the photograph: "William Carlos Williams asked Martha and Barbara Morgan to make an illustration for a poem he was writing on the Spanish Loyalist war so we collaborated and created this as if a Bomb [sic] was going to descend." Morgan added and underscored, "This is not a 'dance.' It was a 'study.'" The photographer, writer and dancer met in Graham's studio, where Morgan arranged the lighting in such a way that it would appear as if a bomb were exploding. In other words, Morgan utilized the studio lighting to enhance volume, seize movement and express an idea, in much the same way that Graham used her body to inform space.

Barbara Morgan first met Graham in 1935, shortly after she had started to take photographs, marking the beginning of an intense and highly productive collaboration. Graham's unorthodox dance style inspired Morgan to produce her most compelling images. Born Barbara Brooks Johnson in Buffalo, Kansas, in 1900, Morgan began her artistic career as a painter. She studied art from 1919 to 1923 at the University of California, Los Angeles, joining the faculty in 1925. She became interested in photography during the period from 1925 to 1930 when teaching at UCLA and helped mount an exhibition of Edward Weston's prints in one of the university's galleries. Living in New York in 1935, she experienced her first Martha Graham performance, "Primitive Mysteries," at the 95th Street YMCA and started her fifty-year collaboration and friendship with the dancer. Even in the non-photographic work she continued to produce, her aesthetic evolved from figurative to abstract, a development that one might attribute, to her engagement with essential movement in dance.

Graham summed up the significance of this body of Morgan's work in the following passage, noting how the photograph provides a permanent record of a transient experience:

> The only record of a dancer's art lies in the other arts. A dancer's instrument is his body bounded by birth and death. When he perishes his art perishes also. The art of dance is not arrested, but the world has only a legend about the individual, and the quality that has made him an artist…. Photographs present more tangible evidence of a dancer's career. Photographs, when true to the laws that govern inspired photography, reveal facts of feature, bodily contour, and some secret of his power.[2]

50   Arnold Newman

New York 1918–2006 New York
Alfred Stieglitz and Georgia O'Keeffe 1944
Gelatin silver print, 24.1 × 19.4 cm
32322

Inscriptions   secondary support, l.l., graphite, *Steiglitz and O Keefe Spring '44*, l.r., graphite, *Arnold Newman*

Annotations   secondary support, verso, u.c., green ink, *Georgia O'Keeffe and Alfred Stieglitz*; u.c., graphite, *6* [circled];
c. black ink stamp, repeated, *PHOTOGRAPH BY / ARNOLD NEWMAN / NEWMAN STUDIOS / 311 LINCOLN ROAD / MIAMI
BEACH 39, FLA.*; c. graphite, *1944*; l.c., grey ink stamp, twice, *© ARNOLD NEWMAN / THIS PHOTOGRAPH CANNOT
BE USED FOR / THE REPRODUCTION IN ANY FORM WITHOUT THE / EXPRESSED AND WRITTEN PERMISSION / OF THE
PHOTOGRAPHER, IT CAN BE USED / FOR EXHIBIT PURPOSES ONLY.*

Provenance   gift of Dorothy Meigs Eidlitz, St. Andrews, New Brunswick, 1968

Portraiture was Arnold Newman's métier. After spending two years from 1936 to 1938 studying painting
at the University of Miami Beach, Newman took up a position in Philadelphia working as an assistant in
the portrait studio of Leon Perskie.[1] This double portrait was made three years after Newman relocated to
New York, where, in 1946, he would open his own studio.[2]

As someone with training in art and with early aspirations to practice as a painter,[3] Newman would quite
naturally come to pioneer aesthetically in photography once he chose it as his medium. He was consequently
credited with having created the genre of "environmental portraiture," which eliminated the formality of
portraits posed in the impersonal setting of a studio and replaced it with a context familiar to the sitter.

Newman was particularly drawn to photographing artists. "I'm interested in people who do things," he said,
"and the hardest working people I know are creative people: artists, musicians, writers."[4] Many of his
portraits of artists were photographed in their workplaces, allowing their personalities to be more fully
expressed by the inclusion of objects that they had made, such as in the portrait of Jackson Pollock
(fig. 50.1) or tools central to the execution of their art, as in his legendary Stravinsky portrait.

Oddly, this likeness of two of America's most accomplished artists of the twentieth century was made in
one of the most neutral of environments, focussing attention exclusively on their dramatically cloaked
and darkly robed figures. The corner of the stark white room in which they appear serves to enhance the
blackness of their silhouettes and confers a memorial mood upon the picture.

Arnold Newman made this portrait just two years before Alfred Stieglitz's death. At the time of the sitting,
although still technically married, the couple were living separate lives and had been doing so since about
1933 when O'Keeffe could no longer tolerate Stieglitz's infidelities. If Newman did not consciously place
the two celebrated artists in this pose in order to construct a narrative of their disintegrating relationship,
but had some other intent in mind, this portrait is now the beneficiary, or victim, of hindsight. Facing two
different directions, Stieglitz stands and O'Keeffe is seated. He dominates the foreground while she is
half-obscured in the background. This portrait shows them, if somewhat grimly, as two strongly independent
individuals, to the degree that they seem scarcely to register one another's presence. During the same sitting, Newman set up other configurations of the pose even more extreme in illustrating their separateness
(fig. 50.2). Newman has effectively used the space between his subjects as part of the environment to draw
a telling portrait of the complex psychology of the two artists.

Stieglitz and O'Keefe Spring '44   Arnold Newman

Fig. 50.1 Arnold Newman, *Jackson Pollock*, 1949. Arnold Newman Collection/Getty Images (53466599)

Fig. 50.2 Arnold Newman, *Portrait of O'Keefe and Stieglitz*, 1944, gelatin silver print. Arnold Newman Collection/Getty Images (113464606)

51   Irving Penn
Plainfield, New Jersey 1917–2009 New York
Colette (1873–1954) 1951, printed 1972
Platinum and palladium print, mounted on aluminum, 50.3 × 50 cm, sheet 63.3 × 55.9 cm
32593

Inscriptions   secondary support, verso, paper backing, all in graphite, c., *1054* [circled] *19/50* [circled] / *Wiggins –
tease[?] paper on aluminum / multiple coating and printing / 1* [circled] *Palladium / 2* [circled] *Platinum – palladium /
Print made summer 1972 / I Penn* [circled]

Annotations   secondary support, verso, c., black ink stamp, *Hand-coated by the photographer*, c., typewritten in black
ink, *COLETTE* [underlined] / *Photograph by Irving Penn / Copyright © 1960 by / The Conde Nast Publications Inc. /
Not to be reproduced without written / permission of the copyright owner.*, c., stamped in black ink, *Deacidified to pH
8.5-9.5*, c., stamped in black ink with graphite additions, *In addition to 50 numbered prints of this image / in platinum
metals, unnumbered, but signed, silver / prints not exceeding a total of 25 may exist.*

Provenance   purchased from David Mirvish Gallery, Toronto, 1978

Irving Penn earned a reputation as one of America's premier advertising and fashion photographers. He
also made a considerable contribution to the field of photography through his personal images. As a
student of renowned art director Alexey Brodovitch (1898–1971) at the Philadelphia Museum School of
Industrial Art, from 1934 to 1938, Penn learned how to make images that invite immediate attention and
close scrutiny.

Applying his talents in the early 1940s to various aspects of commercial work, including magazine production with *Vogue* and *Junior League* and advertising work for Saks Fifth Avenue, he undertook his
first significant photographic assignments in 1943, when Alexander Liberman hired him as an assistant
at *Vogue* and published one of his photographs on the cover of the October issue. This was followed by
photographic portraits and fashion work a year later.[1]

This likeness of Colette is best appreciated in the context of his portraits of artists made from the late 1940s
into the 1960s. Early on Penn was particularly fond of posing his subjects in the corner of his studio, such
as in the portrait of Igor Stravinsky with his hand to his ear, but in time he adopted a less rigid approach,
going so far as to make close-up views in which the sense of context is completely removed, as in a later
portrait of Anaïs Nin from 1971. In *Colette*, his flair for pared down, elegant composition and his feel for
textures much in evidence, Penn produced an unconventional portrait of Colette that shows a flamboyance
in keeping with the personality of his subject.

Showing Colette draped in richly textured, tactile fabrics – she is reputed to have been wearing her dress-
ing gown and night dress – Penn emphasizes her sensuality without glamorizing her. The light that falls
across her features is soft but nonetheless delineates with unforgiving clarity the signs of age. Colette's
third husband, Maurice Goudeket, describes the ways in which the Penn portrait departed from the typical
photographs of Colette: " … Penn made a truly stupefying portrait of her.… It was simply a head and shoulders. There was nothing between Colette and posterity but Colette herself: no apartment, and no legend."[2]

Reviled and celebrated during her lifetime for her sexually liberal ways that included numerous and simul-
taneous, bisexual affairs, three marriages, and a scandal-riddled liaison with her stepson from her second
marriage, Colette (born Sidonie-Gabrielle Colette) was a prolific fiction writer with occasional spells of
working in Paris music halls as a performer.[3] In this portrait, Colette, nearing her eightieth birthday, strikes
a pose that is full of challenge. With her chin propped on her right hand and her gaze directed forthrightly
at the photographer, Penn's portrait conveys her spirited sense of social defiance. The exaggerated foreshortening suggests that Penn lowered his shooting angle considerably to show the petite and courageous
woman as a powerhouse and the object of his intense admiration.

52   Charles Sheeler

Philadelphia 1883–1965 Dobbs Ferry, New York
Side of White Barn 1916–17
Gelatin silver print, 19.3 × 24.3 cm, sheet 20.3 cm × 25.3 cm
32988

Provenance   acquired from the artist by Dorothy Meigs Eidlitz, St. Andrews, New Brunswick; gift of Dorothy Meigs Eidlitz, 1968

Prior to his involvement with photography, Charles Sheeler was establishing himself as a talented painter. Only one year after graduating from the Pennsylvania School of Fine Arts, he exhibited two paintings in its annual exhibition, as he would do again in 1908 when he showed six, and had his first solo exhibition at the McClees Gallery, Philadelphia. He also exhibited five paintings at the William Macbeth Gallery in New York in November of that year.[1]

In 1910 he took the first serious step in his exploration of photography by acquiring a large-format camera. But it wasn't until 1920 that he would have a solo exhibition of his work, including photographs, at Marius de Zayas Modern Gallery in New York.

The vernacular structures in and around Doylestown, in Bucks County, Pennsylvania, where Sheeler and fellow artist and friend Morton Schamberg rented a 1768 house in 1910, were a major source of inspiration. Carefully observed and finely rendered images in both painting and photography provide an in-depth record of the deep attraction that Sheeler felt toward the simple geometric elegance of their Quaker home, while the barns of Doylestown attracted him for their materials.

This sparely eloquent image of the side of a barn in Bucks County would gain iconic status in the history of early twentieth-century modernist American photography. Recognized for its radical composition and sheer beauty, it was awarded fourth prize in the annual Wanamaker Photography contest. But at least one critic, puzzled by the austerity and simplicity of the image stated, "The Barn (Fourth Prize) is texture and nothing more."[2] Witnessing Sheeler's conversion to the more abstract and rule-breaking imperatives of modernism, Alfred Stieglitz, the sole photographer on the jury, must surely have rejoiced in *Side of White Barn*'s[3] expression of pure form, clarity and geometric simplicity, seeing in this its contravention of the very foundations of the Pictorialist aesthetic, with its emphasis on mood and painterliness.

A reviewer of his 1939 show at the Museum of Modern Art admitted to the conundrum that Sheeler's dexterity posed to a true appreciation of his art: "To say that as a painter he is a good photographer and vice versa is too trite to account for his impeccable craftsmanship."[4]

The push and pull from the two media that Sheeler experienced is commemorated in his painting *View of New York* (fig. 52.1),[5] created at a time when, under pressure from his dealer, Edith Halpern, he reduced his photographic practice. Despite this, Charles Sheeler's career in photography left a significant legacy. *Side of White Barn* was chosen for the landmark 1929 *Film und Foto* exhibition held in Stuttgart, along with nine other of his works.[6] While it significantly predates Paul Strand's *Barn Gaspé* (see cat. 66), one cannot help but see this latter image as having been made with *Side of White Barn* in mind despite the estrangement of the two photographers at the time.[7] It is also hard to imagine that *Side of White Barn* was not hovering in Edward Weston's subconscious when he made *Church Door, Hornitos* (fig. 52.2) a year before the two photographers, who had known each other since 1922, would join up for a barn photographing trip to northwestern Connecticut.[8]

Fig. 52.1 Charles Sheeler, *View of New York*, 1931, oil on canvas. Boston Museum of Fine Arts, The Hayden Collection – Charles Henry Hayden Fund (35.69)

Fig. 52.2 Edward Weston, *Church Door, Hornitos*, 1940, printed before July 1969, gelatin silver print. National Gallery of Canada, Ottawa (33667)

53   Aaron Siskind
New York 1903–1991 Providence, Rhode Island
Tabernacle City 1935, printed before March 1965
Gelatin silver print, 34 × 23 cm
32904

Annotations   **verso, secondary support, u.l., black ink, *No-194***
Provenance   **purchased from the artist, Chicago, 1969**

Aaron Siskind, the fifth child of Russian Jewish immigrants, grew up on New York's Lower East Side. Like many young idealists of the time, he joined the Young People's Socialist League (YPSL). In high school he showed a particular interest in contemporary poetry, favouring that of the Imagists and Ezra Pound. At City College, Siskind's love of English literature led him to a teaching career. Until 1947 he taught in the New York public school system and then switched to teaching photography at Trenton Junior College, in New Jersey, until 1949. In 1951 he moved to Chicago to join Harry Callahan on the staff of the Institute of Design as a photography teacher.

His first meaningful encounter with photography began with the gift of a camera from a friend in 1930 on the occasion of Siskind's delayed honeymoon in Bermuda. With his already established interest in literature and music, he was drawn to the way in which photography offered a new language for describing his experience of the world around him.

In 1932 Siskind became involved with the New York Film and Photo League, a highly politicized group from which the still photographers would break away and form the Photo League in 1936. For someone who was largely self-taught in photography, Siskind appears to have been remarkably precocious, creating two significant and sophisticated bodies of photographs before the decade was over: *Tabernacle City* (1932–40) and *Bucks County Architecture* (1935) [fig. 53.1].

Tabernacle City was a Methodist retreat on Martha's Vineyard. "It consisted of numerous small cabins which were constructed around a large simple central tabernacle," writes photographer Carl Chiarenza. "Most of the cabins are individually and ornately decorated in the gingerbread manner. Thus the architecture symbolizes the idea and activity of the retreat: communal sharing and individual meditation."[1] The discovery of this site in the early 1930s was a revelation for Siskind. Just two years into the Depression, many of the cabins had been abandoned or were up for rent or sale. In a surprising move for someone whose political awareness was strongly anchored in socialism, Siskind did not contemplate the impact on the community, but rather, with little to restrict his ability to photograph there, he explored the architecture in its broad and detailed forms.

In this image of a decorative window opening, Siskind delights not only in the simplicity of the architectural structure and the patterning of the applied decoration, but also in the play of the leafy shadows on the surface of clapboard walls. The confident and radical composing of the image recalls Stieglitz's *Grape Leaves and House, Lake George* (fig. 53.2)

The Photo League, in which photography and politics were discussed with equal passion, initially provided Siskind with an environment in which dialogue about the medium and its potential for instigating social change flourished.[2] It was inevitable, however, that Siskind's aesthetic inclinations would eventually clash with the more ideological leanings of his colleagues. In early 1941, after having exhibited *Tabernacle City,* he found himself having to lead a discussion on his work in order to justify the non-political nature of his subject matter. Unable to work within such narrow confines, Siskind left the organization.[3]

Fig. 53.1 Aaron Siskind, *Bucks County 62*, c. 1936–39, printed before March 1965, gelatin silver print. National Gallery of Canada, Ottawa (32897)

Fig. 53.2 Alfred Stieglitz, *Grape Leaves and House, Lake George*, 1934, gelatin silver print. George Eastman House, Part purchase and part gift of An American Place, International Museum of Photography and Film, Rochester, New York

54 Aaron Siskind
New York 1903–1991 Providence, Rhode Island
Maine 1 1949, printed before March 1965
Gelatin silver print, 35.1 × 49.3 cm
32937

Inscriptions   verso, secondary support, u.l., black ink, *No – 97*
Provenance   purchased from the artist, Chicago, 1969

After disengaging from the Photo League in 1941, Aaron Siskind explored the metaphoric and formal values in photography more intensely, going so far as to make images that were either ambiguously representational or abstract. This proclivity was encouraged by the contact he had with some of the New York Abstract Expressionists, one of whom was Barnett Newman, a college friend. Siskind's love of contemporary poetry led him to join City College's literary club, the Clionian Society, where he met Newman and others who would distinguish themselves in New York's art, literary and music scenes between the 1940s and the 1970s. The association with Abstract Expressionist painters was critical to Siskind's evolution as a photographer.

Annual visits to Gloucester and Martha's Vineyard, Massachusetts and the surrounding area in the 1940s were typically spent in the company of Newman, Adolph Gottlieb and Mark Rothko, all of whom provided him with the opportunity to discuss art. This area also offered Siskind a wealth of subject matter ranging from wall surfaces to pieces of discarded rope found on the beach.

By the time that *Maine 1* was made in 1949, Siskind had resigned from teaching in the public school system and had gained recognition in the New York art world by exhibiting his photographs at the Charles Egan Gallery, beginning in 1947 and continuing into the early 1950s.[1] Absorbed by the ways in which found objects of all kinds could suggest anthropomorphic figures, or became totemic (figs. 54.1 and 54.2), Siskind started to work with the pictorial possibilities of the flat plane in the early 1940s. *Maine 1* invites the viewer to contemplate not only the original subject of the photograph, the peeling and bubbling paint surface of a wall, but also the translation of this surface into the rich and seductive tones of the photographic paper. In other works from this period, Siskind introduces a note of spatial ambiguity into the picture (fig. 54.3), an aspect of photographic picture-making he would elaborate on in later work.

In 1951 Siskind joined the teaching staff of the Institute of Design in Chicago, a move that was in synchrony with his now-established practice of examining the structures and surfaces of objects around him, from detritus to fine architecture and experimenting with new ways of expressing and interpreting these forms. His development of a unique picture-making vocabulary owed a significant debt to the painters with whom he associated.

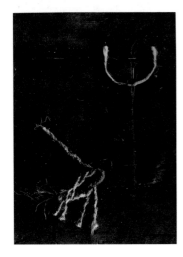  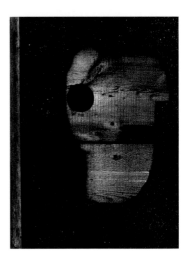

Fig. 54.1 Aaron Siskind, *Gloucester 28*, 1944, printed before March 1965, gelatin silver print. National Gallery of Canada, Ottawa (32910)

Fig. 54.2 Aaron Siskind, *Gloucester 1*, 1944, printed before March 1965, gelatin silver print. National Gallery of Canada, Ottawa (32905)

Fig. 54.3 Aaron Siskind, *Gloucester 16A*, 1944, printed before March 1965, gelatin silver print. National Gallery of Canada, Ottawa (32908)

55 W. Eugene Smith
Wichita, Kansas 1918–1978 Tucson, Arizona
Spanish Wake 1950, printed 1960
Gelatin silver print, 22.5 × 33.7 cm
41284

Inscriptions   l.r., incised with stylus, *W. Eugene Smith*

Annotations   secondary support, verso, u.l., graphite, possibly in different hands, *AY11 / 02 / MEH.MEH674*, u.r., graphite, *KATH. CARTER*, l.c., graphite, *PF47159*, c., grey ink stamp, inverted, *THIS PHOTOGRAPH TAKEN AND COPYRIGHTED / CREDIT / © W. EUGENE SMITH*, grey ink stamp, inverted, *THIS PHOTOGRAPH MAY NOT BE REPRODUCED WITHOUT WRITTEN CONSENT OF W. EUGENE SMITH*

Provenance   purchased from the Howard Greenberg Gallery, New York, 2003

Although attracted to aviation as a possible career early on in his life,[1] Eugene Smith seemed predestined to leave his mark in photography as one of the most significant photojournalists of the twentieth century. His mother, a keen amateur photographer, had a darkroom at home and when he was still in high school he sold his photographs to the *Wichita Eagle* and the *New York Times*.[2] His ability to make professional quality photographs gained him entrance to Notre Dame University on a scholarship in 1936 but he stayed only for a year before moving away to study at the New York Institute of Photography.[3] This was followed by brief employment at *Newsweek*, freelance work for photo agencies and, in 1939, an assignment for *Life*, the newly established illustrated magazine where he would experience a turbulent sixteen years.

Made for one of Smith's last assignments for the magazine, *Spanish Wake*, with its potent message of communal grief, is one of the great icons of twentieth-century photography, reminiscent, in its conscious staging, of Rembrandt's *Anatomy Lesson* (fig. 55.1). Although Smith, his assistant and his interpreter had set off to Spain in May 1950, ostensibly in search of a story about "the struggle for food with political overtones,"[4] the narrative that resulted was a more complex chronicling of life in Deleitosa, a village situated between Salamanca and Madrid. Shaped by poverty and religion and bypassed by any twentieth-century developments, the village was small and medieval in character. Working with 2¼ and 35mm cameras and interrupted only by the occasional visit to Madrid, Smith travelled daily to Deleitosa from Trujillo, forty kilometres away.[5] Photographing the villagers as they went about their daily activities, he was fastidious in ensuring that his reportage be both comprehensive and respectful of his subjects and village life. He would often ask villagers to re-enact gestures he had previously seen until he got the picture he wanted. Of the seventeen photographs that make up the photo-essay, *Spanish Wake* was selected as the closing image, which was spread across two pages. Smith constructed the image with a theatre director's eye for maximizing the drama of the event.[6] "Smith's camera viewpoint," wrote Glenn Willumson, "places the viewer alongside the body as if we, too, were mourning the death of the old man."[7] In this way Smith captured a specific event unfolding at a particular time and place and transformed it into a universal statement about loss and mourning.[8]

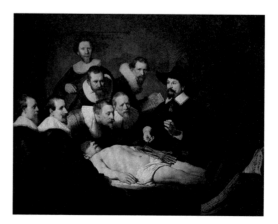

Fig. 55.1 Rembrandt van Rijn, *The Anatomy Lesson of Dr. Nicolaes Tulp*, c. 1632, oil on canvas. Royal Cabinet of Paintings, Mauritshuis, The Hague, Netherlands

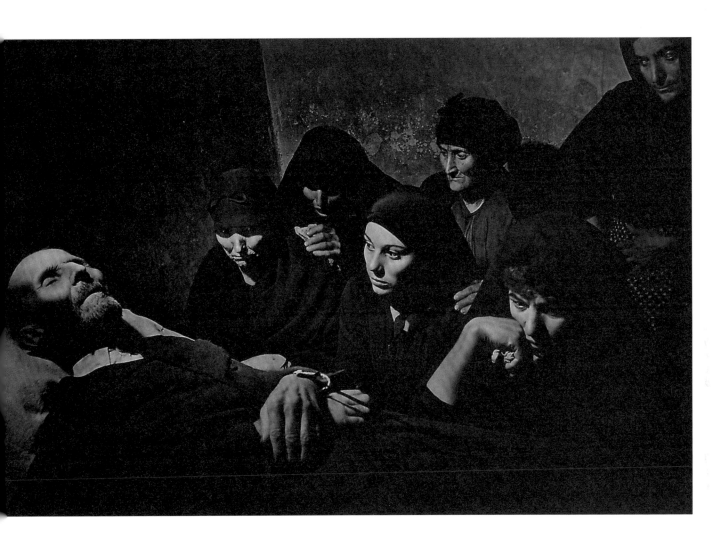

56   Edward J. Steichen

Bivange, Luxembourg 1879–1973 West Redding, Connecticut
Lady and the Lamp 1899
Platinum print, 20.7 × 13.9 cm
42873

Inscriptions   **verso, l.c., graphite,** *1899*

Annotations   **secondary support, verso, l.c., label printed in black ink with typewritten additions,** *MUSEUM OF MODERN ART / 11 WEST 53₀₀ STREET, NEW YORK 19, N.Y. / ARTIST: Edward Steichen / TITLE: Lady and Lamp 1899 / MEDIUM: Platinum print / MOMA - Gift of the Photographer / MUSEUM NO: STORAGE SPACE: / 145.61* **[crossed out]** */ COLLECTION OF PHOTOGRAPHS,* **l.r., graphite,** *65/72*

Provenance   **gift of the artist to Museum of Modern Art, New York; purchased by Hans P. Kraus Jr., New York, through Sotheby's, New York, 22 October 2002; purchased from Hans P. Kraus, New York, 2009**

Lady and the Lamp is one of the few remaining images from Edward Steichen's early years practicing photography. Steichen's career as a photographer would come to embrace all the significant cultural and technological shifts that shaped the medium as an art form in the late nineteenth century and early twentieth century. Steichen and his family immigrated to the United States from Luxembourg in 1881, eventually settling in Milwaukee.[1] In 1895, while serving a four-year apprenticeship as a lithographer at Milwaukee's American Fine Art Company, Steichen bought his first camera.[2] Soon, he was teaching himself both to paint and to take photographs and, with a group of friends, founded the Milwaukee Art Students League.[3] He thus came to the practice of photography with a picture-making sensibility formed from his experience of painting and printmaking. Steichen began exhibiting his romantic Pictorialist photographs in photographic salons, including the landmark exhibition, "The New School Of American Photography," shown in Paris and London. By 1901, he was elected a member of the Linked Ring.[4] For at least twenty years Steichen brought to his photography practice a romantic and symbolist sensibility that privileged soft focus, silhouette and diffused light over a uniform distribution of tones. Suffused with a quiet but evocative moodiness, his paintings and photographs were intimate and accomplished.

Symbolism had a strong influence on what was known as the Secessionist movement in photography, inspiring photographers to make images that resembled painting rather than transcriptions of reality. In *Lady and the Lamp*, a full length, three-quarter profile of a young woman dominates the picture. Wearing a cape of shimmering fabric she gazes into the light of a standing lamp, a symbol of knowledge and enlightenment. The light from the lamp, itself a strong point of illumination, gives vague definition to the lamp stand and the rippling folds of her clothing and, although it floods her face, her features remain in soft focus. The rest of the picture is obscured by shadow and darkness.

It is worth noting that in the same year he made the platinum print of *Lady and the Lamp,* Steichen successfully exhibited, at the Second Philadelphia Salon of Pictorial Photography, *Lady in the Doorway, Milwaukee* (1898) [fig. 56.1], a gelatin silver print of similar composition and mood. The acclaim that this work received might well have inspired Steichen to create *The White Lady*, another figurative study of similar arrangement and mood (fig. 56.2).

Fig. 56.1 Edward J. Steichen, *Lady in the Doorway, Milwaukee*, 1898, gelatin silver print. Museum of Modern Art, New York, Gift of the photographer (141.61)

Fig. 56.2 Edward J. Steichen, *The White Lady*, before April 1906, half-tone. National Gallery of Canada, Ottawa, Gift of Dorothy Meigs Eidlitz, St. Andrews, New Brunswick, 1968 (34999.74)

57 Edward J. Steichen
Bivange, Luxembourg 1879–1973 West Redding, Connecticut
Nocturne – Orangerie Staircase, Versailles 1908
Gum bichromate print, 29.5 × 38.3 cm
33361

Annotations secondary support, verso, c. vertical, in graphite, *16 ᶜᵐ / to reproduce from this / in case you can't make / it from negative / Stieglitz*

Provenance purchased at Sotheby Parke Bernet (#3918), New York, through Daguerreian Era, Pawlet, Vermont, 1976

Nocturne – Orangerie Staircase, Versailles was made during Edward Steichen's second stay in France from 1906 until the outbreak of World War I in 1914. If he made his first trip, from 1900 to 1902, as a fledgling painter and photographer, this one was undertaken as a rising star. In the four years between visits, the aspiring young artist from Milwaukee had set up a studio at 291 Fifth Avenue – the future site of the Little Galleries of the Photo-Secession, also known as "291" – and became closely associated with Alfred Stieglitz, editor of *Camera Notes* magazine and doyen of the Photo-Secessionist movement.[1] He had also made some of his most iconic portraits, nudes, landscapes and urban views, including *J. Pierpont Morgan, Esq.* (1903), *In Memoriam* (1901), *The Pond – Moonrise* (fig. 57.1), and *The Flatiron* (1904).

Popularized in the 1870s paintings of James McNeill Whistler (fig. 57.2), the nocturne referred to the veil of darkness that marks the deepening shadows of nightfall or night itself. A visual trope for artists drawn to metaphysical renditions of reality, it permitted them to orchestrate the extremes of silhouetted areas and sharp glimmers of light in their compositions and to maintain an enigmatic quality in their pictures. Acutely aware of the graphic language of picture-making, Edward Steichen was well acquainted with the ways of executing visual images in a lower tonal register, both in his landscape paintings and in his photographic work. He had already demonstrated this in 1904 in making *The Pond – Moonrise*, also a platinum-based print. Prudently placing a single accent of light on the pediment of the orangery in *Nocturne – Orangerie Staircase, Versailles*, Steichen draws attention to the upper centre portion of the print in this otherwise murky and deeply silhouetted scene. Being thus drawn into the picture surface, the eye takes in the extreme subtleties of light and dark that are played out against each other.

During his first stay in France, Steichen had developed a friendship with the French sculptor Auguste Rodin, whom he greatly admired, photographing him and his work in his studio in Meudon. During a later, longer stay in France, Steichen repeated his visit and on one occasion encouraged Rodin to move his monumental plaster of the French writer Honoré de Balzac outdoors at night so that he could capture it under moonlight in a series of gum-platinum prints. Steichen's passion for the mysterious and enclosing atmosphere of night time is expressed in both his iconic *Balzac, The Silhouette – 4 a.m* and *Nocturne – Orangerie Staircase, Versailles*.

Made in the same year, both of these works are virtuoso performances in the exploration of the stylistic and syntactical scope offered by the nocturne and evidence of its great attraction to Steichen. "The romantic and mysterious quality of moonlight, the lyric aspect of nature made the strongest appeal to me," he would write in his autobiography.[2] *Nocturne - Orangerie Staircase, Versailles* was exhibited in the landmark International Exhibition of Pictorial Photography, held at the Albright Art Gallery in Buffalo, New York, in 1910.

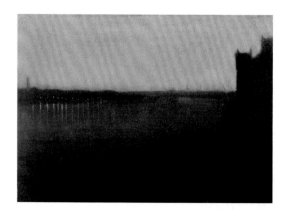

Fig. 57.1 Edward Steichen, *The Pond – Moonrise*, 1904, Platinum print with applied colour, Metropolitan Museum of Art, New York, Alfred Stieglitz Collection, 1933 (33.43.40)

Fig. 57.2 James Abbott McNeill Whistler, *Nocturne in Grey and Gold Westminster Bridge*, c 1871–72, oil on canvas. The Burrell Collection, Glasgow Museums (35.642)

58 Edward J. Steichen
Bivange, Luxembourg 1879–1973 West Redding, Connecticut
Sunburn, New York 1925
Gelatin silver print toned, 24 × 19.4 cm, sheet 25 × 20 cm
40068

Inscriptions   verso, l.c., graphite, *34 / Sunburn*

Annotations   secondary support, verso, u.c., grey ink stamp, *PHOTOGRAPH BY STEICHEN / 80 WEST 40ᵀᴴ STREET / NEW YORK*, c., stamped in grey ink, *COPYRIGHT / Conde Nast Publications, Inc.*, l.c., graphite, *PF22738*

Provenance   Joanna Steichen; Howard Greenberg Gallery, New York, 1998; purchased from Howard Greenberg Gallery, 1999

Edward Steichen's career as a photographer came to embrace almost all the significant cultural and technological shifts that shaped the medium as an art form in the late nineteenth and early twentieth centuries. Joel Smith, chronicler of Steichen's early years, aptly describes him as "forging his rich patois of aesthetic intuitions."[1]

Even a superficial comparison of *Sunburn* and his portrait of Eleanora Duse (fig. 58.1), made in 1903, provides ample evidence of this stylistic adaptability. An accomplished Pictorialist photographer who experimented with the Autochrome colour process in the first decade of the century, he turned, in the 1920s, to an aesthetic more closely aligned to "straight" photography and to the decidedly more lucrative business of fashion photography. A gifted printmaker capable of executing the highest quality gum bichromate and platinum prints – and a combination of both processes – he came to reject the materials and techniques associated with his earlier more gestural printmaking. Instead he opted for the cleaner definition and crisp surfaces of the gelatin silver print.

Steichen's decision to accept the position of chief photographer to the Condé Nast publishing empire, in 1923, strained his relationship with Alfred Stieglitz. While much of Steichen's commercial work was driven by the necessity of making money – he had substantial alimony payments[2] – he also wanted his images to reach a wider audience. "Photographic prints," he said, "are too slow and don't reach far, but the printed page goes all over the world."[3]

Steichen would serve his extended audience over the years with a dynamic range of portraits of celebrity sitters for *Vanity Fair* and *Vogue*. His characteristic emphasis on the face is evident in the portraits of Duse, Gloria Swanson (fig. 58.2), and in *Sunburn*. In the latter two, this tight framing suggests he intended to gain greater psychological insight into his sitter by forcing attention to what he considered the sole arena of expressive gesture. The Duse portrait is parsed in soft and gauzy terms that disembody the subject and expel any sense of personality, while the graphically powerful and unyielding portraits of Swanson and the sitter in *Sunburn* suggest a different recognition of female identity.

The subject of *Sunburn* was an "unknown." Published in a layout with other Steichen images[4] in the 15 May 1950 issue of *Life* to accompany an article on the photographer, the caption describes her as "a visitor who came to the photographer's New York studio after a day on the beach. Steichen was struck by the peculiar, almost wild, look that the sunburn gave to her eyes."[5]

Possibly Steichen was indeed simply responding to the possibilities in the contrast between her skin tone and the whites of her eyes, but the radical composition, which reduces the head to an almost Brancusi-like shape,[6] suggests a more complex set of responses, including a desire to show that he was both progressive as an artist and capable of making a portrait infused with passion and intimacy, as Stieglitz and Strand had done respectively in their series of portraits of Georgia O'Keeffe and Rebecca Strand.

Fig. 58.1 Edward J. Steichen, *Duse*, 1903, photogravure. National Gallery of Canada, Gift of Dorothy Meigs Eidlitz, St. Andrews, New Brunswick, 1968 (34999.68)

Fig. 58.2 Edward J. Steichen, *Gloria Swanson*, 1924, gelatin silver print. The Museum of Modern Art, New York, gift of the photographer (219.1961)

59 Ralph Steiner
Cleveland, Ohio 1899–1986 Hanover, New Hampshire
Model T 1929, printed later
Gelatin silver print, 24.2 × 19.2 cm, sheet 25 × 20 cm
35955

Inscriptions   secondary support, l.r., black ink, *1929 Ralph Steiner / neg. and print*, verso, c., black felt pen, *Ralph Steiner / negative and print / 1929*

Annotations   secondary support, verso, l.r., red felt pen, *EP*; tertiary support, c., typewritten label, *Ralph Steiner / Model T / 1929*, l.l., graphite, *GC953 / -16*

Provenance   purchased from Christie's New York ("19th and 20th Century Photographs," lot 406), 1991

Ralph Steiner claimed to have been completely innocent of the concept of abstract art in the early phase of his career as a photographer. Writing in 1980 about a group of proof prints depicting the geometry and cast shadows of an egg-beater (fig. 59.1), visual exercises in lighting and form undertaken at the Clarence White School between 1921 and 1922, Steiner made the following comment about the place of abstraction in his vision: "I knew nothing at the time of Vorticism, and may not have know[n] the word 'abstraction.' At Dartmouth I'd take[n] 'Modern Art I and II.' It began, modern-ly with Jan and Hubert Van Eyck … Although the Nude had already Descended the Stairs, we never heard one word of *even* the Impressionists – don't know if the Professor approved."[1]

It was undoubtedly during his year under Clarence White in New York that Steiner's awareness of non-figurative art was nurtured. The emphasis placed on the non-representational aspects of picture-making in the Clarence White School curriculum tended toward – as Steiner is reputed to have complained later – "Design, design, design."[2] In his composition of *Model T,* Steiner makes evident not only his fascination with geometric forms, but also his ability to transform the essence of everyday objects into images that excite a level of contemplation detached from functionality. This radically framed image of the car's front fender, wheel and part of its axel shows Steiner's delight in curves, round forms and radiating spokes, as well as in the play of the shadows cast by the wheel. As tedious as photographing egg beaters may have seemed to Steiner when he was a student, there is no doubt that his appreciation of abstract form would manifest itself when making *Model T* and other images later in the early 1930s.

By 1929, the year he made *Model T* and the related images in the National Gallery's collection – *Ford Car* 1929/1979 and *Saratoga Coal Makes Warm Friends* (1929/1979) – Steiner had met and come under the influence of Paul Strand. It is highly likely that he would have seen Strand's *Wire Wheel*, a much earlier silver platinum print of the same type of subject matter (fig. 59.2). There is a marked difference between Strand's stronger aestheticization of the object's lines and Steiner's inclusion of part of the licence plate, which grounds the object in mundane reality. Steiner and Strand eventually collaborated in the making of two films: *The Plow that Broke the Plains* (1936) and *The City* (1939).

Steiner had begun to exhibit his photographs in the late 1920s and would be the first photographer invited to the Yaddo artists' colony in Saratoga Springs, New York, where he likely made this image.[3] By 1932 his photographs would be exhibited alongside those of Walker Evans and Margaret Bourke White. From the mid-1930s, his work would be characterized by strong material description, vernacular subject matter and the use of light to reveal shapes and structures.

Fig. 59.1 Ralph Steiner, *Untitled*, c. 1921–22, gelatin silver print, National Gallery of Canada, Ottawa, Gift of the artist, Thetford Hill, Vermont, 1980 (PSC80:823:6)

Fig. 59.2 Paul Strand, *Wire Wheel*, 1917, silver platinum print. Aperture Foundation, Paul Strand Archive

60 Alfred Stieglitz
Hoboken, New Jersey 1864–1946 New York
Miss S.R., Vienna 1904
Carbon print, 20.8 × 14 cm
42914

Inscription   verso, u.c., black crayon, *Miss R. – Vienna / 1904*

Provenance   **Christie's East, 8 November 1982 (Sale 5215, Lot 219); Sotheby's New York, 15 October 2008; unidentified owner; purchased from Hans P. Kraus, Jr., New York, 2009**

In the summer of 1904 while travelling in Europe, Alfred Stieglitz took three different views of a young woman in Vienna. We know her only as "Miss S.R." One of the portraits shows the sitter with her head slightly tilted in a three-quarter right pose (fig. 60.1) and it is this one that is well known because of its publication as a photogravure in two issues of *Camera Work*.[1] While the strong graphic qualities of the published version certainly make it a captivating and almost decorative image, this rare variant of *Miss S.R.* is a bolder and more natural portrait of the young woman. It is also a rare carbon print from this series. In this half-length portrait the sitter holds her body at a similar angle, but glances over her shoulder, past the photographer. Her coat fills the bottom half of the picture space in a way that makes the image more arresting and less decorative than the better-known view.[2] An intimate portrait and a very fine print, it might well be one of Stieglitz's last experiments with the carbon print.[3]

For Stieglitz photography was a medium that allowed him to explore the world around him in all its manifestations. He photographed people, buildings, street scenes and landscapes, bringing to all of these subjects a keen sense of picture-making and an eye for how the camera could record the incidental and accidental in a way that animated the picture. His portraits of artists John Marin, Arthur Dove, and of his second wife, Georgia O'Keeffe, are recognized for their directness and, in the case of the latter, for their intensity and passion. His portraits of unidentified sitters, such as Miss S. R., however, also enjoy an important place in his oeuvre. As photographer Dorothy Norman observed, Stieglitz was "moved to photograph a face reflecting an innocence, a state of becoming, a search, a struggle, a feeling of wonder."[4] Among his many contributions to the field was Stieglitz's commitment to keeping photography alive to all the possibilities of aesthetic expression that the medium was capable of exploring. Stieglitz explored fresh approaches to almost all aspects of photography, including the genre of portraiture. One of his statements worthy of repeating in the context of a sitting that produced variant views was his assertion that "to demand *the* portrait that will be a complete portrait of any person is as futile as to demand that a motion picture be condensed into a single still."[5]

Fig. 60.1 Alfred Stieglitz, *Miss S.R*, 1904, photogravure. National Gallery of Canada, Ottawa, Gift of Dorothy Meigs Eidlitz, St. Andrews, New Brunswick, 1968 (34999.59)

61 Alfred Stieglitz
Hoboken, New Jersey 1864–1946 New York
The Steerage 1907, printed 1915
Photogravure, 33.3 × 26.4 cm, sheet 46.6 × 31.9 cm
39132

Provenance   Yarlow/Salzman Gallery, Toronto; Alan Walker, Toronto; Rosemary Speirs, Ottawa; gift of Rosemary Speirs, Ottawa, 1997, in memory of Alan John Walker, Toronto

This photograph was taken by Alfred Stieglitz while aboard the *SS Kaiser Wilhelm II* en route to Europe, in May 1907. As a first class passenger Stieglitz, who was travelling with his wife and daughter, had the freedom to roam the upper decks of the boat, and it was probably during the ship's anchoring in Plymouth that he encountered the scene depicted here.[1] He described with vivid recall his response to seeing the clusters of people on the lower decks – travellers who had either gone to America to work temporarily, or who had been hopeful immigrants, turned away for some reason and now returning to the countries of their birth:

> The scene fascinated me: a round straw hat; the funnel leaning left, the stairway leaning right; the white draw-bridge, its railings made of chain; white suspenders crossed on the back of a man below; circular iron machinery; a mast that cut into the sky, completing the triangle. I stood spellbound for a while. I saw shapes related to one another – a picture of shapes, and underlying it, a new vision that held me: simple people; the feeling of ship, ocean, sky …[2]

A skilfully composed image that unites complex formal elements, *The Steerage*, like other seminal images in Stieglitz's oeuvre (see figs. 61.1 and 61.2), represents his ongoing reformulation of photographic seeing.[3] It is also an image that apparently elicited strong responses at the time of its making and continues to exist surrounded by a swirl of re-examination and debate.[4]

In 1914 Stieglitz asked Mexican artist Marius de Zayas, who was going to Paris, to take a print of *The Steerage* with him to show Pablo Picasso. De Zayas reported back to him that, upon seeing the print, Picasso concluded that Stieglitz was "the only one who has understood photography."[5] Picasso's endorsement of Stieglitz, and of *The Steerage* in particular, inspired even greater interest in the image. In 1915 de Zayas and Paul Haviland wrote brief texts to accompany its publication as a large format photogravure in the magazine *291*. De Zayas felt that in *The Steerage,* Stieglitz had "obtained the verification of a fact,"[6] an interesting, if curious, assessment of a work that is such a virtuoso expression of how the camera can radically transform our perception of reality by favouring formal structure. Stieglitz thus casts into doubt the notion of photography as a transmitter of "facts."

Fig. 61.1 Alfred Stieglitz, *Paula, Berlin*, 1889, gelatin silver print. George Eastman House, Rochester, New York, Part purchase and part gift of An American Place, ex-collection Georgia O'Keeffe (74:0052:0040)

Fig. 61.2 Alfred Stieglitz, *The "Mauretania,"* 1910, photogravure. National Gallery of Canada, Ottawa, Gift of Dorothy Meigs Eidlitz, St. Andrews, New Brunswick, 1968 (34999.98)

62 Alfred Stieglitz
Hoboken, New Jersey 1864–1946 New York
Equivalent c. 1930
Gelatin silver print, 11.2 × 8.8 cm
41925

Provenance   purchased from Lee Gallery, Winchester, Massachusetts, 2006

On the shores of Lake George, in New York's Adirondack Mountains, Alfred Stieglitz's summer home Oaklawn brought a measure of tranquillity to his life.[1] It also provided him with the stimulus to explore connections between nature and his own thoughts about human existence in his photographic studies of clouds, trees, portraits, or nudes. Some bodies of work, most specifically those of clouds, reached a metaphoric height previously unattained in his work. His decision to orient his camera upward and capture – under all kinds of weather and lighting conditions – the ever-changing play of clouds sweeping up from behind the hills of Lake George grew out of a range of competing ideas and emotions that he recorded as visual *equivalents*.[2] First embarked upon in the fall of 1922,[3] a year of significant turmoil and change for him, Stieglitz found solace in the constant manifestations and rhythms of nature as they are embodied in cloud forms. Working with an 8 × 10 camera, he rendered the horizon line visible in these earliest cloud studies. In 1923 he turned to working with a 4 × 5, eliminating all evidence of the landscape and titling the series of images *Songs of the Sky*.

Stieglitz first saw these photographs as analogous to passages of music and called the first grouping *Music – A Sequence of Ten Cloud Photographs*. He reinforced this concept by exhibiting them a year later as *Clouds in Ten Movements* and naming new photographs of clouds from that year *Songs of the Sky*. This exploration became a body of more than 350 images celebrating the abstract values of light and dark and more importantly, represented what Stieglitz called *Equivalents*, or later simply *Equivalent*, meaning that each photograph of a cloud formation stood for his state of mind at the time of its capture.

A comparison of this image with *Equivalent* (fig. 62.1) shows Stieglitz's penchant at this time for working with a sky that is a darkened field punctuated only sparingly by light. Stieglitz, once again in a melancholic mood, was identifying with its oppressive darkness. Even so, the shifting skies must have provided Stieglitz with the consolation that whatever his own trials, they were outmatched by nature on a far more dramatic scale. Stieglitz would end the series in 1935.[4]

Stieglitz travelled to Europe frequently in the first decades of his career as a photographer, publisher and gallerist, visiting London on several occasions. Although he attributed his interest in this subject to his student days in Germany in the late 1880s,[5] it is tempting to speculate that he might have seen the paintings of John Constable, who a hundred years earlier made his first studies of clouds (fig. 62.2). Constable also recognized their relationship to music and their emotional appeal. Skies, he wrote "must and always shall with me make an effectual part of the composition. It will be difficult to name a class of Landscape, in which the sky is not the "key note," the standard of "Scale," and the chief "Organ of Sentiment.""[6]

Fig. 62.1 Alfred Stieglitz, *Equivalent*, 1929, gelatin silver print. National Gallery of Canada, Ottawa (41561)

Fig. 62.2 John Constable, *Cloud Study*, 27 August 1822, oil on paper relaid on synthetic board, presented anonymously 1952. Tate Gallery, London (N06065)

63   Alfred Stieglitz
Hoboken, New Jersey 1864–1946 New York
Poplars, Lake George 1932
Gelatin silver print, 23.9 cm × 18.8 cm
37978

Provenance   purchased from the Andrew Smith Gallery, Sante Fe, New Mexico, 1995

When Alfred Stieglitz made *Poplars, Lake George*, he was preoccupied with nature as poetic metaphor. Unlike artists focused on the rugged properties of the grand landscape,[1] he was drawn to the isolation of details in natural forms. His metaphorical association of natural forms with either music or internal psychological moods places Stieglitz in a closer relationship to Symbolist painters than to any of his contemporaries in photography. Peter C. Bunnell eloquently summarizes Stieglitz's personal identification with the outside world: "Every image came from deep within him, and his goal was to manifest this depth on the outside, and to have others awakened by it as if by his presence itself."[2]

With its tranquil setting, Lake George inspired in Stieglitz a desire to translate reality in a more metaphysical manner. If his cloud sequences (see cat. 62) are his visual equivalents of musical passages, Stieglitz's studies of trees, which date from the early 1920s through to his last years of photographing, represent time in a corporeal manner, alluding, as they do, to the cycle of life and death.[3]

In *Dancing Trees* (fig. 63.1) the limbs and trunks of two healthy trees embrace, whereas in *Poplars*, taken eleven years later, an old tree with tangled dead branches dominates the foreground, obscuring the young, living tree behind it. Among the best of Stieglitz's images, *Poplars* is rich in its expression of form and light; eloquent and radical at the same time in its exploration of the photographic vocabulary and, most importantly, expressive of the photographer's deepest feelings as he nears the end of the cycle of his own life. Stieglitz and his father had together planted the poplars, which had become "advanced in age, dead and dying by the 1930s."[4]

As director, from 1929 to 1946, of An American Place, on Madison Avenue, Stieglitz continued to advocate for photography, although his influence had diminished significantly by this time. It is possible that this image was made during the spring or summer of 1932, when the artist was experiencing severe personal conflict. The economic depression was intensifying and many respected colleagues such as Paul Strand were moving away from making only photographs and working in film. They were also rejecting imagery expressive of individual concerns, in favour of an engagement with larger collective political issues. This was a position antithetical to Stieglitz and his vehemence on this topic, as with other issues, led to bitter break-ups of friendships. His relationship with O'Keeffe had also deteriorated into harsh disputes. As he described the meaning of his photographs, his vision of the world bordered on apocalyptic and his photographs permitted him to introduce some order. "My photographs," he wrote, "are a picture of the chaos in the world and of my relationship to that chaos. My prints show the world's constant upsetting of man's equilibrium and his eternal battle to re-establish it."[5]

Whereas nature and trees appear in Stieglitz's earlier work as silhouetted, moody elements (fig. 63.2), here in this 1930s image he is delineating their forms in sharp realism.

Fig. 63.1 Alfred Stieglitz, *Dancing Trees*, 1921, palladium print. San Francisco Museum of Modern Art, Purchase, Alfred Stieglitz Collection

Fig. 63.2 Alfred Stieglitz, *Life and Death*, c. 1927, gelatin silver print. George Eastman House, Rochester, New York, Gift of Dorothy Norman

New York 1890–1976 Orgeval, France
Percé Beach, Gaspé 1929, printed c. 1945
Gelatin silver print, 11.9 × 14.7 cm, sheet 12.6 × 15.3 cm
41145

Inscriptions   secondary support, verso, c., blue ink, *Gaspé – 1929 / Percé beach – / Paul Strand*

Annotations   secondary support, verso, u.l., graphite, *#11*[?] *n group*, u.r., graphite, *GSP – SEA – 319 T III*

Provenance   **Paul Strand Archive, Millerton, New York; purchased by Kaspar Fleischmann, Galerie zur Stockeregg, Zurich, 1984; purchased with the support of the Members and Supporting Friends of the National Gallery of Canada and its Foundation, 2003**

Percé Beach, Gaspé is a picture about land, sky, weather and people at work. The beach occupies the foreground, rising from the lower right corner at a slight angle. A boat is brought ashore by fishermen who appear as small, silhouetted forms bent over the vessel's hull. The sails of already beached vessels remain rigged, while out in the middle distance the relatively smooth plane of water is dotted with the outlines of four other boats. The colossal outline of Percé Rock is etched sharply against the sky, the unmistakable profile of the headland looming over the ocean. The far shore appears as a misty, horizontal band of grey, while the sky is a subtle field of cloud cover, pale silvery light and soft clouds. Together the components are balanced in an exquisitely composed and executed picture. Art critic Belinda Rathbone noted that such photographs by Strand "evoke the physicality of clouds, a feeling of weather and seasonal effect, and a sense that these things are matters of daily consequence."[1]

Paul Strand took this photograph when he and his wife Rebecca Salsbury travelled to the Gaspé Peninsula. The area had recently been made accessible to tourism by the construction, in 1925, of Perron Boulevard, a 553-mile road that ringed the peninsula,[2] and its physical and cultural virtues were extolled by writers in numerous popular American magazines. Being there in the fall, Strand responded to the cool slate grey of the northern light, noting that it had necessitated switching processes to express its particularity. "Certain things," he wrote, "require a different kind of treatment. For instance, these things of the Southwest are platinum prints…. Then when I went up to the north to Gaspé in 1929, I couldn't print my pictures on platinum paper. I felt that, photographically speaking, though platinum was a much superior paper, it was the wrong paper. The north is cold, the colour that best showed this was something with a black overtone …"[3]

In keeping with his observation Strand slightly enlarged this image from a 4 × 5 negative and consciously printed it on a gelatin silver paper obtaining the softer, cooler tones.[4] It is not only the quality of light that Strand so effectively communicates in his 1929 Gaspé Peninsula pictures, but also the sense of relative scale, as demonstrated in other views of the beach at Percé, where the figures of fishermen and a horse are dwarfed by the immense open expanses of sea and sky (fig. 64.1).[5] In the catalogue of the 1945 Museum of Modern Art retrospective of Strand, Nancy Newhall emphasizes his ability to unite all the elements of his 1929 Gaspé experience into his pictorial structure: "he began composing with all landscape elements, developing an exquisite sense for the moment when the moving forces of clouds, people, boats are in perfect relation with the static forms of houses and headlands."[6] This is as much in evidence in his studies of Percé as it is in his miniaturized views of the villages dotting the Peninsula, such as the one taken at Saint-Maurice-de-l'Échouerie in 1929 (fig 64.2).

Fig. 64.1 Paul Strand, *Black Horse on the Beach, Percé Gaspé*, 1929, gelatin silver print. Philadelphia Museum of Art (1980-21-80)

Fig. 64.2 Paul Strand, *Village, Gaspé*, 1929, gelatin silver print. National Gallery of Canada, Ottawa, Purchased 1979 with the assistance of a grant from the Government of Canada under the terms of the Cultural Property Export and Import Act (33310)

65 Paul Strand
New York 1890–1976 Orgeval, France
Gaspé Fisherman, Hilaire Cotton (1865–1959) 1936, printed July 1937?
Gelatin silver print, 14.8 × 11.7 cm
41141

Inscriptions   verso, u.c., graphite, *Gaspé fisherman*, c., graphite, *Photograph by / Paul Strand*

Annotations   verso, u.l., blue pencil, *51* [circled], c.r., vertical, blue pencil, *6902*, l.l. vertical, graphite, *2751B* [circled], l.c., graphite, *7/1/37*

Provenance   from the artist to Cipe Pineles, early 1940s; Carole Fripp (née Pineles), Toronto; Stephen Bulger Gallery, Toronto; purchased with the support of the Members and Supporting Friends of the National Gallery of Canada and its Foundation, 2003

This is a rare and iconic portrait that Paul Strand made of Hilaire Cotton on his second trip to the Gaspé Peninsula in 1936. It is distinguished from the handful of other portraits made over the course of this visit by its complexity. Cotton stands in a patch of light just inside the door of what might be a fishing hut. Although fully facing Strand, his gaze is turned toward something lying outside the frame, the strong light causing him to furrow his brow. The unusual inclusion in this portrait of a sagging chicken wire fence between Strand and his subject misleadingly suggests a casualness of intent, but it is far from being a snapshot. The attention paid to the detailing of Cotton's shirt, braces and pants as well as the framing of his figure against a dark background and in relationship to the architecture, are all conscious picture-making strategies that we see Strand using in his celebrated earlier Mexican portraits of 1933–34 (fig. 65.1).

What are we to make of the photographer's intent? Does it reflect a prevailing sentiment labelled "anti-modernist" by those who understood the touristic attraction of places like the Gaspé Peninsula as an escape from a rapidly changing urban America, or was it an expression of solidarity with the worker? Given Strand's level of intellectual sophistication, it seems unlikely that he would have bought into the stereotype of the "habitant" or the "authentic French Canadian" popular among some English-speaking tourists to the Gaspé (both American and Canadian).[1]

By this time strongly politicized, Strand returned to the Gaspé in 1936 with a far greater interest in photographing people, whose absence in his previous pictures had been noted by Moscow theatre director Boris Alpers during a 1935 trip that Strand made with Harold Clurman to the Soviet Union.[2]

If this image contains any notion of a stereotype, it is because of the subject's status as a worker. Its use to illustrate a book review of M.J. Coldwell's *Left Turn Canada* in the Marxist publication *New Masses* would also suggest that both the photographer and the readership recognized its potential political import.[3]

Strand gives further expression to the relationship between people and their culture and environment – and to the political nature of this relationship – in his extraordinary publication *Time In New England*. The doorway which frames Hilaire Cotton in this picture is a trope repeated in many of Strand's portraits from the Gaspé trip, as well as in those taken over the next few decades in New England (fig. 65.2), Mexico, France and the Scottish Hebrides. It not only acts as an effective formal device to isolate his subjects, but also retains a material context for our better understanding of their social origins and reiterates their status as individuals.

In all likelihood, this gelatin silver print was made in 1937 and gold-toned by Strand to give it warmth and richness.

Fig. 65.1 Paul Strand, *Men of Santa Anna, Michoacan*, 1933, printed 1967, photogravure, from *The Mexican Portfolio* (1967). National Gallery of Canada, Ottawa (33306.5)

Fig. 65.2 Paul Strand, *Susan Thompson, Cape Split, Maine*, 1945, gelatin silver print. Philadelphia Museum of Art, The Paul Strand Retrospective Collection, 1915–1975. Gift of the Estate of Paul Strand, 1980 (1980-21-161)

66 Paul Strand
New York 1890–1976 Orgeval, France
Barn, Gaspé 1936
Platinum print, varnished, 11.8 × 15 cm, sheet 12.4 × 15.7 cm
41146

Inscriptions   secondary support, verso, l.l., graphite, *VIN/PLAT / 1st / class - P.S. 815A FII X*

Provenance   **Paul Strand Archive Millerton, New York; Galerie zur Stockeregg, Zurich, 1984; Purchased from Galerie zur Stockeregg with the support of the Members and Supporting Friends of the National Gallery of Canada and its Foundation, 2003**

Paul Strand's photographs of barns surpass mere documentation of their subject matter to become part of a complex mosaic of variations on a theme. It was not only the vernacular nature of their structures that interested him, or their form-follows-function aesthetic. Rather, it was something more layered and complex that embraced both of these aspects and gave the photographer the opportunity to explore materiality, geometry and pure abstraction. Carefully framed in the 4 × 5-inch or 5 × 7-inch screen of Strand's Graflex cameras, barn facades, with their often asymmetrical arrangement of doors, windows and shutters, became rhythmic arrangements of dark and light, solids and voids. The rectangles, squares and triangles of their windows, doors and roofs became compositional elements that he could use in a more overarching way, framing vistas and generally adding a strong visual dynamic to his picture-making (figs. 66.1 and 66.2).

It is tempting also to see, within Strand's repertoire of sheds, barns, fishing huts and simple wooden house fronts – deliberate quotations not only of other photographers' images but also of his own works. Strand likely met Charles Sheeler (see cat. 52) in 1918 when their work was exhibited at Marius de Zayas Modern Gallery in New York City. In 1920 they collaborated on the film *Manhatta*.

Sheeler's *Side of White Barn* left a strong impression on those who viewed it. In 1918 it won fourth prize in the John Wanamaker photography exhibition, with Alfred Stieglitz at the head of the jury.[1] Strand likely saw the print around this time and one imagines him paying close attention, not only committing its visual details to memory, but also mining it for the intelligence it offered on photographic vision and the future evolution of the medium. When Strand made *Barn, Gaspé* almost twenty years later, he was almost certainly entering into a visual dialogue with Sheeler's series of barns.

Photo historian Steve Yates points out that for Strand, "the front of wooden buildings became a concentrated subject that would continue to be utilized in numerous variations."[2] He effectively supports his observation by drawing our attention to the close relationship between *Barn, Gaspé* and *Ghost Town, Red River, New Mexico*, an image made six years earlier.

A varnished platinum print – and one of only two known prints of this image[3] – *Barn, Gaspé* is a rare and superb example of its kind.

Fig. 66.1 Paul Strand, *Trois-Rivières, Quebec*, 1936, gelatin silver print, toned. National Gallery of Canada, Ottawa, Purchased 1979 with the assistance of a grant from the Government of Canada under the terms of the Cultural Property Export and Import Act (33311)

Fig. 66.2 Paul Strand, *Village Gaspé*, 1936, gelatin silver print. San Francisco Museum of Modern Art, Collection of the Sack Photographic Trust

67 Paul Strand

New York 1890–1976 Orgeval, France
Closed Door, New England 1945
Gelatin silver print, 24.5 × 19.4 cm, sheet 25.4 × 20.2 cm
33307

Inscriptions   verso, all in graphite u.c., *Closed door / New England. 1945 / 26*, c., *Paul Strand H.S.*
Annotations   verso, in several hands, graphite, u.l., *#227 / 4*, u.c., *Closed door / New England 1945 / 26 / Paul Strand H.S.*, c., black ink stamp with graphite additions, *L 77.048*, l.c., graphite, *1no + [?] 5 [?]*
Provenance   purchased from the David Mirvish Gallery, Toronto, 1978

Closed Door, New England is an elegiac image. It appears in the fourth and final part of the 1950 publication *Time in New England*, by Paul Strand and Nancy Newhall.[1] This collaborative project consisted of a tandem gathering of photographs made by Strand – mainly in Maine and Vermont – in 1927–28 and again from 1944 to 1946, with text passages and poems selected by Newhall. Some of the texts date as far back as 1620. *Closed Door* is found opposite Thomas Wentworth Higginson's diary entry for 19 May 1886, in which he chronicles Emily Dickinson's funeral. On first read, the text seems oddly dissociated from Strand's image. "To Amherst," he wrote, "to the funeral of that rare and strange creature, Emily Dickinson." Higginson describes the country as "exquisite," the day as "perfect," and her appearance in death youthful and peaceful. Yet, moving between text and image, our appreciation of Strand's photograph deepens. The blackness of the door and central placement of the urn-shaped finial transcend the conventions of domestic architectural style. Just as they lend a solemn air to the image, so the light reflected off the glass panes of the transom and sidelights introduces an ethereal quality.

Time in New England comprises four parts with eighteen thematic sections.[2] While *Closed Door* is found in the section "Ebb," *Open Door* (fig. 67.1) appears earlier on in the book in the section "Hill and Town." Focusing on the partly open door leading into the vestibule, with its staircase and a chair on the landing visible, Strand has composed this photograph with equally exquisite precision. The two images evoke beginnings and endings.

Strand was fascinated by almost all aspects of quotidian life and this included the architectural setting in which the small dramas of daily human existence are played out. For Strand, New England was the stage upon which the ideals and struggles of American life were enacted. He wrote:

> New England has and I think will always have a special meaning for Americans. The land and its people, their cities and towns, their factories and mills, the villages surrounded by frames, the long coast and the sea whipping against it – all these are New England, …in this region, in these six states of the Union, were born many of the thoughts and actions that have shaped America for more than three hundred years…it was this concept of New England that, like a scenario, gave the clues to the photographs in this book and brought them into relationship with the text. I was led to try to find in present-day New England images of nature and architecture and faces of people that were either part of or related in feeling to its great tradition.[3]

Fig. 67.1 Paul Strand, *Open Door, Maine*, 1945, gelatin silver print.
Paul Strand Archives

New York 1882–1934 New York
Portrait of a Girl c. 1930
Platinum print, 20.6 x 15.6 cm, sheet 21.4 x 16.4 cm
39163

Provenance   from John Jacob Niles estate to Charles Isaacs, Malvern, Pennsylvania; Purchased from Charles Isaacs, Malvern, Pennsylvania, 1998

Born to a well-to-do New York family, Doris Ulmann had the luxury as a young woman of being able to apply her considerable intellectual curiosity to various fields of enquiry, from law to psychology to photography. The latter might well have remained a hobby, with her making and publishing portraits of her husband's medical colleagues, but instead Ulmann chose in 1913 to establish a professional portrait studio in her apartment on Park Avenue. She later used her photographic skills to investigate and capture the living conditions of rural Appalachian communities. It was undoubtedly under the tutelage of Clarence White, whose family physician was Ulmann's husband, that she came to appreciate the nature of commitment to her chosen field.

As many scholars of Ulmann have observed, she occupied a rather unique place amongst her peers in photography. What was unusual was not the language of her image-making – the soft focus, gentle lighting and frequent choice of platinum and photogravure printing methods, which situated her so solidly in the Pictorialist school – but rather her persistence in a way of working that had lost currency. In spite of this, Ulmann's images avoid the mannerist trap, retaining freshness and integrity. She intuitively understood that this visual vocabulary of yielding edges and a quietly illuminating light allowed her to express, particularly in her Appalachian portraits, the gentleness that she felt toward her subjects.

Portrait of a Girl was possibly taken on the South Carolina plantation of her friend Julia Peterkin (1880–1961), who later published *Roll Jordan, Roll*, a chronicle of the African-American South, illustrated with photographs by Ulmann.[1] This portrait is a sterling example of the quietness of Ulmann's approach, as is another contemporaneous work in the National Gallery's collection (fig. 68.1).

A comparison with the J. Paul Getty Museum's platinum variant of this photograph (fig. 68.2) reveals that Ulmann took more than one image, capturing the slight shifts of her young model, who grasps a pillow behind her and shyly glances over her shoulder, away from the photographer. As conventional as its Pictorialist attributes might be, this picture uses light and its absence in a radical way. The vertical band of darkness down the middle of the girl's body renders her features less legible, but at the same time invites us to look more attentively at her. In this instance the shadow serves not merely to obscure, but also to add tension between its intimations of portent and protectiveness.

Fig. 68.1 Doris Ulmann, *Family, possibly South Carolina*, c. 1929–33, platinum print. National Gallery of Canada, Ottawa (29815)

Fig. 68.2 Doris Ulmann, *Portrait Study, Probably South Carolina or Louisiana*, c. 1929–31, platinum print. J. Paul Getty Museum, Los Angeles (87.XM.89.81)

69   Weegee (Arthur Fellig)
Złoczów, Austrian Galicia (now Zolochiv, Ukraine), 1899–1968 New York
Heat Spell 1941
Gelatin silver print, 34.7 × 26.9 cm, sheet 35.2 × 27.9 cm
26768

Annotations   verso, c.r., black ink stamp, *CREDIT PHOTO BY / WEEGEE / THE FAMOUS*, l.c. inverted, blue ink stamp, *WEEGEE / 451 WEST 47th STREET / NEW YORK CITY, U.S.A. / TEL: 265-1955*, l.l., by Sander Gallery, graphite, *SG/111/X* [?]
Provenance   purchased from the Phyllis Lambert Fund, 1981

Weegee was notorious as an "ambulance chaser" and prowler who hunted sensationalist human interest stories. New York's Lower East Side served as his giant outdoor studio, with heating vents, fire escapes and tenement roof tops providing the backdrops for the human dramas he uncovered. The places and situations that others might have shunned – murder scenes or holding pens in police stations – attracted him. Like Lisette Model, Weegee was drawn to extremes. He became the master of the shocking and grotesque, creating a genre that was so resonant of daily drama that it surpassed the topicality and norms of photojournalism and entered the realm of caricature. Interested in the lives of people ordinary and marginal, and how they coped with their misfortunes (fig. 69.1), he revealed his awareness of social inequities in the sardonic street-talk humour he frequently applied to his titles. In this instance, he captioned this picture "Tenement Penthouse" in his autobiography *Weegee on Weegee*.

Describing how he came to make this photograph of sleeping children nestled together on the landing of a fire escape, Weegee makes reference to its autobiographical content. He had emigrated from Ukraine with his family at the age of ten, at which time his name was changed to Arthur. He never lost sight of his own humble roots, writing:

> During this period, I would ease up a little on my police-beat tour sometime in the early morning hours, and drive around the old neighborhood on the East Side. Strangley enough, I was reliving my early life. I would see a bunch of kids, sleeping on a fire escape. I would go up to the house … the doors were never locked in the tenements … go upstairs and out to the fire escape over the sleeping kids and make a shot of them. Then I would leave five dollars for the folks so that the kids might have candy, ice cream, or a movie. Later, people seeing these pictures in the Museum of Modern Art would wonder how I knew about such things. How did I know about them? Hell! That's the way I had slept.[1]

All variant views of *Heat Spell* published in magazines such as *PM Daily* and *Coronet* in the early 1940s show the same close cropping of the negative compared to a rare print made from what appears to be the full negative shown in fig. 69.2.

Fig. 69.1   Weegee, *Mrs. Henrietta Torres and her Daughter Ada Watch as Another Daughter and her Son Die in Fire*, 15 December 1939, gelatin silver print. National Gallery of Canada, Ottawa, Purchased from the Phyllis Lambert Fund, 1981 (26766)

Fig. 69.2   Weegee, *Tenement Children (children asleep on fire escape)*, 1940s, gelatin silver print. Richard and Ellen Sandor Family Collection

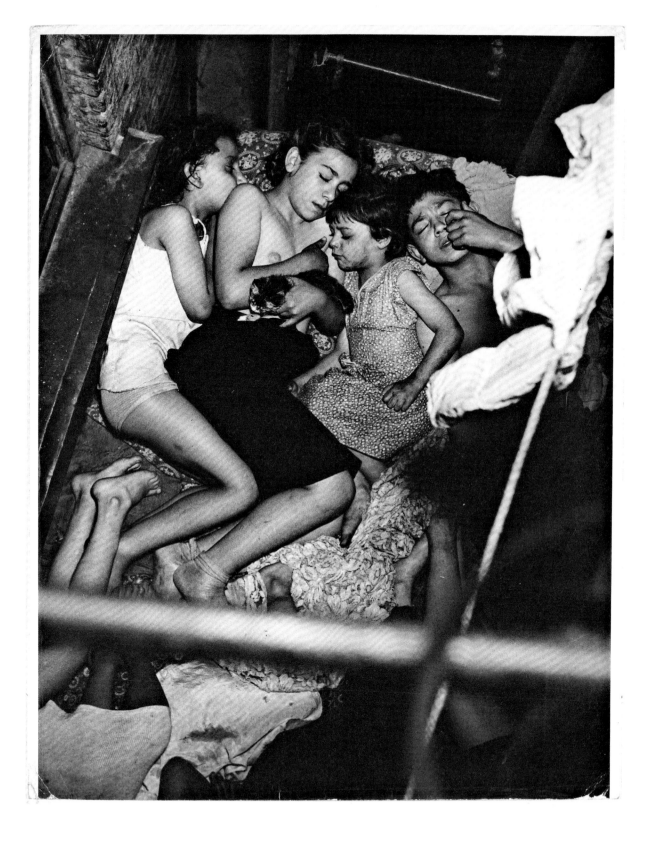

Highland Park, Illinois 1886–1958 Carmel, California
Tina Modotti (1896–1942) 1924
Gelatin silver print, 23.6 × 18.8 cm
33724

Inscriptions   secondary support, l.r., graphite, *Edward Weston 1924*, verso, c., graphite on label, - *Tina Modotti* -

Annotations   secondary support, verso, by David Heath u.r., black ink, *Purchased for $60 June 1960 / from Limelight exhibit / DH*, printed in black ink on label, *EDWARD WESTON / A SPECIAL EXHIBITION AND SALE / MAY 17th through JUNE 26th, 1960 / ON THE OCCASION OF THE SIXTH ANNIVERSARY OF / LIMELIGHT - 91 SEVENTH AVENUE SOUTH AT SHERIDAN SQ, NYC*

Provenance   gift of David M. Heath, Toronto, 1973

Portraiture is arguably the genre that comprises the largest group of Edward Weston's output. It is also the subject matter – favoured since photography was first able to capture the light of day – that allowed him, unlike his nudes or landscapes, to earn a living in the medium. Weston gained experience working in two different studios early in his career. The first job offered only menial chores and the second, which lasted two years, gave him much-needed experience in darkroom work. The effect of observing portrait studio camera operators in action led him ultimately to reject the directorial mode.[1]

This is probably why, in his personal work, he sought to reveal the more faceted dimensions of a subject's identity. It pleased him when he achieved this and provided relief from the standard tedium of commercial portrait work.

We are often told that a photograph "speaks for itself," or that it is "worth a thousand words," and yet, words – the spoken word, in particular – and the photograph do seem at odds. Always on the lookout for ways to make his photographs more emotionally resonant and expressive, on 7 January 1924 in Mexico City, Edward Weston stumbled upon the idea of capturing a sitter in mid-vocalization, either in recitation or in song, and took a profile view of Guadalupe Marín de Rivera with her mouth open (fig. 70.1). In his daybook he told himself to always remember her "singing or talking."[2] This was followed in October of that year by a series of portraits of his lover, Tina Modotti, reciting poetry. "Tina sat to me yesterday morning," he wrote. "We had long planned that I should do her as I have often seen her, quoting poetry – to attempt the registration of her remarkably mobile face in action. There was nothing forced in this attempt, she was soon in a mood which discounted me and my camera – or did she subconsciously feel my presence and respond to it? Within twenty minutes I had made three dozen Graflex negatives and caught her sensitive face with its every subtle change."[3]

Unfortunately, not all of the thirty-six negatives yielded prints that Weston found acceptable. While finding the series of heads the "most significant I have ever made" and "in absolute accord with her emotional crises," he recorded two days later that he had misjudged the timing of the exposures, which meant that a number of images were not printable. "My intellect should not," he berated himself, "have been overwhelmed by my emotions …"[4]

The prints that Weston was able to produce from this sitting, and according to his exacting standards, capture Modotti's animated features and warmth (fig. 70.2).

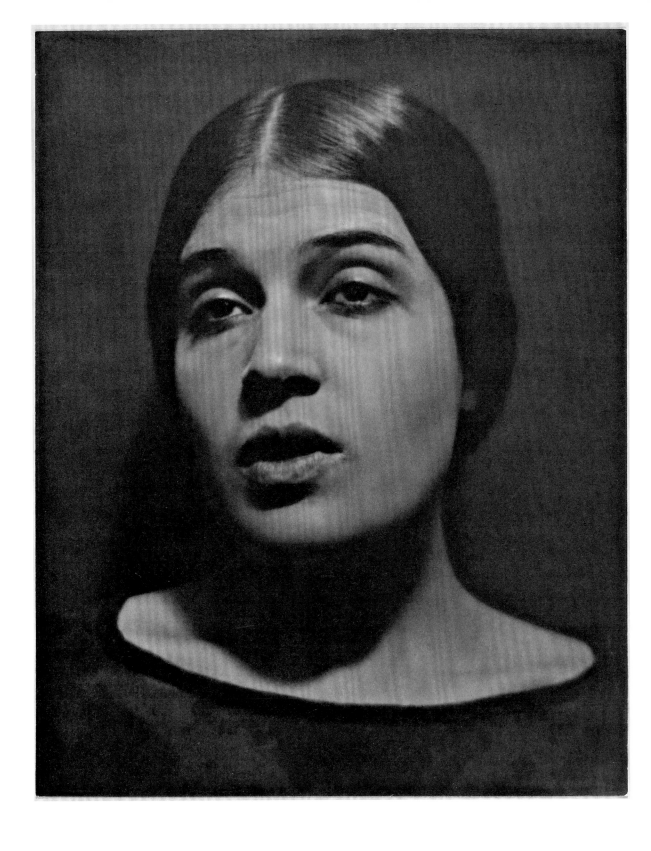

Fig. 70.1 Edward Weston, *Guadalupe Marín de Rivera,*
23 November 1923, printed before July 1969, gelatin silver print.
National Gallery of Canada (33650)

Fig. 70.2 Edward Weston, *Tina Reciting*, 1924, printed before July
1969, gelatin silver print. National Gallery of Canada, Ottawa
(33652)

71 Edward Weston
Highland Park, Illinois 1886–1958 Carmel, California
Heaped Black Ollas June 1926
Gelatin silver print, 18.9 × 23.7 cm
33725

Inscriptions   secondary support, all in graphite, l.l., *11/50*, l.r., *Edward Weston 1926*, verso u.l., graphite, *3Mi / 1926*
Provenance   purchased from Witkin Gallery, New York, 1973

Edward Weston made *Heaped Black Ollas* during his last year in Mexico, a sojourn that would influence his artistic evolution significantly, as well as leave an impact on the development of photography there. Mexico enjoyed a flourishing of the arts in the 1920s, due largely to the progressive social and cultural directives implemented by the relatively stable government of General Álvaro Óbregon. Introduced to the vibrant community of artists whose métiers ranged from painting to writing and pottery, Weston found an environment receptive to the modernist vocabulary that he had started to introduce into his photographs in 1922, after a visit to Alfred Stieglitz in New York.

Like *Piramide del Sol* (fig. 71.1), one of the great remaining Aztec monuments, this image of randomly stored ceramic jars shows Weston responding to the new iconography that accompanied his Mexican experience. It also shows his increasing attraction to photographing objects, an exploration that would result in his iconic series of photographs of peppers and shells (fig. 71.2) made in the late 1920s and early 1930s. In 1928 he indicates having a more profound response to this subject matter than simply an attraction to tactile values. "I have," he wrote, "registered the quintessential quality of the object in front of my lens, without subterfuge or evasions, this holds for the technique and for the spirit, instead of offering an interpretation, a superficial or passing facet."[1]

If the photographing of objects would in time cause Weston to struggle with the notion of the essence of things,[2] and in doing so, to isolate objects and deal with them as he would a portrait, there is little evidence of this kind of ontological struggle in this work. Perhaps this was a first step toward such an enquiry, as Weston seems to respond to the way in which these common household objects, possibly encountered in a market place in Oaxaca, share both commonality and difference. The more concentrated *Tres Ollas de Oaxaca* (fig. 71.3) provoked then Director of the Museum of Modern Art, Rene D'Harnoncourt, to declare, "The Modern painters are all off. They have chosen the wrong medium to express their ideas …. This print is the beginning of a new art."[3]

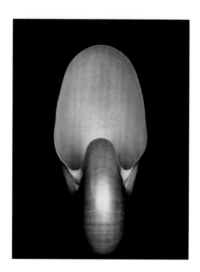

Fig. 71.1 Edward Weston, *Piramide del Sol*, 1923, platinum print. National Gallery of Canada, Ottawa (33718)

Fig. 71.2 Edward Weston, *Nautilus*, 1927, printed before July 1969, gelatin silver print. National Gallery of Canada, Ottawa (33651)

Fig. 71.3 Edward Weston, *Tres Ollas de Oaxaca*, 1926, gelatin silver print. Center for Creative Photography, Tucson, Arizona (81.252.255)

72 Edward Weston
Highland Park, Illinois 1886–1958 Carmel, California
Nude on Sand, Oceano 1936
Gelatin silver print, 18 × 24.2 cm
33721

Inscriptions   secondary support, l.r., graphite, *E W 1936*, verso, u.l., graphite, *235N*, u.c., graphite, *Edward Weston / 1936*
Annotations   secondary support, verso, u.r., graphite, *26 / 14 x 15 5/8*
Provenance   **gift of Dorothy Meigs Eidlitz, St. Andrews, New Brunswick, 1968**

When seen as a group made over the span of his career, Edward Weston's nudes allow us to view his extraordinary evolution as a photographer in a way not always available to us with his other bodies of work. This masterful series of Charis Wilson on the dunes at Oceano, where he reconciles his love of abstraction – in nature and in the human body – shows us how broad his representation of the nude had become. In contrast to his early tentative Pictorialist efforts, exemplified by *Profile* (fig. 72.1), which is perhaps more of a response to a hidebound convention than to genuine artistic exploration, his nudes from 1925 through the late 1930s are revelatory in a complex way. As Wilson aptly expressed it, "No curtain of sensibility hangs between viewer and subject and there is no idealization."[1]

Nobody seems to have understood better than Charis, his model wife, and – perhaps most critically at this point in his life – his collaborator. Uninhibited and more comfortable naked than dressed,[2] Charis came into Weston's life when she was twenty and he just short of fifty. With remarkable maturity she observed his work, and his studies of her, with an unusual detachment. In whatever pose he pictured her, she believed that the narrative behind the image exceeded the boundaries of its simple categorization as a "nude." Their intimate relationship, which began shortly after they met in 1934, was reflected in his regarding her body not as one "an 'audience' sees, but the body a lover knows."[3] Weston's growing preoccupation with abstraction – dating from the early 1920s – intensified following his trip to Mexico in 1923. On 13 November 1925, he wrote in his daybook that, "one must satisfy all desires and at present my tendency seems entirely toward the abstract."[4] This balance between engagement with content and appreciation for its formal expression would prevail until the end of his life.

The morning that Weston and Wilson shared on the sand dunes of Oceano was a defining moment in their working relationship. As Charis recalled in 2005, just a few months shy of her ninety-first birthday, the dunes, which she found to be "magical," "were so isolated in those days – no people, and no noise, and a kind of roar of silence."[5] They set out at dawn from the home of their friend Gavin Arthur, who had established something of an artists' colony at Oceano.[6] Weston was anxious to work with the early morning light, for its subtle delineation of the curves and wind-swept patterns of the sand – "100-feet high ridges of steep-sided bluffs and sculptured peaks"[7] – and Charis was impatient to "whisk off [her] clothes."[8] Undressed, she rolled in abandon down the dunes, while Weston made certain to capture her in various positions (fig. 72.2). It was a productive session in which he made "body portraits" (a term she coined to describe his nudes),[9] explored the sensual and sinuous relationship between the sculpted forms of the dunes and Charis' languorous body, and indulged the same love of abstract form as seen in *Dunes, Oceano* (fig. 72.3).

Fig. 72.1 Edward Weston, *Profile*, 1922, palladium print. National Gallery of Canada, Ottawa, Purchased from the Phyllis Lambert Fund, 1979 (33692)

Fig. 72.2 Edward Weston, *Nude*, 1936, printed 1972, gelatin silver print. National Gallery of Canada, Ottawa (33684.7)

Fig. 72.3 Edward Weston, *Dunes, Oceano*, 1936, gelatin silver print. National Gallery of Canada, Ottawa, Purchased from the Phyllis Lambert Fund, 1979 (33695)

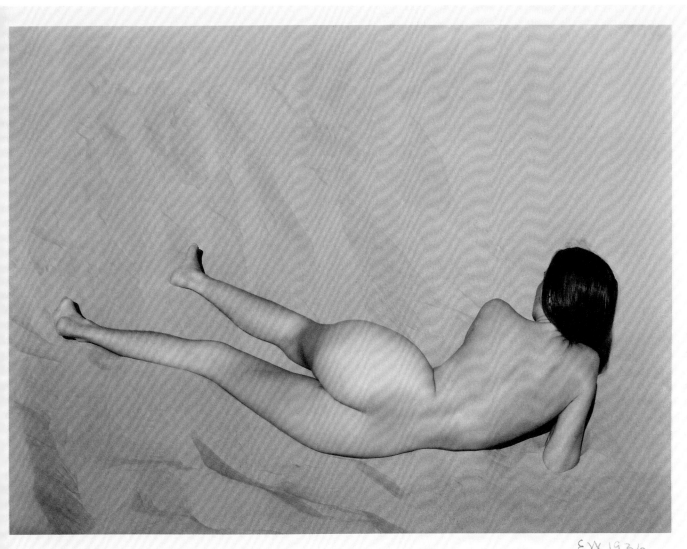

EW 1936

Highland Park, Illinois 1886–1958 Carmel, California
Juniper, Lake Tenaya 1937
Gelatin silver print, 24.2 × 19.3 cm
33730

Inscription   secondary support, l.r. below image, graphite, *Edward Weston 1937*
Provenance   purchased from Myron Wood, Colorado Springs, Colorado, 1979

In spite of the apparent simplicity of this close-up composition of a tree trunk, arriving at its making was a complicated undertaking for Edward Weston. We learn this from an account in Edward Weston's day-books, in which he describes the arduousness of the hike up the mountainside to get this series of pictures. Working with an 8 × 10 camera[1] that necessitated carrying a number of plates and holders, Weston's passion for the subject matter was severely tested by the circumstances. Surrounded by impressive glaciated granite domes, Lake Tenaya is a sparsely forested area and the junipers tended to grow up in the higher, less accessible regions of the landscape. Weston recounted, "Some of my best work that summer was done with the junipers at Tenaya Lake. These wind blasted trees grew well up on the smooth granite cliffs that surround the lake, and climbing them was difficult work. After the first day's work there, climbing up a steep wall of rock to make three negatives, I was prepared to give up. The equipment I carried in the field weighs about fifty pounds … But after some reconnoitring we found an easier incline at a place where the car could be driven back to the base of the slope. From here I would start out before sunrise in the morning, with camera, six holders, and a pocket full of dried fruit, to make the ten or fifteen minute climb to the first junipers. Then for the rest of the day I would progress up and around the mountain from juniper to juniper according to the direction of the sun."[2]

Although highly respectful of Ansel Adams' work, Weston was not as drawn to photographing sublime landscapes as was his friend. He was, however, highly attuned to trees. "A tree, to me, is just as alive and interesting as any human subject."[3] Taut and highly textured, the trunks of junipers presented Weston with the opportunity to examine both nature's massive and more minute forms. They provided him with a comparably undomesticated wildness, but at the same time held themselves up for detailed scrutiny. Their trunks recall the muscular torsions of the naked body of dancer Bertha Wardell, whom he had photographed a decade earlier, in 1927. Analogies between human forms and those in nature were ever present in Weston's imagination, just as he had associated cloud forms with recumbent torsos when photographing in Mexico in 1926 (fig. 73.1), and had related the shapes of turnips to parts of human bodies in 1927. In 1940 he goes so far as to state that photographing trees "is well worth the same time and effort that one devotes to portraiture of people."[4]

A 1938 Guggenheim grant allowed Weston the liberty to concentrate keenly on his chosen subjects and give full and rigorous expression to his vision, and in the case of the juniper trees, to inspect their forms from all sides and a variety of angles (fig. 73.2).

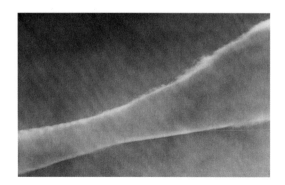

Fig. 73.1 Edward Weston, *Mexico*, 1926, gelatin silver print. National Gallery of Canada, Ottawa, Purchased from the Phyllis Lambert Fund, 1979 (33701)

Fig. 73.2 Edward Weston, *Juniper, Lake Tenaya,* 1937, gelatin silver print. Center for Creative Photography, Tucson, Arizona (81.251.114)

West Carlisle, Ohio 1871–1925 Mexico City
Blind Man's Bluff c. 1898?
Platinum print, 18.9 x 13.8 cm
43202

Provenance   purchased from Lee Gallery, Winchester, Massachusetts, 2010

The word "scopophilia" derives from the Greek "love of looking," and where it crosses over into voyeurism is ambiguous. The act of looking or not being able to look at a given scene is a seminal aspect of all three of the images by Clarence White in this catalogue. In *Boys Wrestling* (see cat. 75) the photographer appears to "spy" on the playing boys. The young boy in *Entrance to the Garden* (see cat. 76) has his back turned to the promise of future worldly experience and does not see what lies ahead; the girl is blindfolded in, *Blind Man's Bluff*. As she participates in this age-old party game (fig. 74.1) – one of the most perverse of the many curious games that children like to play – she appears to be more stricken than entertained. Apparently charged with capturing one or more of her fellow partygoers, she gropes helplessly into the air as an older woman presses into the door jamb to avoid her touch. This image is undoubtedly allegorical and refers in some murky Victorian way to the passage from girlhood into womanhood. It is an electric combination of the warring elements of soft-focus Pictorialist aesthetic and loaded subject matter, at once capable of placating the viewer, with its reticent mellow overtones and innocuous image of childhood games, while inspiring terror, with its depiction of the subject's staggering, fumbling vulnerability.

Women and children were two of White's favourite subjects (fig. 74.2). "It is clear," writes Peter Bunnell, "that even though White was an enthusiastic portraitist of men, his greatest interest lie [sic] in the pictorial depiction of women…. Women were seen as the primary subject of the story-teller's art, of parables, and as the epitome of nature – woman viewed in nature's primordial garden – and it was this literary origin, together with the notion of seriousness in art that concentrated upon notions of truth and beauty that infused White's attitudes."[1] Their representation in his works tends more often than not to be stereotypical and highly romanticized; the women gaze wistfully into space while the children seduce with their freshness and apparent innocence. Every now and then he seems to have ventured into edgier terrain, such as in *Blind Man's Bluff*.

Fig. 74.1 Jean-Honoré Fragonard, *Blind Man's Buff*, 1750–52, oil on canvas. Toledo Museum of Art, Toledo, Ohio, Purchased with Funds from the Libbey Endowment, Gift of Edward Drummond Libbey (1954.43)

Fig. 74.2 Clarence H. White, *The Orchard*, 1902, photogravure. National Gallery of Canada, Ottawa, Gift of Dorothy Meigs Eidlitz, St. Andrews, New Brunswick, 1968 (34999.23)

75 Clarence H. White
West Carlisle, Ohio 1871–1925 Mexico City
Boys Wrestling c. 1905–1908
Platinum print, 24.7 × 19.5 cm, sheet 25.5 × 19.5 cm
43200

Annotations   verso, u.r., graphite, *P1696*

Provenance   purchased from Lee Gallery, Winchester, Massachusetts, 2010

Composed with a sure sense of how to build narrative into a picture and yet retaining an extraordinary lyricism, White's *Boys Wrestling* bears the hallmark of Clarence White's style of photography from the decade between 1898 and 1908. It also exemplifies his masterful handling of the platinum process. This image was almost certainly made during the first summer visit that Clarence White and his family paid to Pictorialist photographer Frederick Holland Day, at Little Good Harbor, Maine, in 1905. Day and White met during the preparations for the 1898 Philadelphia Salon exhibition.[1] Their close friendship, founded on a common passion for the goals of Pictorialist photography and a mutual admiration for one another's work,[2] endured until White's premature death in Mexico City in 1925.

Mysterious and provocative, this image deviates from White's more romantic depictions of women and children (fig. 75.1) by introducing elements of tension and developing a meta-narrative around the herm of Pan. From a dim and hidden vantage point in the lower left corner, Pan appears to be watching over – or perhaps peeking voyeuristically – at the young boys tussling with one another in the light-dappled glade. Indicated by a patch of soft glowing light the world beyond is all but forgotten by the youths lost in their sensuous play.

Boys Wrestling relates to White's Hellenist-inspired *The Pipes of Pan* series (fig. 75.2), made that summer, in which he posed his young sons as woodland gods. There is little question that White was working under the influence of Frederick Holland Day. Day's fascination with the art and mores of classical Greece, and his "intoxication with male beauty"[3] led him to surround himself with related objects and to invoke Hellenist themes and ideals in his work. White in turn responded to the rich allegorical subject matter that Day's obsession offered.

Fig. 75.1 Clarence H. White, *The Readers*, 1897, palladium print. Library of Congress, Washington (LC-DIG-ppmsca-13707)

Fig. 75.2 Clarence H. White, *The Pipes of Pan*, before July 1908, photogravure. National Gallery of Canada, Ottawa (PSC68:039:236)

76 Clarence H. White
West Carlisle, Ohio 1871–1925 Mexico City
Entrance to the Garden c. 1908
Gum bichromate print, 24.4 × 20.1 cm
43201

Inscriptions   secondary support, b.l. below image, graphite, [illegible] *Clarence H. White*

Annotations   verso, b.c., in graphite, *PF86059*; secondary support, verso, b.c., graphite, *PF86059*, b.r., *89:428*

Provenance   purchased from Lee Gallery, Winchester, Massachusetts, 2010

Entrance to the Garden is another of White's virtuoso Pictorialist renditions, in which form and light are expressed in a very limited range of tonalities. Photographs historian Beaumont Newhall noted White's exceptional contribution to the history of the medium: "What he brought to photography was an extra-ordinary sense of light."[1]

Employing gum bichromate, a process that allows for a dense, rich, almost painterly surface texture, White made a print that is tactile and endowed with a strong presence. It is an image permeated with a mood of reverie and contemplation. A young boy lounges at the entrance of a garden that in all likelihood repre-sents the world of experience. Enclosed and sheltered by darkness, the boy's forms are subtly outlined by light falling on him like a theatrical spotlight. White's masterful handling of composition and manipulation of light suggest a play between consciousness and the unconscious, between inner and outer worlds, between being and becoming.

Known as a highly accomplished printmaker, particularly of platinum prints, Clarence White excelled in his handling of the gum bichromate process in *Entrance to the Garden*, integrating with superb skill the meaning of his image and the medium of its expression.

The July 1908 issue of *Camera Work* was primarily devoted to Clarence White's work, all as photogravures, with *Entrance to the Garden* appearing along with *Boys Wrestling* (see cat. 75) and *Portrait – Master Tom* (fig. 76.1). Presenting no less than sixteen images by White, it was also the issue that provided him with the greatest exposure that he would receive in *Camera Work* over its fifteen-year run.

Portrait – Master Tom is of the same young boy lying on the grass in *Entrance to the Garden*. Young chil-dren – particularly his own three sons – were among White's favourite subjects, providing him with the opportunity to explore the theme of innocence, but in this instance he appears to have posed a friend's child. *Boy with Camera Work* (fig. 76.2) is at once a portrait of White's second son and an affirmation of the photographer's deep involvement with Stieglitz's newly formed Photo-Secession group.

Fig. 76.1 Clarence H. White, *Portrait – Master Tom*, before July 1908, photogravure. National Gallery of Canada, Ottawa (PSC68:039:234)

Fig. 76.2 Clarence H. White, *Boy with "Camera Work"*, before January 1905, photogravure. National Gallery of Canada, Ottawa (PSC68:039:76)

Minneapolis, Minnesota 1908–1976 Boston
Sun in Rock (San Mateo County, California) c. October – November 1947, printed 1960
from *Song Without Words*
Gelatin silver print, 9.1 × 11.8 cm
33736.5

Inscriptions   secondary support, l.r. below image, graphite, *Minor*, verso, l.l., graphite, #5
Provenance   purchased from the Phyllis Lambert Fund, 1979

As a student of botany in 1927, Minor White learned photography basics by making photo-micrographic transparencies of algae. He returned to the medium in 1938–39 when he was employed by the Works Progress Administration Oregon Art Project to document Portland's waterfront and historic nineteenth-century cast-iron facades, slated for demolition. White later taught photography workshops.

By 1940 White, had come to believe that the medium could serve as a language for self-expression, and had committed himself to the art, publishing his newly formulated ideas about photography in "When is Photography Creative?"[1] He referred to photographs taken in 1940 as "things for what they are." Ten years on, he alluded to them as "things for what Else they are." This seemingly insignificant change reveals much about the spiritual nature of White's personal and professional evolution. It illustrates his conviction that the meaning we extract from photographs is mutable and deeply metaphoric, dependent not only upon what the viewer brings to the image but also upon the context in which it is viewed.

A major influence on White, in terms of both making and interpreting photographs, was the publication *America and Alfred Stieglitz*, in which he first saw Stieglitz's *Equivalent* (see cat. 62).

White created *Song without Words* in 1947 as a sequence with twenty-four prints. Over the next decade he reworked the grouping, creating several sets of fifteen prints titled *These Images*. The sequence of *Song without Words* which includes *Sun in Rock* was re-composed in 1961.[2] It consists of fourteen images made along the coast a few miles south of San Francisco. It is an elusively romantic sequence, with each image celebrating the expression of light in its various manifestations, from harshly defining, as in *Sun in Rock*, to softly reflecting, as in *San Mateo County Coast* (fig. 77.1). Other images show the dissolution of form and absence of light when the landscape is enshrouded by fog. In his reading of Princeton University's thirteen-print variant, scholar John Pultz sees *Song without Words* as an expression of sexual longing and consummation, with the figure of the young man (fig. 77.2), who appears in two of the images, as the object of desire.[3]

Minor White's greatest contribution may well have been his ability to illustrate complex and often inchoate emotions through the juxtaposition of judiciously selected images.

Although there are strong links between his work and that of other American photographers of his time – particularly Edward Weston, Ansel Adams, and Paul Strand – it is perhaps more meaningful to see him issuing from a longer tradition of American art, one that took the union of man with nature as one of the highest ideals, as epitomized in the writings of Ralph Waldo Emerson. "The feat of the imagination," wrote Emerson, "is in showing the convertibility of everything into every other thing. Facts which had never before left their stark common sense suddenly figure as Eleusinian mysteries. … All the facts in nature are nouns of the intellect and make the grammar of the eternal language."[4]

Fig. 77.1 Minor White, *San Mateo County Coast*, 1947, printed 1960. National Gallery of Canada, Ottawa (33736.12)

Fig. 77.2 Minor White, *Robert Bright*, 1947, gelatin silver print. National Gallery of Canada, Ottawa, Purchased from the Phyllis Lambert Fund, 1979 (33736.6)

Notes

Introduction

1 "Notes Made by Stieglitz," in *Stieglitz on Photography: His Selected Essays and Notes*, ed. Richard Whelan, (New York: Aperture Foundation, 2000), p. 23.

2 Dorothy Norman, *Alfred Stieglitz: An American Seer* (New York: Random House 1960, 1973), p. 47.

3 De Kay was also editor and arts editor of the *New York Times* and ran an article in his newspaper announcing the forthcoming exhibition. See Stieglitz, "The Origin of the Photo-Secession and How it Became 291 (I)" in *Stieglitz on Photography*, p. 120.

4 Alfred Stieglitz "An Apology," in *Camera Work*, no. 1 (January 1903), in Jonathan Green, *Camera Work: A Critical Anthology* (New York: Aperture, 1973), p. 26.

5 Stieglitz had a business partnership with his friends Louis Shubart and Joseph Obermeyer known as the Heliochrome Company (later Photochrome Engraving Company) from 1890 to 1895. Steichen served a four-year apprenticeship as a lithographer at the American Fine Art Company, a period in which he founded the Milwaukee Art Students League.

6 Cited by Constance Rourke in *Charles Sheeler: Artist in the American Tradition* (New York, 1938), pp. 121–122.

7 Dow had been White's mentor at Columbia University's Teachers College in 1907. White hired Max Weber, who was also highly influenced by Dow, to teach at Seguinland School of Photography. See Bonnie Yochelson, "Clarence H. White, Peaceful Warrior," in *Pictorialism into Modernism: The Clarence H. White School of Photography* (New York: Rizzoli, 1996), pp. 26, 56–58.

8 Frederick James Gregg, "Letting in the Light," in *Documents of the 1913 Armory Show: The Electrifying Moment of Modern Art's American Debut*, ed. Kenyon Cox (Tucson, AZ: Hol Art Books, 2009), p. 7.

9 Sarah Greenough, "How Stieglitz Came to Photograph Clouds," in Peter Walch and Thomas F. Barrow, eds., *Perspectives on Photography: Essays in Honor of Beaumont Newhall* (Albuquerque: University of New Mexico Press, 1986), p. 160.

10 See Christian A. Peterson, *After the Photo-Secession: American Pictorial Photography, 1910–1955* (New York: W.W. Norton, 1997) for an elaboration on this.

11 Cited in *Camera Work: A Pictorial Guide,* ed. Marianne Fulton Margolis (New York: Dover, 1978), p. x.

12 Alfred Stieglitz, "How I Came to Photograph Clouds," in *The Amateur Photographer & Photography* (19 September 1923), p. 255.

13 *Manuscripts* was a modest publication issued by Stieglitz, Herbert J. Seligman, and Paul Rosenfeld from 1922–23. See Sarah Greenough, "Chronology," in *Alfred Stieglitz: Photographs and Writings* (Washington: National Gallery of Art and Callaway Editions), p. 240.

14 Cited by Norman in *Alfred Stieglitz*, p. 35.

15 His two-year sojourn in Mexico in 1932–34 affirmed his leftist leanings as made evident in his passionate avowals in letters to friends. See Rebecca Bussell and Trudy Wilner Stack, *Paul Strand Southwest* (New York: Aperture, 2004), p. 106.

16 His Doylestown and Pennsylvania Barn photographs notwith-standing, Sheeler was known principally for his painting through-out the 1910s and would return to the medium in the 1930s. Six of his still lifes and landscape paintings were exhibited in the Armory Show in 1913. Expanding from painting into film and photography, he was the consummate modernist.

17 Sheeler and Strand may have first met during the 1918 exhib-ition at Marius de Zayas Modern Gallery in New York City where their work was shown along with that of Morton Schamberg. In 1919 Sheeler moved to New York and within a year he and Strand began collaborating on the film, *Manhatta*. The nine-minute film celebrated the architecture, sites and people of New York City, and included excerpts from Walt Whitman's poem "Mannahatta." For an account of their friendship and eventual estrangement, see Theodore E. Stebbins and Norman Keyes, Jr., *Charles Sheeler: The Photographs* (New York: New York Graphic Society and Boston: Little, Brown, 1987), p. 17.

18 As cited in Therese Thau Heyman, *Seeing Straight: The f.64 Revolution in Photography*, exh. cat. (Oakland, CA: The Oakland Museum, 1992), p. 55.

19 Ibid., p. 23.

20 Weston, "Letter Regarding Pictorialist Practices in Response to Comments by F. H. Evans: 1922," reprinted in Peter C. Bunnell, ed., *Edward Weston on Photography* (Salt Lake City, UT: Gibbs, 1983), p. 24.

21 See Richard Lorenz, *Imogen Cunningham: The Modernist Years* (Tokyo: Treville, 1993), n.p.

22 Much of this biographical information comes from Richard Lorenz, "Cunningham, Imogen," Oxford Art Online, www.oxford-artonline.com (accessed 22 March 2011) and the *International Center of Photography Encyclopedia of Photography* (New York: Crown Publishers, 1984), pp. 125–126.

23 Peter C. Bunnell, ed., *Minor White: The Eye that Shapes*, exh. cat. (Princeton, New Jersey: Princeton University Art Museum, 1989), p. 5.

24 "White eventually formed a classification system for all photo-graphs: documentary, pictorial, informational and Equivalent. To him, a photograph became an Equivalent when it transcended its original and customary purposes, such as the other categories, and more specifically when it evoked a heightened emotion. He compared the significance of an Equivalent to the 'intimations of immortality' of William Wordsworth (1770–1850) and suggested that curiosity and courage were prerequisites for the discovery of such images. His equivalence concept was a form of spiritual discipline for the photographer as well as for the active viewer, and the process of photographing and interpreting photographs became a search for a cosmic essence." Richard Lorenz, "White, Minor (Martin)," Oxford Art Online at www.oxfordartonline.com (accessed 8 April 2011).

25 Lloyd C. Englebrecht, "Educating the Eye: Photography and the Founding Generation at the Institute of Design 1937–1946," in David Travis and Elizabeth Siegel, eds., *Taken by Design: Photographs from the Institute of Design, 1937–1971*, exh. cat. (Chicago: Art Institute of Chicago, 2002), p. 17.

26 Sarah Greenough, *Harry Callahan*, exh. cat. (Washington: National Gallery of Art, 1996), p. 180.

27 Ibid., p. 182.

28 Grace M. Mayer, "Chronology," in Paul Sherman, ed., *Harry Callahan*, exh. cat. (New York: Museum of Modern Art, 1967), p. 76.

29 "Ansel's wave sequence influenced me the most. I later forgot about that sequence and started doing series myself – I thought I was doing something original. I had sort of run out of gas and didn't know what to do next so I started making a series of three. The idea of change really fascinated me – to keep the camera in the exact spot and just put in another sheet of film to show the changes. I started doing all kinds of pictures like this and worked on the series for years. …

"I never made a picture that was strong enough to hold up before Ansel's visit. After I had seen Ansel I didn't care about s-curves or the camera club criticism. I was free to go out and look and photograph what I wanted to." Cited by Keith Davies in *Harry Callahan, Photographs: An Exhibition from the Hallmark Collection of* Photographs, exh. cat. (New York: Hallmark Cards, 1981), p. 51.

30 Ibid., p. 53.

31 As cited by Sherman in *Harry Callahan*, p. 6.

32 Hine also made extensive notes that were published with his photographs and, in 1907, began studies in sociology at Columbia University.

33 Riis photographed New York tenements for *The New York Times* in 1888–89. Anne Ehrenkranz, "Riis Jacob A(ugust)," Oxford Art Online at www.oxfordartonline.com (accessed 8 April 2011).

34 Lewis Hine, "The Silhouette in Photography," in *The Photographic Times* 38 (November 1906), p. 488, cited in Michael Sundell "Golden Immigrants at the Gold Door: Lewis Hine's Photographs of Ellis Island," *Social Text*, no. 16 (Winter 1986–87), pp. 170–172.

35 Anne Tucker, *Photographic Crossroads: The Photo League*, no. 25 (Ottawa: National Gallery of Canada, 1978), pp. 3–4.

36 Naomi Rosenblum, "Photo League," Oxford Art Online at www. oxfordartonline.com (accessed 28 February 2011).

37 The Resettlement Administration was established under the direction of Rex Tugwell, whose book *American Economic Life and the Means of Its Improvement* (1925) had been illustrated with photographs by Lewis Hine. Concerned that criticism of him as "Rex the Red" had made him a liability, Tugwell resigned in 1936. The administration was incorporated into the Department of Agriculture, which, with the passing of the 1937 Farm Security Act, was re-named the Farm Security Administration (FSA). The FSA had broader powers to aid poor farmers and would eventually help 800,000 families. Beverly W. Brannan, "To Make a Dent in the World," in Gilles Mora and Beverly W. Brannan, *FSA: The American Vision* (New York: Abrams, 2006), pp. 9, 11, 15; Charles Hagen, "Things Which Should be Photographed as an American Background," in *American Photographers of the Depression* (New York: Pantheon, 1985), pp. 6, 10; Alan Lawson, "Farm Security Administration," www.answers.com/topic/farm-security-administration (accessed 8 April 2011).

38 Linda Gordon, *Dorothea Lange: A Life Beyond Limits* (New York: W.E. Norton, 2009), p. 202.

39 Roy Stryker, 17 October 1963, in "Oral history interview with Roy Emerson Stryker, 1963–1965," conducted by Richard Doud for Archives of American Art. Transcript published online at www.aaa.si.edu/collections/interviews/oral-history-interview-roy-emerson-stryker-12480 (accessed 8 April 2011).

40 The FSA photography project resulted in an extensive pictorial record of American life between 1935 and 1944. Photographers such as Walker Evans, Dorothea Lange, Russell Lee, Arthur Rothstein, Ben Shahn, Jack Delano, Marion Post Wolcott, Gordon Parks, John Vachon, and Carl Mydans – also represented in the National Gallery of Canada's photographs collection – initially documented the administration's cash loans to farmers and the construction of suburban communities. Later they turned their lenses on the lives of sharecroppers in the South and migratory agricultural workers in the mid-western and western states. "Farm Security Administration/Office of War Information Collection," Library of Congress website at www.loc.gov/rr/print/coll/052_fsa.html (accessed 8 April 2011).

41 James R. Mellow, *Walker Evans* (New York: Basic Books, 1999), p. 269.

42 Cited in ibid., p. 224.

43 Roy Stryker, 23 January 1965, interview with R. Doud.

44 Anne Whiston Spirn, *Daring to Look: Dorothea Lange's Photographs and Reports form the Field* (Chicago: The University of Chicago Press, 2008), pp. 29–30.

45 Gordon, *Dorothea Lange*, pp. 119, 357, 358.

46 Cited in Leslie Katz, "Interview with Walker Evans," *Art in America* (Mar–Apr 1971), p. 83.

47 Cited in Mellow, *Walker Evans*, p. 214.

48 Ibid., p. 213.

Cat. 1

1 "Chronology," in *Berenice Abbott: Photographs*, with Muriel Rukeyser and David Vestal (Washington: Smithsonian Institution Press, 1970, 1990), p. 163.

2 Isamu Noguchi et al., *Isamu Noguchi: Sculptural Design* (Weil am Rhein, Germany: Vitra Design Museum, 2001), p. 72.

3 Masayo Duus, *The Life of Isamu Noguchi: Journey without Borders*, trans. Peter Duus (Princeton, NJ: Princeton University Press, 2004), pp. 111, 122.

Cat. 2

1 Berenice Abbott, *New Guide to Better Photography* (New York: Crown Publishers, Inc., 1953), p. 1.

2 Ann Thomas, *Beauty of Another Order: Photography in Science* (Ottawa: National Gallery of Canada; New Haven: Yale University Press, 1997), p. 109.

3 Her photographs of penicillin mould, soap bubbles, leaves, the inner workings of a fob-watch, and magnetism were made using a macroscopic lens and a flash. Dating from 1946, they are excellent examples of her signature balance of sheer beauty and factual clarity. She also experimented as early as 1940 with making photograms of wave motion with liquid in a glass through which she projected a light source. Thomas, *Beauty of Another Order*, p. 110.

4 The committee was based at the Massachusetts Institute of Technology, Cambridge and funded by the National Science Foundation with assistance from the Ford and Sloan foundations. Hank O'Neal, *Berenice Abbott: American Photographer* (New York: McGraw-Hill, 1982), p. 27.

5 I. Bernard Cohen, "Some Recollections of Berenice Abbott." An expanded text of a eulogy given at the Berenice Abbott memorial at the New York Public Library, Saturday, 8 February 1992, unpublished manuscript, p. 11, curatorial files, National Gallery of Canada.

6 Francis Lee Friedman, *Introduction to Physics,* 2nd edition (Lexington, MA: D.C. Heath and Company, 1960) and *Physics: Laboratory Guide* (Lexington, MA: D.C. Heath and Company, 1960).

7 O'Neal, *Berenice Abbott: American Photographer*, p. 27.

Cat. 3

1 Ansel Adams, *Examples: The Making of 40 Photographs* (Boston: Little Brown, 1983), p. 23.

2 John Szarkwoski, "Photography: A New Kind of Art," in *Dialogue* 9: 3 (1975), p. 50. Reprinted from John Szarkowski, "A Different Kind of Art," in *New York Times Magazine* (13 April 1975).

3 Adams, *Examples*, p. 26.

4 Ibid., p. 27.

5 A trained musician, Adams supported himself until 1930 by teaching the piano. "Adams, Ansel (Easton)," www.oxfordartonline.com (accessed 7 April 2011).

6 Adams, *Examples,* p. 23.

Cat. 4

1 While Adams did not record the date he made this photograph, Dr. David Elmore of the High Altitude Observatory in Boulder, Colorado, analysed the moon's position in the image and suggested that it was made at approximately 4:05 pm on 31 October 1941. Sean Callahan, "Short Takes: Countdown to Moonrise," in *American Photographer* (January 1981), pp. 30–31. However, astronomer Dennis di Cocco, after further analysis, determined that it was taken at 4:49 pm on 1 November 1941. Dennis Di Cocco, "Dating Ansel Adams's Moonrise," in *Sky & Telescope* (November 1991), pp. 480, 520. Both sources are cited in Karen E. Haas and Rebecca A. Senf, *Ansel Adams* (Boston: Museum of Fine Arts, 2005), p. 69.

2 Ansel Adams, *Examples: The Making of 40 Photographs* (Boston: Little, Brown, 1983), p. 41.

3 Geoffrey Batchen, *Each Wild Idea: Writing, Photography, History* (Cambridge, MA: MIT Press, 2002), p. 152.

4 Adams, *Examples*, p. 42.

5   Mary Street Alinder, *"Ansel Adams: Some Thoughts About Ansel And About Moonrise"* (Alinder Gallery, Gualala, CA, 1999), cited online at http://photo.net/bboard/q-and-a-fetch-msg?msg_id=001Wam (accessed 14 March 2011).

6   Thanks to National Gallery of Canada Photographs Conservator John McElhone for his input on this entry.

Cat. 5

1   Sean Callahan, *The Photographs of Margaret Bourke-White* (New York: New York Graphic Society, 1972), p. 5.

2   Stephen Bennett Phillips, *Margaret Bourke-White: The Photography of Design, 1927–1936* (New York: Rizzoli in association with The Phillips Collection, 2003), p. 14.

3   Ibid., p. 18.

4   Bourke-White's mother bought her a 3 ¼ × 4 ¼ Icas Reflex camera with a cracked lens. Callahan, *The Photographs of Margaret Bourke-White*, p. 29.

5   Bourke-White wrote: "The articles which so frequently appear in our American magazines, debating the relative merits of women in the home as against women in business would be incomprehensible to her. She is working, as the men work, to advance the great industrial program of which she feels she is part." Idem., "Silk Stockings in the Five Year Plan," in *New York Times Magazine*, 14 February, 1932, p. SM4.

6   Ibid.

7   In Bourke-White's 1931 book *Eyes on Russia*, this image is titled *Verblud: 272,000 Acres. An American Disc-Harrow. A Storehouse, State Farm no. 2.*

8   When applying for a visa, she was told by the head of the Soviet Information Bureau in Washington that her photographs possessed "Russian style." Vicki Goldberg, *Margaret Bourke-White: A Biography* (Reading, MA: Addison-Wesley, 1987), p. 126.

9   Robert E. Snyder, in "Margaret Bourke-White and the Communist Witch Hunt," *Journal of American Studies* 19 (April 1985), notes that Bourke-White claimed to be politically disinterested and not well informed (p. 21). He details the investigations into her political affiliations, and her eventual removal from the Custodial Detention Index and the Security Index, while the FBI continued to maintain files on her (p. 24).

Cat. 6

1   "Port of New York Authority," *Fortune*, vol. 8, no. 3. (Sep. 1933), pp. 22–31, 118.

2   In 1929–30 Chrysler hired Bourke-White to photograph its new skyscraper under construction in Manhattan. She took photographs "800 feet above the street … on a tower that swayed 8 feet in the wind, often in sub-freezing temperatures." Margaret Bourke-White, *Portrait of Myself* (New York: Simon and Schuster, 1963), p. 77, reprinted in Stephen Bennett Phillips, *Margaret Bourke-White: The Photography of Design, 1927–1936* (New York: Rizzoli in association with The Phillips Collection, 2003), p. 12.

3   Letter from Ralph McAllister Ingersoll to Margaret Bourke-White, January 1933, as reprinted in Phillips, *Margaret Bourke-White: The Photography of Design, 1927–1936*, p. 183.

4   Le Corbusier, *When the Cathedrals Were White: A Journey to the Country of Timid People*, trans. Francis E. Hyslop (New York: McGraw-Hill, 1964), p. 75.

Cat. 8

1   Harry Callahan, "Harry Callahan: A Life In Photography," in Keith F. Davies, *Harry Callahan Photographs: An Exhibition from the Hallmark Collection of Photographs* (New York: Hallmark Cards, 1981), p. 51.

2   Paul Sherman, *Harry Callahan* (New York: Museum of Modern Art, 1967), p. 7.

Cat. 9

1   The Bauhaus opened in Weimar in 1919 and in Dessau in 1925. Moholy-Nagy taught there from 1923–28. Fleeing Europe for the United States in 1936, he opened a comparable school in Chicago the following year, which he named the New Bauhaus. In 1938 when funding dried up he closed the school temporarily, re-opening it the following year as as a self-funded venture. Intially called the Chicago School of Design, it became the Institute of Design in 1944 and would later become part of the Illinois Institute of Design and Technology. Charles Traub, *The New Vision: Forty Years of Photography* (Millerton, New York: Aperture, 1982), p. 19.

2   *Telehor*, vol. 1, no. 2 (1936), cited in Traub, *The New Vision*, p. 15.

3   On music, Callahan wrote: "I had a really big collection of classical records … I thought if I was a composer I'd want to compose it so that when someone played it, it would all be there." Harry Callahan, "Harry Callahan: A Life in Photography," in Keith F. Davies, *Harry Callahan Photographs: An Exhibition from the Hallmark Collection of Photographs* (New York, Hallmark Cards: 1981), p. 55.

Cat 10.

1   Callahan, "Harry Callahan: A Life in Photography," in Keith F. Davies, *Harry Callahan Photographs: An Exhibition from the Hallmark Collection of Photographs* (New York, Hallmark Cards: 1981), p. 55.

2   Ibid., p. 54.

Cat. 11

1   Coburn had a studio in Boston by age 12, and one in New York on Fifth Avenue by age 20. John Pultz and Catherine B. Scallen, *Cubism and American Photography, 1910–1930* (Williamstown, MA: Clark Art Institute, 1981), p. 12.

2   Ibid.

3   Margaret Harker, "Coburn, Alvin Langdon," Oxford Art Online, www.oxfordartonline.com (accessed 14 March 2011).

4   Robert Doty, *Photo Secession: Photography as a Fine Art* (Rochester, NY: The George Eastman House, 1960), p. 34.

5   Käsebier, who employed Coburn in her Boston studio in 1903, encouraged him to partake in Arthur Wesley Dow's summer art schools in Ipswich, Massachusetts. There he learned about design, arts and crafts and the elements of composition. Barbara Michaels, "Arthur Wesley Dow and Photography," in Nancy E. Green et al., *Arthur Wesley Dow (1857–1922): His Art and His Influence* (New York: Spanierman Gallery, 1999), p. 86.

Cat. 12

1   Alvin Langdon Coburn, "The Future of Pictorial Photography," in *Photograms of the Year, 1916*, pp. 23–24, reprinted in *Photography: Essays & Images; Illustrated Readings in the History of Photography*, ed. Beaumont Newhall (New York: Museum of Modern Art, 1980), p. 205.

2   As these titles suggest, Coburn adopted a radical vantage point, shooting down at the streets from the tops of the city's skyscrapers, creating a perspective that he described as Cubist. It has been proposed that Coburn's photograph *The Thousand Windows, New York*, of 1912 influenced the work of the artist Wyndham Lewis, particularly his *New York* of 1914. Bruce Burgess, "Coburn and Vorticism: An Image of the Future," in *The British Journal of Photography* (1 February 1979), p. 94.

3   Pound dubbed it the "Vorticist movement" (to which both Coburn and Pound belonged), and the resulting images "Vortographs." While Coburn's prints are the only known use of the Vortoscope for photographs, it is known that Pound introduced the device to Fernand Léger, who apparently used it in the making of his film *Ballet mécanique* in 1923–24.

4   Ezra Pound, *"The Little Review": The Letters of Ezra Pound to Margaret Anderson,* ed. Thomas L. Scott, et al. (New York: New Directions, 1988), p. 17

5   Alvin Langdon Coburn, *Alvin Langdon Coburn Photographer: An Autobiography* (New York: Frederick A. Praeger, 1966), p. 102.

6   Nancy Newhall, "Alvin Langdon Coburn – The Youngest Star," in *Alvin Langdon Coburn: Photographs 1900–1924*, ed. Karl Steinorth (Zurich: Edition Stemmle, 1998), p. 43. Originally published in *A Portfolio of Sixteen Photographs by Alvin Langdon Coburn*, intro. Nancy Newhall (Rochester, NY: George Eastman House, 1962).

7   Ibid.

8   Ibid., p. 42.

Cat. 13

1   "Chronology of Imogen Cunningham," online at www.imogen-cunningham.com (accessed 22 March 2011).

2   Much of the biographical information in this entry comes from Richard Lorenz, "Cunningham, Imogen," Oxford Art Online, www.oxfordartonline.com (accessed 22 March 2011) and the *International Center of Photography Encyclopedia of Photography* (New York: Crown Publishers, 1984), pp. 125–126.

3   Cunningham was strongly represented in the landmark international modernist exhibition *Film und Foto*, held in Stuttgart in 1929.

4   Lorenz, "Cunningham, Imogen."

Cat. 14

1   Curtis was "initiated into the Hopi Snake Dance religious society by Shipaulovi Snake Pries Sikyaletstiwa" in August 1906. "Edward S. Curtis and The North American Indian: A Detailed Chronological Biography," online at www.soulcatcherstudio.com (accessed 11 March 2011).

2   Brian Thom, "Aboriginal Intangible Property in Canada: An Ethnographic Review," Section 2.3.3, Industry Canada, online at www.ic.gc.ca (accessed 11 March 2011).

Cat. 15

1   After receiving his engineering degree, Edgerton worked for a year at the General Electric plant in Schenectady, New York. In 1926 he enrolled at M.I.T., receiving both his masters degree and doctorate there, and becoming a permanent member of the faculty. He would soon gain recognition for his contribution to the world of art and photography after various scientific and photography magazines published his photographs taken with a strobe flash. In 1933 and 1934 his photographs were accepted in the annual Royal Photographic Society exhibition in London. In 1941 he received an award from the Franklin Institute for the invention of a high-speed motion picture camera that "increased knowledge in the fields of pure and applied science." Marie Dagata, "Biographical Outline: Harold Eugene Edgerton," in Estelle Jussim, *Stopping Time: The Photographs of Harold Edgerton*, ed. Gus Kayafas (New York: Abrams, 1987), pp. 152–154.

2   The stroboscope was invented by Belgian physicist Joseph Plateau and Austrian mathematician Simon Stampfer, both "inspired by some investigations of Michael Faraday." James R. Killian, Jr., "Papa Flash and His Magic Lamp," in Harold E. Edgerton and James R. Killian, Jr., *Moments of Vision: The Stroboscopic Revolution in Photography* (Cambridge, Massachusetts: MIT Press, 1979), p. 8. William Henry Fox Talbot's first photograph made with a flash in 1851 has also been noted in this respect. Joyce E. Bedi, "The Man Who Stopped Time," in *Invention & Technology* (Summer 1997), p. 37.

3   Edgerton applied his ultra-high-speed light to the testing of motors and regulation of industrial clothing looms. His inventions were used for airplane landing lights and warning lights atop towers, and his high-intensity strobe lamps were used by Allied forces during the Second World War to track enemy movements at night. Jussim, *Stopping Time*, pp. 16, 35.

4   Ibid., p. 18.

5   Dagata, "Biographical Outline," p. 154.

Cat. 16

1   Turner Browne and Elaine Partnow, *Macmillan Biographical Encyclopedia of Photographic Artists and Innovators* (New York: Collier Macmillan Publishers London, 1983), p. 173.

2   Rudolf Eickemeyer, "My First Photograph," in *The Photo Era*, vol. 47, no. 2 (August 1921), p. 76, as cited in Mary Jean Madigan, "Rudolf Eickemeyer, Jr. – A Biographical Appreciation," in *Photography of Rudolph Eickemeyer Jr.*, (Yonkers, New York: Hudson River Museum, 1972), n.p.

3   Although his career declined sharply after his wife died in 1916, Eickemeyer had a retrospective at Anderson Galleries in 1922, won the Emerson Medal in 1925, participated in his last international salon in 1926, and in 1929 donated 100 medalled photographs, plus awards and trophies, to the Smithsonian. Roger Hull, "The Traditional Vision of Rudolf Eickemeyer, Jr.," *History of Photography*, vol. 10, no. 1 (Jan–Mar 1986), p. 56. Madigan, "Rudolf Eickemeyer, Jr., n.p.

Cat. 17

1   Ulrich Pohlmann, "Beauty is Soul: The Life and Work of the Photographer Frank Eugene Smith," in *Frank Eugene: The Dream of Beauty* (Munich: Nazraeli Press, 1995), p. 21.

2   Ibid., p. 35.

3   Michèle and Michel Auer, "EUGENE, Frank," *Encyclopédie Internationale des photographes de 1839 à nos jours/ Photographers Encyclopedia International 1839 to the Present*, vol. 1. (Geneva: Éditions Camera Obscura Switzerland, 1985), n.p.

4   In the fall of 1900, Eugene sat on the jury of the third Photographic Salon in Philadelphia with Käsebier, White and Stieglitz. At the end of 1900, he spent Christmas in Paris with Day and Steichen, then travelled with Day to Egypt for about four months in early 1901. Pohlmann, *The Dream of Beauty*, p. 51.

5   Auer, n.p.

6   Ibid., n.p.

7   Dallett Fuguet, "By a photographer," in *Camera Notes*, vol. 3, no. 4 (April 1900), p. 213, cited in Pohlmann, *The Dream of Beauty*, p. 43.

8   This portrait is not made from any of the 260 FE negatives housed in the Deutsches-Museum, Munich, all of which post-date Eugene's American period. E-mail correspondence from Cornelia Kemp, Curator, Film and Photography Department, Deutsches-Museum, Munich, 13 July 2010.

Cat. 18

1   Maria Morris Hambourg, "A Portrait of the Artist," in Maria Morris Hambourg et al., *Walker Evans* (New York: Metropolitan Museum of Art and Princeton: Princeton University Press, 2000), p. 6.

2   Ibid., p. 10.

3   Ibid., p. 13.

4   Doug Eklund, "Exile's Return: The Early Work, 1928–34," in Hambourg et al., p. 29.

5   Mia Fineman, "Notes from Underground: The Subway Portraits," in Hambourg et al., p. 110.

6   The exhibition took place from 2 May to 2 June 1932. James R. Mellow, *Walker Evans* (New York: Basic Books, 1999), p. 167.

7   *The New York Times*, 8 May 1932, cited in ibid.

8   Evans visited Ben Shahn and family in Truro, Cape Cod, Massachusetts, that summer and might have made *Roadside Gas Sign* at that time. Notation on the negative sleeve indicates that the photograph was taken en route to Truro. Mellow, *Walker Evans*, p. 115.

9   Ibid, p. 127.

Cat. 19

1   A full transcript of a taped interview with the artist, conducted 4 August 1971, appears in Jerry L. Thompson, *Walker Evans at Work: 745 Photographs Together with Documents Selected from Letters, Memoranda, Interviews, Notes* (New York: Harper & Row, 1982), p. 82.

2   Ibid., p. 88.

3   Ibid., p. 82.

4   This was the July–September issue.

5   In discussing Evans' avowed desire to remain apolitical in his work, John Szarkowski observes that "Evans' unfortunates have not yet learned to lose themselves in their role: they are still individuals, and might even be mistaken … for someone we know." John Szarkowski, in *Photography Until Now* (New York: Museum of Modern Art, 1989), p. 276. This is especially true of images such as *Citizen of Havana*.

Cat. 20

1   James R. Mellow, *Walker Evans* (New York: Basic Books, 1999), p. 135.

2   Ibid., p. 131.

3   Jeff L. Rosenheim, "'The Cruel Radiance of What Is': Walker Evans and the South," in Maria Morris Hambourg et al., *Walker Evans* (New York: Metropolitan Museum of Art and Princeton: Princeton University Press, 2000), p. 59.

4   Ibid.

5   Ibid., p. 65.

6   Mellow, p. 115.

7   Rosenheim, "The Cruel Radiance of What Is," p. 84.

8   Walker Evans, "Primitive Churches," in *Architectural Forum* (December 1961), p. 103.

9   Walker Evans, "The Thing Itself is Such a Secret and So Unapproachable," interview in *Yale Alumni Magazine* (February 1974), reprinted in *Image*, vol. 17, no. 4 (December 1974), p. 18.

Cat. 21

1   Colin Westerbeck and Joel Meyerowitz, *Bystander: A History of Street Photography* (Boston: Little, Brown, 1993), p. 284.

2   In January 1937, the Farm Security Administration absorbed most of the programs of the Resettlement Administration, including the Division of Information. Jeff L. Rosenheim, "'The Cruel Radiance of What Is': Walker Evans and the South," in Maria Morris Hambourg et al., *Walker Evans* (New York: Metropolitan Museum of Art and Princeton: Princeton University Press, 2000), p. 101, note 96.

3   James R. Mellow, *Walker Evans* (New York: Basic Books, 1999), p. 265.

4   Members of the Burroughs family later expressed bitterness that their privacy had been invaded and their poverty laid bare by the publication of the book. Christina Davidson, "Let Us Now Trash Famous Authors," *The Atlantic* (April 2010), www.theatlantic.com/magazine/archive/2010/04/let-us-now-trash-famous-authors/7994/ (accessed 15 March 2011).

Cat. 22

1   Lincoln Kirstein, interview with James R. Mellow, 20 June 1991, cited in James R. Mellow, *Walker Evans* (New York: Basic Books, 1999), p. 138.

2   While Evans had planned to use his 1940 Guggenheim fellowship to document the "American scene," a bout of appendicitis interrupted this plan and he used the money instead to focus on the subway photographs, receiving a six-month extension to the grant in 1941. Mia Fineman, "Notes from Underground: The Subway Portraits," in Maria Morris Hambourg et al., *Walker Evans* (New York: Metropolitan Museum of Art and Princeton: Princeton University Press, 2000), p. 109.

3   Mellow, *Walker Evans*, pp. 624, 626–627.

4   Walker Evans, "Along the Right of Way," in *Fortune,* vol. 42 (September 1950), p. 106.

5   "The U.S. Depot: A Portfolio by Walker Evans, in *Fortune*, vol. 47 (February 1953), p. 138.

6   Walker Evans, "The Unposed Portrait," *Harper's Bazaar*, vol. 95 (March 1962), p. 120, cited in Fineman, "Notes from Underground," p. 107.

7   Evans, "The Unposed Portrait," p. 120, cited in ibid., p. 115.

8   Fineman, "Notes from Underground," p. 107.

9   Ibid.

10 Ibid., pp. 107–119.

11 Mellow, p. 166. This image, according to Evans biographer, James R. Mellow, was likely included in the exhibition "Modern Photography at Home and Abroad," held at the Albright Art Gallery, Buffalo, 7–25 February 1932. Ibid.

12 The book was published by Houghton Mifflin, Boston, in conjunction with the first exhibition of Evans' subway portraits, held at the Museum of Modern Art, New York, in 1966. Fineman, "Notes from Underground," p. 115.

Cat. 23

1   Thomas Buchsteiner, "The Language of the Image – What You See Is What You Get," in *Andreas Feininger: That's Photography*, ed. Thomas Buchsteiner and Otto Letze (Ostfildern-Ruit, Germany: Hatje Cantz, 2004), p. 10.

2   Marcel Franciscono, *Walter Gropius and the Creation of the Bauhaus in Weimar: The Ideals and Artistic Theories of its Founding Years* (Urbana, IL: University of Illinois Press, 1971), pp. 3, 5.

Cat. 24

1   According to Feininger's son, Tomas, the artist built the radio in about 1927. E-mail from Tomas Feininger to Katherine Stauble, curatorial assistant, 25 January 2011.

Cat. 25

1   Thomas Buchsteiner, "The Language of the Image – What You See Is What You Get," in *Andreas Feininger: That's Photography*, ed. Thomas Buchsteiner and Otto Letze (Ostfildern-Ruit, Germany: Hatje Cantz, 2004), p. 10

2   Andreas Feininger, *Shells: Forms and Designs of the Sea*: *152 Photographs with Text* (New York: Dover, 1983), p. 46.

Cat. 26

1   Robert Frank, quoted by Edna Bennett, "Black and White are the Colors of Robert Frank," *Aperture* 9, no. 1 (1961), p. 22.

2   Sarah Greenough refers to the principles of composition that Frank learned from Michael Wolgensinger, to whom he was apprenticed in 1942 when still living in Zurich: "when attempting to impart a sense of immediacy and action, he [Frank] utilized abruptly cropped, sometimes slightly out-of-focus forms at the edges of his pictures, suggesting that the viewer like Frank himself, was a participant in the event," "Zurich to New York 1924–1954," in *Looking In: Robert Frank's The Americans* (Washington: National Gallery of Art, 2009), p. 11.

3   *Black, White and Things* consisted of thirty-four photographs divided into three parts: "Black" (12), "White" (8) and "Things" (14).

4   Greenough, *Looking In*, p. 16, note 53.

5   An early supporter of Frank's work, Walker Evans encouraged the younger photographer to apply for a Guggenheim grant in 1955 and provided a reference. Ibid., p. 36. Frank carried Evans' book with him in 1955–56 while making the road trip that resulted in the publication of The Americans. Jeff L. Rosenheim, "Robert Frank and Walker Evans," in *Robert Frank's The Americans*, p. 150.

Cat. 27

1   Philip Brookman, *Robert Frank: London/Wales* (Washington: Corcoran Gallery of Art), p. 5.

2   The longest stretch spent in London was from November 1952 to March 1953.

3   Brookman, *Robert Frank: London/Wales*, p. 10.

4   Sarah Greenough, "Resisting Intelligence: Zurich to New York," in Greenough, et al., *Looking In*, p. 8. In 1942, Frank worked as a still photographer for the film *Steibruch*, directed by Sigfrit Steiner. Ibid., p. 9.

5   His first attempts in the medium of moving images was in the summer of 1958 when he, his wife Mary Allan Kaprow, Richard Bellamy, and Miles Forst worked on a short film using an 8mm camera. Sarah Gordon and Paul Roth, "Map and Chronology," in Greenough, *Looking In*, p. 368.

Cat. 28

1   Martha A. Sandweiss, *Laura Gilpin: An Enduring Grace* (Fort Worth, TX: Amon Carter Museum, 1986), p. 16.

2   Ibid., pp. 41–42.

Cat. 29

1   Largely self-taught, Grossman was highly regarded at the school. His students included Lisette Model, Helen Gee, Arthur Leipzig, and Louis Stettner, who called him the "Ghandi" of photography for his great authority. Walter Rosenblum, also a student, called him "the organizational genius at the league." Lili Corbus Bezner, *Photography and Politics in America: From the New Deal into the Cold War* (Baltimore: John Hopkins University Press, 1999), pp. 73, 76.

2   Grossman served in the Air Force Public Relations section. Bezner, *Photography and Politics in America*, pp. 91–92.

Cat. 30

1   Elizabeth McCausland, "Hine's Photo Documents," in *Photo Notes* (September 1940), p. 3. Hine likely overestimated the number of daily arrivals in his title for the image *When 10,000 to 12,000 Passed Through Each Day*.

2   Ibid., pp. 3–4.

Cat. 31

1   Thomson's *Street Life of London* was published in 1878.

2   Cited in Elizabeth McCausland, "Portrait of a Photographer," in *Survey Graphic* (October 1938), p. 503.

3 "Hine began by using 5 × 7 glass plates and then added 4 × 5 plates. He later carried a Graflex camera that used 4 × 5 film." Marianne Fulton in *Lewis Hine: Passionate Journey: Photographs 1905–1937*, ed. Karl Steinorth (Zurich: Stemmle in association with Rochester: George Eastman House, 1996), p. 11. According to Naomi Rosenblum, the plates made for the NCLC are held by the Library of Congress. Rosenblum, "Biographical Notes," in Walter Rosenblum et. al, *America & Lewis Hine: Photographs 1904–1940* (New York: Aperture, 1977), p. 19.

4 Lewis W. Hine, "The Silhouette in Photography," in *The Photographic Times* 38 (November 1906), p. 488, as cited in Michael Sundell, "Golden Immigrants at the Gold Door: Lewis Hine's Photographs of Ellis Island," in *Social Text*, no. 16 (Winter 1986–1987), pp. 170–172.

5 Elizabeth McCausland, "Hine's Photo Documents," in *Photo Notes* (September 1940), p. 4.

Cat. 32

1 It was incorporated by an Act of Congress in 1907. See NCLC website www.nationalchildlabor.org/ (accessed 14 March 2011).

2 Judith Sealander, *The Failed Century of the Child: Governing America's Young in the Twentieth Century* (New York: Cambridge University Press, 2003), p. 137.

Cat. 33

1 Käsebier began taking photographs of her family members in the 1880s but it was only in the early 1890s that she became aware of the expressive potential of the medium for the making of art. Having discovered photography as her vocation in 1893 while in France, where she took a painting course, she moved to Germany for a year to study photographic chemistry. She opened a portrait studio in New York in 1897, which she operated until 1927.

2 Her studio address was 273 Fifth Avenue. Joel Smith, *Edward Steichen: The Early Years* (Princeton, NJ: Princeton University Press and New York: Metropolitan Museum of Art, 1999), p. 21.

3 "From 1898 until about 1912, she intermittently played hostess to Indian friends, at home as well as at her studio." Barbara L. Michaels, *Gertrude Käsebier: The Photographer and Her Photographs* (New York: Harry N. Abrams, Inc., 1992), p. 30.

4 Ibid.

5 *The Red Man* "was difficult to print, and could not have been produced in quantity …" Michaels, *Gertrude Käsebier*, p. 34.

Cat. 34

1 The hamlet of Serbonne is just outside of Voulangis.

2 Sister of Clara, Steichen's first wife. Käsebier was chaperoning the two Smith sisters on their trip to Paris from their home in Missouri. Penelope Niven, *Steichen: A Biography* (New York: Clarkson Potter, 1997), p. 119.

Cat. 35

1 "Florodora Girls" were the chorus girls who were part of Broadway's first major musical comedy hit, *The Florodora Girl*, 1930.

Cat. 36

1 This was probably Käsebier's third studio, which she operated from 1907 to mid-1914. She opened her first at 12 East 30th Street, in 1897. By 1899 she had opened a second second studio at 273 Fifth Avenue. Barbara L. Michaels, *Gertrude Käsebier: The Photographer and Her Photographs* (New York: Harry N. Abrams, 1992), pp. 28, 56, 58.

2 Gertrude Käsebier, "Enthusiasm from Mrs. Käsebier," in *Bulletin of Photography*, no. 267 (18 September 1912) p. 419.

3 "Art at Home and Abroad," in *The New York Times*, part 7 (13 October 1912), p. 7, cited in Michaels, *Gertrude Käsebier*, p. 140.

Cat. 37

1 Sally A. Stein contends that it was made in the fall of 1932 or winter of 1933. "Future Evidence: The Photographs of Dorothea Lange," in Judith Keller, *Dorothea Lange: Photographs from the J. Paul Getty Museum* (Los Angeles: The J. Paul Getty Museum, 2002), p. 99. The White Angel Jungle soup kitchen ran from 12 January 1931 to 19 February 1933, which suggests that the image was made no later than winter 1933. John Freeman, "Lois Jordan, The Shadowy White Angel," in *San Francisco Bay Area Postcard Club Newsletter*, vol. XXIII, no. 10 (November 2008), pp. 9–10.

2 Milton Meltzer, *Dorothea Lange: A Photographer's Life* (New York: Farrar Straus Giroux, 1978), p. 22; see also Karin Becker Ohrn, *Dorothea Lange and the Documentary Tradition* (Baton Rouge: Louisiana State University Press, 1980), p. 4

3 Linda Gordon, *Dorothea Lange: A Life Beyond Limits* (New York: W.E. Norton, 2009), p. 33.

4 This biographical background information owes a great deal to Linda Gordon's *Dorothea Lange.*

5 Gordon, ibid., p. 106.

6 Ohrn, *The Documentary Tradition*, p. 24.

7 "It was the first day that I ever made a photograph on the street." Dorothea Lange, interviewed by Richard Doud for the Archives of American Art, 22 May 1964. http://www.aaa.si.edu/collections/interviews/oral-history-interview-dorothea-lange-11757 (accessed 15 March 2011).

8 Dorothea Lange, "Dorothea Lange in Perspective," interviewed by Nat Hertz, in *Infinity*, vol. 12, no. 4 (April 1963), pp. 9–19, cited in Meltzer, *Dorothea Lange*, p. 71.

Cat. 38

1 Linda Gordon in Milton Meltzer, *Dorothea Lange: A Photographer's Life* (New York: Farrar Straus Giroux, 1978), pp. 126, 128.

2 Ibid., p. 105. Her colleagues in 1935 included Arthur Rothstein, Carl Mydans, Walker Evans, and Ben Shahn. Meltzer, *Dorothea Lange*, p. 106.

3 Anne Whiston Spirn, *Daring to Look: Dorothea Lange's Photographs and Reports from the Field* (Chicago: The University of Chicago Press, 2008), p. 300.

4 Dorothea Lange, "The Assignment I'll Never Forget: Migrant Mother," in *Popular Photography* (February 1961), pp. 42–43, 128, cited in Meltzer, *Dorothea Lange*, pp. 132–133.

5 Ibid., p. 133.

6 Ibid.

7 Roy Stryker, cited in Roy Emerson Stryker and Nancy Wood, *In This Proud Land: America 1935–1943 as Seen in the FSA Photographs* (Greenwich, Connecticut: New York Graphic Society, 1973), p. 19.

Cat. 39

1 "I came to photography quite by accident…. I worked in a glass factory where I sustained a serious injury to my right hand. I lost the use of my hand for fourteen months. It was during that period that I began looking for a new way to make a living. When a friend suggested that I study photography at the Photo League and perhaps be able to get a job as a darkroom technician, I decided it was worth a try. … Two weeks after the class began I knew with absolute certainty that photography would be my life's work." Arthur Leipzig, "Introduction," in *Arthur Leipzig: A Retrospective* (Brookville, New York: Hillwood Art Gallery, 1989), p. 2.

2 Leipzig apparently spent most of his spare time at the Photo League but took only two classes, one with Sid Grossman and the other with Paul Strand. He asserted that it was from Grossman that he learned "the photography basics – technique, composition and aesthetics," and that Grossman introduced him to "the world of Art." Ibid. From Strand, he learned "to adhere to exacting standards. Strand taught his students the sometimes painful lesson that a nearly good photograph was not a good photograph." Bonnie Yochelson, in Hillwood Art Gallery, *Arthur Leipzig*, p. 3.

3 Leipzig, "Introduction," p. 2.

4 Dorothy Norman, *Stieglitz* (New York: Aperture, 1976), p. 161, cited in Sarah Greenough, Juan Hamilton, *Alfred Stieglitz: Photographs & Writings* (Washington: National Gallery of Art, 1983), p. 26.

Cat. 41

1 Maria Morris Hambourg, "Helen Levitt: A Life in Part," in Sandra S. Phillips and Maria Morris Hambourg, *Helen Levitt* (San Francisco: San Francisco Museum of Modern Art and New York: Metropolitan Museum of Art, 1991), p. 47.

2 Ibid.

3 Sandra Phillips writes that Levitt recalled being stunned by the originality and beauty of this exhibition. Phillips, "Helen Levitt's New York," in Phillips and Hambourg, *Helen Levitt*, pp. 28, 41, note 35.

4   Hambourg, "Helen Levitt: A Life in Part," Ibid., p. 54. Hambourg says Levitt probably saw both Cartier-Bresson's and Evans' work at Julian Levy in 1935 – see p. 63, note 1 – but that she didn't meet Evans until 1938.

5   Agee wrote the introductory essay to *Ways of Seeing*, the first major publication of Levitt's work. Prepared for publication in 1946, it did not see the light of day until 1965. Ibid., p. 58.

6   Evans and Levitt also shared a darkroom in 1938–39, and he lent her his 4 × 5 view camera, with which she made a number of photographs. Ibid., pp. 54–55.

7   Phillips, "Helen Levitt's New York," p. 17.

8   There is a wonderful tension between the immediacy of Levitt's images from this period and the sense of timelessness in her photographs. On the latter, Sandra S. Phillips writes: "As if to underscore the perpetual nature of what she sees, Levitt avoids observation of a specific time or place. We find no suggestion, for instance, of season; except for the children who are ecstatically running into the spraying water hydrant or the four little girls with soap bubbles who are sparingly clad, we would scarcely know it was summer. There are no rainstorms, no snow heaps; there is no sense of time of day, much less time of year. Most of the pictures have a pearly light, an unspecified, general illumination." Ibid., p. 16.

9   Max Kozloff, "A Way of Seeing and the Act of Touching," in *Observations: Essays on Documentary Photography*, from the series *Untitled*, no. 35, (Carmel, California: The Friends of Photography, 1984), p. 68. Kozloff adds, "her off-hand framing … conducted such volatile and lyric energy." Ibid., p. 70.

10   "… she most frequently finds children for her subjects, since they assume imaginative characters with more ease than adults." Phillips, "Helen Levitt's New York," p. 16.

11   Adam Gopnik, "Improvised City: Helen Levitt's New York," *The New Yorker* (19 November 2001), pp. 88–91.

Cat. 42

1   Christopher Mele, *Selling the Lower East Side: Culture, Real Estate, and Resistance in New York City* (Minneapolis: University of Minnesota Press, 2000), pp. 97–103. See also Phillip Lopate, *Waterfront: A Walk Around Manhattan* (New York: Anchor Books, 2005), pp. 275–278, 362.

2   Ben Maddow, *Faces* (Boston: New York Graphic Society, 1977), p. 336.

3   John Szarkowski, "A Different Kind of Art," in the *New York Times Magazine* (13 April 1975), p. 241, reprinted in "Photography: A New Kind of Art," in *Dialogue*, vol. 9, no. 3 (1976), p. 48.

4   Likely referring to *Butterfly Boy*, she elaborates: "In other words, there came the discovery that he had strong aesthetic inclinations which would have to be reconciled with his equally strong social preoccupations. The tension between these two inclinations reveal themselves [sic] superbly in his study of a little black boy …" Estelle Jussim, *Jerome Liebling: Photographs 1947–1977* (Carmel, California: Friends of Photography, 1978), p. 6.

5   Ibid.

6   Claire Cass, "Jerome Liebling," in *This Was the Photo League: Compassion and the Camera from the Depression to the Cold War* (Chicago: Stephen Daiter Gallery and Houston: John Cleary Gallery, 2001), p. 165.

7   Jussim, *Jerome Liebling*, p. 6.

8   Claire Cass, "Jerome Liebling," p. 165.

Cat. 44

1   Ann Thomas, *Lisette Model* (Ottawa: National Gallery of Canada, 1990), p. 102.

2   Ibid., p. 95.

3   Ibid., p. 164.

4   Diane Arbus, in Thomas, *Lisette Model*, p. 149.

Cat. 45

1   Lisette Model, Lisette Model fonds (Series 6, Notebook 2, page 11), National Gallery of Canada, Ottawa

2   Lisette Model, lecture at Boston Photographic Resource Center, Boston, 16 February 1979.

3   The Photo League comprised members who not only accommodated Model's left-leaning social philosophy, but also shared her passion for New York's vital street life. It was also an organization with a strong didactic mission that whole-heartedly supported Model's vision of photography as a way of learning, and it was there that she formulated her position vis-à-vis photography as a tool of intellectual exploration.

Cat. 46

1   Alfred Eisenstadt, "Sammy's Bowery Follies: Bums and Swells Mingle at Low-Down New York Cabaret," *Life*, vol. 17, no. 23 (4 December 1944), pp. 57–60.

Cat. 47

1   Diane Arbus, *Diane Arbus: An Aperture Monograph* (New York: Aperture, 1972), p. 1.

Cat. 48

1   Martha Graham, "1980 Perspectives," in Barbara Morgan, *Martha Graham: Sixteen Dances in Photographs*, revised edition (Dobbs Ferry, New York: Morgan and Morgan, 1980), p. 8.

Cat. 49

1   George Beiswanger, "Martha Graham: A Perspective," in Barbara Morgan, *Martha Graham: Sixteen Dances in Photographs*, revised edition (Dobbs Ferry, New York: Morgan and Morgan, 1980), p. 144.

2   Martha Graham, "Dancer's Focus," in ibid., p. 10.

Cat. 50

1   In 1939 Newman returned to Florida to run a photographic studio in West Palm Beach, and opened his own studio in Miami Beach in 1942. Andy Grundberg, "Arnold Newman, Portrait Photographer Who Captured the Essence of His Subjects, Dies at 88," *New York Times* (7 June 2006), online at www.nytimes.com (accessed 29 March 2011).

2   Newman moved to New York temporarily in 1941, and permanently in 1946. "Arnold Newman (1918–2006): Chronology," in *Sitters and Signatures: Autographed Portraits by Arnold Newman* (New York: Howard Greenberg Gallery, 2007), p. 46.

3   James Danziger and Barnaby Conrad, III, *Interviews with Master Photographers: Minor White, Imogen Cunningham, Cornell Capa, Elliott Erwitt, Yousuf Karsh, Arnold Newman, Lord Snowdon, Brett Weston* (New York and London: Paddington Press, 1977), p. 112.

4   Interview with Arnold Newman in ibid., p. 115.

Cat. 51

1   Cameron Shaw, "Chronology," in *Irving Penn: Platinum Prints* (Washington: National Gallery of Art and New Haven and London: Yale University Press, 2004), p. 167.

2   Maurice Goudeket, *Près de Colette* (Paris: Flammarion, 1956), pp. 58, cited in, and trans. by, Rosamond Bernier, "Some Early Portraits by Irving Penn," in *Irving Penn: A Career in Photography*, ed. Colin Westerbeck (Chicago: The Art Institute of Chicago and Boston: Bullfinch Press/Little, Brown and Company, 1997) pp. 135, 137. Bernier points out the discrepancy between Goudeket's dating of the sitting to 1953, and the correct date of 1951 detailed in Penn's notes. In his account, Goudeket continues: "Her forehead was almost entirely open to view. It was huge, meaningful, touched with genius. It was a startling image, but it was also an act of treachery, an intrusion upon her inmost being. It laid bare all that Colette liked to conceal – and doubtless something about herself of which not even she was aware." Goudeket, Ibid., p. 58, cited in, and trans. by, Philip Gefter, "Irving Penn," *Slate*, http://www.slate.com/toolbar.aspx?action=print&id=2185054 (accessed 29 February 2008).

3   Laurel Cummins, *Colette and the Conquest of Self* (Birmingham, Alabama: Summa, 2005), p. 21.

Cat. 52

1   Theodore E. Stebbins, Jr. and Norman Keyes, *Charles Sheeler: The Photographs* (Boston: Little, Brown, and Company, 1987), p. 161.

2   Ibid., p. 12

3   Stebbins and Keyes note that it was called *Bucks County Barn* in this exhibition, but that one "can be reasonably certain that the photograph … was *Side of White Barn*." Ibid.

4   James Lane, "Of Sheeler's Immaculatism: The Modern Museum's One Man Show," in *Art News* 38 (7 October 1939), p. 10.

5   Carol Troyen, "Photography, Painting, and Charles Sheeler's View of New York" *Art Bulletin* 86, no. 4 (December 2004), p. 731.

6   The image appears in the 1979 catalogue commemorating the exhibition with the title and date *Pennsylvania Barn, 1915*. Ute Eskildsen and Jan-Christopher Horak, *Film und Foto: der zwanziger Jahre: eine Betrachtung der Internationalen Werkbundausstellung "Film und Foto" 1929* (Stuttgart: Württembergischer Kunstverein Stuttgart, 1979), p. 96.

7   Strand and Sheeler began collaborating on the film *Manhatta* in 1920. They later had a falling out as a result of Sheeler's comments concerning an exhibition of Stieglitz's work at the Anderson galleries in 1923. Charles Brock, *Charles Sheeler: Across Media* (Washington: National Gallery of Art, 2006), p. 51.

8   Ibid., p. 173.

Cat. 53

1   Carl Chiarenza, "Form and Content in the Early Work of Aaron Siskind," in *Massachusetts Review*, vol. 19, no. 4. (Winter 1978), p. 824.

2   A presentation by Paul Strand at the League influenced his decision to become a photographer. As a member, Siskind readily took on the job of leading the Features Group, which meant that he would conduct photography excursions to various parts of New York City with League photographers.

3   Lili Corbus Bezner, *Photography and Politics in America: From the New Deal Into the Cold War* (Baltimore: Johns Hopkins University Press, 1999), p. 47.

Cat. 54

1   Aaron Siskind, interviewed by Barbara Shikler, 1982, on American Suburb X: Photography and Culture website, www.americansuburbx.com/2009/01/theory-interview-with-aaron-siskind.html (accessed 22 March 2011).

Cat. 55

1   Eugene Smith, cited in Paul Hill and Thomas Cooper, "Interview with W. Eugene Smith: 1977: An Exerpt," in *Photography in Print: Writings from 1816 to the Present*, ed. Vicki Goldberg (Albuquerque: University of New Mexico Press, 1988), p. 432.

2   Glenn G. Willumson, *W. Eugene Smith and the Photographic Essay* (New York: Cambridge University Press, 1992), p. 24.

3   Ibid.

4   Jim Hughes, *W. Eugene Smith: Shadow and Substance: The Life and Work of an American Photographer* (New York: McGraw-Hill Publishing Company, 1989), p. 254.

5   Willumson, *W. Eugene Smith*, p. 107.

6   Smith used bleach on the final print to heighten the whites of some of the women's eyes, and to slightly change the direction of their gaze. Hughes, *Shadow and Substance*, p. 265.

7   Willumson, *W. Eugene Smith*, p. 115.

8   Smith recounted that a day earlier the son of the deceased had given him permission to photograph the scene: "So I went in with one assistant. The only light in there was a candle about three feet over (the dead man's) head, and with all that black that they were wearing, it was *very* difficult. But I wanted to hold that same mood of lighting, so it was one of the few times I used a flashbulb. I took the reflector off and just used the bare bulb. By hand signals alone I motioned to my assistant to work his way around behind the people to a position where he could hold the bulb over the candle so that it would simulate the candle lighting.

"I made one exposure and immediately realized that it was no good, that the picture was all out of rhythm. I made one more and I thought I had at least a good picture. I would have loved to stay there and photograph for a couple of rolls, but then I saw the son standing in the doorway peering in. I again motioned without words for my assistant to go through the other doorway so that mourners in the other room and the son in the doorway could be seen, made one more exposure, and then very reluctantly I left. All this time never having said a word, hoping I never created much of a disturbance." W. Eugene Smith, cited in Hughes, *Shadow and Substance*, pp. 256–257.

Cat. 56

1   Grace M. Mayer, "Biographical Outline," in Edward Steichen, *A Life in Photography: Edward Steichen* (Garden City, N.Y.: Doubleday, 1963), n.p.

2   Penelope Niven, *Steichen: A Biography* (New York: Clarkson Potter, 1997), p. 29.

3   The friends rented space, paid a model for life drawings and convinced some local artists, including Richard Lorenz and Robert Schode, to give them informal lessons and evaluate their work. Niven, *Steichen*, p. 42.

4   From 1947 to 1962, Steichen was director of the department of photography at the Museum of Modern Art, New York. Steichen, *A Life in Photography*, pp. 283, 285–286.

Cat. 57

1   He had also collaborated with Stieglitz on the creation of *Camera Work* magazine and contributed to two all-Steichen issues. The first, published in 1903, contained seven photogravures and four half-tone reproductions. For an analysis of the subject representation of Steichen's work in this publication and in the Photo-Secession's 1904 touring exhibition, see Joel Smith, *Edward Steichen: The Early Years* (Princeton, NJ: Princeton University Press in association with the Metropolitan Museum of Art, 1999), p. 22.

2   Edward Steichen, *A Life in Photography: Edward Steichen* (Garden City, N.Y.: Doubleday, 1963), n.p.

Cat. 58

1   Joel Smith, *Edward Steichen: The Early Years* (Princeton, New Jersey: Princeton University Press and New York: Metropolitan Museum of Art), 1999, p. 23.

2   Carol Squiers, "Edward Steichen at Condé Nast Publication," in *Edward Steichen: In High Fashion, the Condé Nast Years, 1923–1937* (Lausanne: Musée de l'Élysée, Foundation for the Exhibition of Photography, 2008), p. 109.

3   Edward Steichen, interviewed by A. D. Coleman, 7 July 1969, published in *Photograph* (New York), vol. 1, no. 2 (1976), p. 33, cited in Smith, *Edward Steichen*, p. 38.

4   *George Bernard Shaw*, 1907; a later portrait of *Greta Garbo* taken at MGM in 1927; and *H.L. Mencken*.

5   *Life*, vol. 28, no. 20 (15 May, 1950), p. 119.

6   Sarah Greenough notes that Steichen had a close familiarity with Brancusi's work: "Brancusi deputized Steichen to take charge of the installation, the first at 291 to consist entirely of sculpture. In the Armory Show, Brancusi's work had been clustered atop a rectangular pedestal … At 291, Steichen carefully choreographed the placement of sculpture [sic] in a presentation known through a photograph by Alfred Stieglitz"in *Modern Art and America: Alfred Stieglitz and his New York Galleries* (Washington: National Gallery of Art, 2000), pp. 157–158.

Cat. 59

1   Ralph Steiner, letter to James Borcoman, 16 January 1980, in curatorial files, National Gallery of Canada, Ottawa.

2   Patricia Johnston, "Steiner, Ralph," in *The Oxford Companion to the Photograph,* ed. Robin Lenman (Oxford: Oxford University Press, 2005) p. 598.

3   John Raeburn, *A Staggering Revolution: A Cultural History of Thirties Photography* (Chicago: University of Illinois Press, c. 2006), p. 25. Walker Evans later said he had been influenced by Steiner's *American Baroque* wicker chair and Ford automobile studies created at Yaddo. Ibid.

Cat. 60

1   *Camera Work*, no. 12 (1905) and *Camera Work*, no. 41 (1913).

2   A third variant view – closer in composition to the Camera Work image – exists in gelatin silver form in the collection of the National Gallery of Art, Washington.

3   According to Sarah Greenough, Stieglitz moved away from carbon printing around this time. He was most active with this process from the 1880s to the mid-1890s. E-mail correspondence to Ann Thomas, 23 July 2009.

4   Dorothy Norman, *Alfred Stieglitz: Introduction to an American Seer* (New York: Duell, Sloan and Pearce, 1960), p. 30.

5   Ibid.

Cat. 61

1   Beaumont Newhall, "Alfred Stieglitz: Homeward Bound," in *Art News*, vol. 87, no. 3 (March 1988), p. 142.

2   Cited in *Alfred Stieglitz: Photographs from the J. Paul Getty Museum*, ed. Weston Naef (Malibu, California: The J. Paul Getty Museum, 1995) p. 20.

3   James S. Terry cites Stieglitz: "Had I gotten my picture? I knew if I had, another milestone in photography would have been reached, related to the milestone of my Car Horses made in 1892 and my Hand of Man made in 1902, which had opened up a new era of photography, of seeing," in "The Problem of the Steerage," *History of Photography*, vol. 6, no. 3 (July 1982), pp. 212.

4   The lukewarm reception of *The Steerage* in 1907 was likely based on its lack of narrative appeal. More recent questioning has not been about the importance of the work, but rather querying why Stieglitz did not immediately recognize the advance that it represented – he waited four years to publish it, another six to exhibit it – and why he took credit for recognizing its groundbreaking quality, when this discovery was reputedly made by the painter Max Weber, while examining Stieglitz's prints in 1910. For further discussion, see Terry "The Problem of the Steerage," pp. 218–220.

5   Newhall, "Alfred Stieglitz: Homeward Bound," p. 45. De Zayas felt compelled to leave the print with Picasso since he was so admiring of it.

6   Marius De Zayas, in *291*, no. 8 (October 1915), reprinted in *291: no. 1–12:1915–1916*, with an introduction by Dorothy Norman (New York: Arno Press, 1972), n.p.

Cat. 62

1   The family sold Oaklawn in 1919, as maintenance costs became prohibitive, but retained a thirty-six-acre farm and house up the hill, and a strip of waterfront. Roxana Robinson, *Georgia O'Keeffe: A Life* (Lebanon, New Hampshire: University Press of New England, 1989), pp. 224–225.

2   Sarah Greenough asserts that the location of work took second place to the ideas that Steiglitz was exploring at the time: "The ideas embodied in the early 1920s photographs, especially those of clouds, have little or nothing to do with Lake George specifically and everything to do with Stieglitz's understanding of the nature and function of art and photography." Sarah E. Greenough, "Alfred Stieglitz's Photographs of Clouds." PhD diss., University of New Mexico, 1984 (Ann Arbor, Michigan: UMI), p. 4.

3   Sarah E. Greenough, "How Stieglitz Came to Photograph Clouds," in *Perspectives on Photography: Essays in Honor of Beaumont Newhall*, ed. Peter Walch and Thomas F. Barrow (Albuquerque: University of New Mexico Press, 1986), p. 151.

4   Greenough, "Alfred Stieglitz's Photographs of Clouds," p. 175.

5   "Thirty-five or more years ago I spent a few days in Murren (Switzerland), and I was experimenting with ortho[chromatic] plates," he wrote. "Clouds and their relationship to the rest of the world, and clouds for themselves, interested me, and clouds which were most difficult to photograph – nearly impossible. Ever since then clouds have been in my mind most powerfully at times, and I always knew I'd follow up the experiment made over thirty-five years ago." Cited by Greenough, *Perspectives on Photography*, p. 152, fn 35.

6   John Constable, letter to Bishop John Fisher, 23 October 1821, reproduced in *John Constable's Correspondence VI*, ed. R.B. Beckett (Ipswich, U.K.: Suffolk Records Society, 1968), p. 77.

Cat. 63

1   Ansel Adams, Edward Weston and other West Coast artists come to mind.

2   Peter C. Bunnell, *Alfred Stieglitz: Photographs from the Collection of Georgia O'Keeffe* (New York: Pace/MacGill Gallery and Santa Fe: Gerald Peters Gallery, 1993), p. 20.

3   Stieglitz made observations about the chestnut trees at Lake George: "My mother was dying, our estate was going to pieces. The old horse of thirty-seven was being kept alive by the seventy-year-old coachman … I, full of the feeling of today: all about me disintegration – slow but sure: dying chestnut trees." Alfred Stieglitz, "How I Came to Photograph Clouds," *Amateur Photographer and Photography* (19 Sep., 1923), p. 255.

4   Bunnell, *Alfred Stieglitz*, p. 53.

5   As quoted by Sarah Greenough in *Alfred Stieglitz: Photographs and Writings* (Washington: National Gallery of Art and New York: Callaway Editions, 1983), p. 26.

Cat. 64

1   Belinda Rathbone, "Paul Strand: The Land & Its People," in *The Print Collector's Newsletter*, vol. XXI, no. 1 (March–April, 1990), p. 3.

2   Wilfrid Bovey wrote in 1935, "With completion of the Perron Boulevard in 1925, the rugged Gaspé Peninsula was opened to motorists around its entire area – about ten times that of Rhode Island.… Ten years ago only a few outsiders had any idea of the interest and beauty of the Gaspé area, for it was difficult of access. The last few years, however, have seen astonishing changes. By a remarkable feat of highway engineering, a broad, safe, 553-mile road, linked with the general systems of Quebec and New Brunswick, and so with those of New England, has encircled the entire peninsula." Wilfrid Bovey, "The Gaspé Peninsula Wonderland," in *National Geographic*, vol. 68, no. 3 (August 1935), pp. 209, 211.

3   Paul Strand, lecture at the Chicago Institute of Design, 1 August 1946, pp. 87–88, 91, in *Paul Strand: Sixty Years of Photographs: Excerpts from Correspondence, Interviews, and Other Documents* (Millerton, NY: Aperture, 1976), p. 164.

4   According to Anthony Montoya, Director of the Paul Strand Archive, the paper appears to be B7 (Bromide 7), a paper Strand used in the 1940s.

5   Anne Lyden notes that although the prints were small, "the landscapes depicted were often vast in scope." Anne Lyden, *Paul Strand: Photographs from the J. Paul Getty Museum* (Los Angeles: The J. Paul Getty Museum, 2005), p. 38.

6   Nancy Newhall, *Paul Strand* (New York: Museum of Modern Art, 1945), p. 6.

Cat. 65

1   "American travel writers, for example, consciously sought what they understood to be an authentic experience or … 'the true French Canadian' … it is puzzling that these American travel writers should have been convinced that the 'dying race' of the habitant in twentieth-century Quebec represented the authentic French Canadian. After all, demographic and economic indicators between 1920 and the 1950s pointed to the relative yet steady decline of the rural population in the province." Nicole Neatby, "Meeting of Minds: North American Travel Writers and Government Tourist Publicity in Quebec, 1920–1955," in *Social History*, vol. 36, no. 72 (2003), p. 478.

2   "… looking at Strand's 'tragic landscapes,' he [Alpers] asked the photographer why there were no people in them. When Strand returned to the United States this criticism rankled enough to make him want to re-photograph the Gaspé area, this time with fishermen." Mike Weaver, "Dynamic Realist," in *Paul Strand: Essays on his Life and Work* (New York: Aperture, 1990), p. 199.

3   "*New Masses* reviewer Charles Green singled out 'among the outstanding photos in the show' … the incredible golden geometry of the fishing village, number 57 in the Gaspé series." Bruce Hugh Russell, "The Other Place on the Map: Paul Strand & Georgia O'Keeffe in Québec," (May 1999), p. 19.

Cat. 66

1   One of Sheeler's Doyelstown interiors won first prize, Strand took second for another photograph and third was claimed by Morton Schamberg. In appreciation, Stieglitz dubbed them the "trinity of photographers." Gilles Mores, "Charles Sheeler: A Radical Modernism," in *The Photography of Charles Sheeler: American Modernist* (Boston: Bulfinch Press, 2002), p. 79.

2   Steve Yates, *The Transition Years: Paul Strand in New Mexico* (Santa Fe, NM: Museum of Fine Arts, Museum of New Mexico), p. 16.

3   The other print is in the collection of the San Francisco Museum of Modern Art.

Cat. 67

1   Paul Strand and Nancy Newhall, *Time in New England* (New York: Oxford University Press, 1950).

2   The 18 themes in the book are: Part One (plates 1–20): New World, Wilderness, Foothold, Quakers, Savages, Heaven and Hell, Witchcraft; Part Two (plates 21–33): Native Earth, Prophecies, Revolution; Part Three (plates 34–68): Hill and Town (*Open Door* is plate 37), The Sea, Fine Auroras, Protest, Abolition; Part Four (plates 69–106): Ebb (*Closed Door* is plate 72), Tenacious Roots, and Affirmations.

3   Strand, *Time in New England*, p. vii.

Cat. 68

1   Julia Peterkin won the Pulitzer Prize for her 1928 novel *Scarlet Sister Mary*, inspired by the lives of the African-American workers on the cotton plantation she shared with her husband. Their fifteen hundred-acre farm, outside Columbia, South Carolina, employed some three hundred workers. Ulmann visited Peterkin on a number of occasions to photograph the workers. Philip Walker Jacobs, *The Life and Photography of Doris Ulmann* (Lexington: University of Kentucky, 2001), p. 62.

Cat. 69

1   Weegee, *Weegee by Weegee: An Autobiography* (New York: Ziff-Davis Publishing Company, 1961), p. 95.

Cat. 70

1   Edward Weston, "Thirty-Five Years of Portraiture," Part I, in *Camera Craft*, vol. 46, no. 9 (September 1939), pp. 399–408, reprinted in *Edward Weston on Photography*, ed. Peter C. Bunnell (Salt Lake City: Gibbs M. Smith, 1983), p. 104.

2   Edward Weston *The Daybooks of Edward Weston,* vol. 1, *Mexico,* ed. Nancy Newhall (Rochester, New York: George Eastman House, 1961), p. 42.

3   Ibid., p. 95.

4   Ibid.

Cat. 71

1   Edward Weston, "Conceptos del Artista," in *Forma*, vol. 2, no. 7 (1928), pp. 15–18, reprinted in "Concepts of the Artist: 1928," in *Edward Weston on Photography,* ed. Peter C. Bunnell (Salt Lake City: Gibbs M. Smith, 1983), p. 47.

2   For a fuller discussion of Weston's photographing of objects see Estelle Jussim, "Quintessences: Edward Weston's Search for Meaning" and Mike Weaver, "Curves of Art," in *EW 100: Centennial Essays in Honor of Edward Weston,* ed. Peter C. Bunnell and David Featherstone (Carmel: The Friends of Photography, 1986).

3   Cited in Jean S. Tucker, *Group f.64* (St. Louis: University of Missouri Press, 1978), p. 4, note 7.

Cat. 72

1   Charis Wilson, *Edward Weston Nudes: His Photographs Accompanied by Excerpts from the Daybooks & Letters* (Millerton, New York: Aperture, 1977), p. 9.

2   Ibid., p. 7.

3   Ibid., p. 9.

4   Weston, *The Daybooks of Edward Weston*, vol. 1, p. 136.

5   Charis Wilson, interviewed in *The Eloquent Nude: The Love and Legacy of Edward Weston and Charis Wilson,* (Portland, Oregon: NW Documentary, 2008)

6   Wilson, *Edward Weston Nudes*, p. 12.

7   Ibid., p. 13.

8   Wilson, interviewed in *The Eloquent Nude.*

9   Wilson, *Edward Weston Nudes*, p. 7.

Cat. 73

1   Edward Weston, *Edward Weston on Photography*, p. 94.

2   Weston, "Photographing California: 1939," Part II,, in *Camera Craft*, vol. 46, no. 3 (March 1939), pp. 99–105, reprinted in Ibid.

3   Edward Weston, "I Photograph Trees: 1940," in *Popular Photography*, vol. 6, no. 6 (June 1940), pp. 20–21, 120–123, reprinted in *Ibid*, p. 115.

4   Ibid.

Cat. 74

1   Peter C. Bunnell, *Clarence H. White: The Reverence for Beauty* (Athens, Ohio: Ohio University Gallery of Fine Art, 1986), p. 7.

Cat. 75

1   Peter C. Bunnell, *Clarence H. White: The Reverence for Beauty* (Athens: Ohio University Gallery of Fine Art, 1986), p. 24.

2   According to Estelle Jussim, Day considered White a genius. Estelle Jussim, *Slave to Beauty: The Eccentric Life and Controversial Career of F. Holland Day, Photographer, Publisher, Aesthete* (Boston: Godine, 1981), p. 153.

3   Jussim, *Slave to Beauty*, p. 8.

Cat. 76

1   Letter from Beaumont Newhall to Maynard P. White, Jr., 14 September, 1973. Cited in Maynard P. White, *Clarence H. White* (Millerton, NY: Aperture, 1979), p. 8.

Cat. 77

1   Published in *American Photography*, vol. 37 (January, 1943), pp. 16–17.

2   Letter from Peter Bunnell, curator of the Minor White Archive, to Andrea Fajrajsl, reproduction and rights staff, National Gallery of Canada, Ottawa, 1 February 1993.

3   John Pultz, "Equivalence, Symbolism, and Minor White's Way into the Language of Photography," in *Record of the Art Museum*, Princeton University, vol. 39, no. 1/2 (1980) pp. 28–39.

4   Ralph Waldo Emerson, as quoted in Barbara Novak, *American Painting of the Nineteenth Century: Realism, Idealism and the American Experience* (Praeger: New York et al., 1969), p. 22.